TWENTIETH CENTURY ETHICS

TWENTIETH CENTURY ETHICS

ROGER N. HANCOCK

1974
Columbia University Press
New York and London

The Andrew W. Mellon Foundation, through a special grant, has assisted the Press in publishing this volume.

Library of Congress Cataloging in Publication Data

Hancock, Roger N.   1929–
    Twentieth century ethics.

    Bibliography: p.
    1. Ethics—History—Great Britain.   2. Ethics—
History—United States.   I. Title.
BJ319.H27   170'.9   74-12023
ISBN 0-231-03877-1

CONTENTS

INTRODUCTION   1

  1 Aim and Scope of This Book   1

  2 Normative Ethics and Meta-Ethics   3

  3 Types of Ethical Theory   11

I MOORE AND THE REFUTATION OF NATURALISM   18

  1 Three Assumptions of Moore's Ethical Theory   18

  2 Moore's Refutation of Naturalism   27

  3 Moore and the Problem of Ethical Knowledge   32

II INTUITIONISM   41

  1 Sidgwick and the Irreducibility of "Ought"   42

  2 Prichard: The Attack on Utilitarianism   46

3 Ross: The Meaning of "Right"   50

4 Some Problems for Intuitionists   52

III   NATURALISM   58

1 The Meaning of "Naturalism"   59

2 Santayana and Subjectivism   64

3 Perry's Theory of Value   68

4 Dewey's Theory of Valuation   74

5 The Ideal Observer Theory   80

6 Some Problems for Naturalists   82

IV   NON-COGNITIVISM: THE EMOTIVE THEORY   87

1 Ayer's Pure Emotive Theory   87

2 Stevenson: The Meaning of "Meaning" and the
Concept of Emotive Meaning   97

3 Stevenson's Theory of Ethical Disagreement   109

V   NON-COGNITIVISM: HARE   118

1 Hare's Refutation of Naturalism   119

2 Prescriptivism   123

3 The Universalizability Principle   133

VI   THE GOOD REASONS APPROACH   144

1 Ethical Reasoning as *Sui Generis*   145

2 Could a Moral Principle Be Anything?   156

**VII   THE RETURN TO NORMATIVE ETHICS:
SINGER AND RAWLS**   164

1 The Generalization Argument   165

2 Singer on the Status of Moral Principles — 177

3 Rawls: Goodness as Rationality. — 181

CONCLUSION — 188

1 Normative Ethics and Meta-Ethics Again — 188

2 Fact and Value: An Untenable Dualism? — 197

3 ''Is'' and ''Ought'' — 213

4 Can Ethical Disagreement Be Resolved? — 221

REFERENCES — 231

BIBLIOGRAPHICAL NOTE — 235

INDEX — 237

ACKNOWLEDGMENT

SEVERAL CHAPTERS IN THIS BOOK contain material I have revised from previously published articles. I should like to thank the publishers of the following for their permission to use them in the present book: "The Refutation of Naturalism in Moore and Hare," *The Journal of Philosophy,* Vol. LVII, No. 10 (May 12, 1960); "A Note On Hare's *The Language of Morals,*" *The Philosophical Quarterly,* Vol. 63, February, 1963; "A Note On Naturalism," *Ethics,* Vol. LXXVII, No. 1, October, 1966.

TWENTIETH CENTURY ETHICS

INTRODUCTION

1 Aim and Scope of This Book

THE PRIMARY AIM OF THIS BOOK is to give a critical presentation of the main types of ethical theory developed in the course of the twentieth century. Insofar as it defends a particular viewpoint, it is a defense of naturalism in a sense explained in this Introduction and in Chapter III—a sense in which naturalism is the thesis that ethical judgments can be derived from non-ethical statements of fact by ordinary inductive and deductive reasoning. The argument for this thesis is contained in the Conclusion, in particular in section 3 of the Conclusion.

In the light of the above aims, something should be said about three self-imposed limitations of this book. First, it deals only with recent work in ethics in the English-speaking countries, a limitation that partly reflects the author's interests and competence, but also reflects the fact that, unfortunate as it may be, work in ethical theory in the English-speaking countries in recent times has been done independently of work outside these areas. No suggestion is being made that the work of Nicolai Hartmann or Max Scheler, for example, is less important than the work of, say, G. E. Moore or Charles Stevenson. The suggestion is simply that the recent work of English-speaking philosophers is in some important sense autonomous and can therefore be treated in a book such as this by itself.

Second, the book is limited in that it deals with work by men who are exclusively or primarily philosophers in the present academic sense of the term, and not, for example, with work by men who are primarily theologians or social scientists. Thus, there is no discussion of what is currently called "situation ethics," partly again a reflection of the author's interests and competence, but also because this development is largely the work of men whose interests and orientation are primarily theological, not philosophical in the current academic sense. Similarly, there is no discussion of the recent development (actually beginning in the nineteenth century in the work of men such as Edvard Westermarck) currently called "cultural relativism," a development which, although of great interest to many philosophers, is itself primarily a theory within social science.

Third, and most important, this book is largely limited to what philosophers have come to call "meta-ethics" as contrasted with "normative ethics." For purposes of this book, ethical theory is to be understood as inquiry concerning the meanings or functions of ethical terms and ethical judgments, the status of ethical judgments (e.g. whether *a priori* or in some sense empirical), the justification of ethical judgments and in particular the question of the relation of ethical judgments to non-ethical factual statements (the so-called "is-ought" question), the nature of ethical disagreement (e.g. whether primarily disagreement in belief or disagreement in attitude), and the related question of the ways, if any, in which ethical disagreement can be resolved. All these questions, presently regarded as meta-ethical by most philosophers, are theoretical questions, as opposed to substantive moral questions such as "Should abortion be permitted?" or "Are there any just wars?" It is certainly not suggested that the meta-ethical questions are more important than the substantive moral questions such as those cited, even in the sense that to answer the normative questions satisfactorily (whatever that may come to) one must first answer the meta-ethical questions. The limitation to meta-ethics is simply a reflection of the fact, arguably an unfortunate one, that the meta-ethical questions have increasingly dominated philosophical discussion (again in the academic sense of "philosophical") in the twentieth century in English-speaking countries. This book in effect simply acknowledges this fact without subscribing to it, or indeed without even conceding that the very distinction between normative ethics and meta-ethics is entirely clear-cut. It is in fact the author's view that this distinction, itself a crucial development in recent ethics, should be regarded as itself controversial, not as something to be simply taken for granted. In the following section I shall briefly discuss some of the problems involved in the distinction as currently understood by philosophers, and sketch briefly the history of the distinction in twentieth century ethics.

2   Normative Ethics and Meta-Ethics

The distinction between normative ethics and meta-ethics was defined above, in effect, by enumeration: certain questions were said to be meta-ethical, others were said to be normative. Can the distinction be defined in a general way so as to give a clear way of deciding whether a given question is meta-ethical or normative? It is not easy to say. One obvious candidate would be that a normative ethical judgment is one in which an ethical predicate (such as "right," "wrong," "good," "bad," "obligatory," etc.) is *used* in the sense that it is actually ascribed to some subject, as in "Killing in self-defense is not wrong." A meta-ethical statement, by contrast, might be defined as a statement *about* a normative statement which is not itself a normative statement. (It is clear that some statements about normative statements are themselves normative statements in the above sense: e.g. the statement "One ought not to make general statements in ethics," is itself an ethical judgment—and a general one at that!) But while such a characterization of the distinction between normative ethics and meta-ethics, in terms of the kind of statements made in each, does do something to explain the distinction in a general way, it is not entirely satisfactory. For there are countless statements, not themselves normative, which one could make about normative statements but which no one would regard as meta-ethical. Thus "Smith said 'Killing is wrong' " is a statement, not itself a normative statement, about a normative statement. But it belongs to biography or history, not to meta-ethics. Nor is it simply a question of generality: some very general statements about normative statements could be made which few would consider meta-ethical. Thus "All moral judgments reflect the speaker's upbringing" belongs to psychology rather than to ethics, although possibly it has implications for ethics.

Roughly speaking, meta-ethical statements are statements which answer general logical and epistemological questions about normative ethical judgments; in particular, questions about their meanings and about the sense, if any, in which they can be known to be true or false. But this is only a rough characterization. One might, for example, concern oneself with the logical validity of arguments which happen to contain normative ethical premises and conclusions, but if one's purpose were simply to assess the formal validity of the reasoning, one would be doing formal logic and not meta-ethics. Hence it is perhaps a mistake to look for some general characteristic of meta-ethical statements which clearly and sharply divides them from all other kinds of statements.

Historically, it would appear that the origin of the current distinction between normative ethics and meta-ethics lies in the work of G. E. Moore, as so much of recent ethical theory does in one way or another. In *Principia Ethica* (Sections 3-5) Moore distinguished in effect two fundamentally different ways of interpreting what he took to be the basic question of ethics, namely the question "What is good?" The question "What is good?," Moore pointed out, could mean either (a) "What particular thing, or general kind of thing, is good?" in which case it would be answered by e.g. "What Smith did yesterday was good" or "Books are good," or (b) "What is the meaning of the term 'good'?" or, as Moore prefers to phrase it, "How is good to be defined?" In insisting on the importance of distinguishing these two senses of the question "What is good?" Moore in effect introduced the distinction between normative ethics and meta-ethics as now understood: either (a) the question "What is good?" belongs to normative ethics, or (b) it belongs to meta-ethics. Moore himself, in *Principia Ethica,* was concerned with both questions. But it was his discussion of the second question that has been by far the more influential in the history of recent ethics. And the second question, generalized as the question of the meaning of ethical terms and statements, came to be the main if not the sole concern of many philosophers writing on ethics.

Moore himself did not make a general distinction between normative ethics and meta-ethics, in these or any other terms; this was done, however, in two influential books, A. J. Ayer's *Language, Truth, and Logic* and C. L. Stevenson's *Ethics and Language*. Ayer distinguished (a) "propositions which express definitions of ethical terms, or judgments about the legitimacy or possibility of certain definitions," (b) "propositions describing the phenomena of moral experience," (c) "exhortations to moral virtue," and (d) "actual ethical judgments"; only the first, Ayer argued, is the proper concern of ethical philosophy. Stevenson distinguishes "normative ethics" from what he describes as "a narrowly specialized part" of ethics which seeks to "clarify the meaning of the ethical terms" and to "characterize the general methods by which ethical judgments can be proved or supported"—inquiries which he terms respectively "analysis" and "methodology." The present conception of meta-ethics is essentially Stevenson's conception of analysis and methodology as, in a sense, defined by what he discusses in *Ethics and Language*.

Ayer's view that "ethical philosophy" should confine itself to definitions of ethical terms or judgments about such definitions may serve to raise certain problems in the meta-ethical/normative ethical distinction as currently understood. First, it seems clear that Ayer confines the scope of ethical philosophy very narrowly indeed, much more narrowly than Stevenson does, for example. It may be true that meta-ethics as presently understood is "narrowly specialized," to use Stevenson's phrase. But it is considerably broader than Ayer's conception of ethical philosophy. Ayer limits ethical philosophy to "analysis" in Stevenson's sense, whereas the current conception of meta-ethics, following Stevenson himself, includes considerably broader questions about the justification of ethical judgments, the nature of ethical disagreement, and the methods available for the resolution of ethical disagreement. It is true that to an important extent one's views on these broader questions are determined by one's views concerning the narrower question of the analysis of ethical terms and statements. Yet, views concerning the meaning of ethical terms are not univocally associated with views about the justification of ethical judgments. And one can deal with the latter question without committing oneself on the former question, as indeed a number of recent philosophers have done. Hence, the questions of meta-ethics cannot be entirely reduced to questions concerning the meaning of ethical terms. But if more is included, it is not clear where the line is to be drawn. For example, one might raise the question of what it is that makes a certain kind of ethical argument a good argument: this seems to fall within the scope of meta-ethics as currently understood, and yet there is also an important sense in which this question, given certain meta-ethical views such as Stevenson's own, becomes a psychological question. In general, once one gives up Ayer's narrow conception of the role of the philosopher in ethics, it becomes difficult to draw a sharp line between meta-ethical questions and questions belonging to other inquiries such as psychology.

A further question raised by Ayer's conception of ethical philosophy is whether, assuming there is a clear distinction between normative ethics and meta-ethics, philosophers should limit themselves to meta-ethics. Ayer held that they should: "A strictly philosophical treatise on ethics," he argued, "should . . . make no ethical pronouncements," presumably meaning no normative ethical pronouncements. Ayer and others who hold this view seem to support it by two main arguments. (1) It is argued that philosophers as such are not especially qualified to answer normative ethical questions. There is no reason to think, for example, that philosophers as such have an especially acute moral sense, or are well informed on ethically relevant factual questions. Hence even granting there are moral experts in some sense, philosophers cannot claim to be such experts. (2) It is a consequence of non-cognitivist meta-ethical theories such as Ayer's own that normative ethical judgments are not, at least not primarily, statements that are true or false, but rather expressions of feelings and attempts to influence the feelings of others (Ayer and Stevenson) or imperatives (Hare). But if normative ethical judgments are not statements that are true or false, they cannot be a part of philosophy, since philosophy purports to be a cognitive activity aiming at the discovery of truth. How sound are these arguments? They are certainly not conclusive. As regards the first argument, it is not clear that to do normative ethics is necessarily to make a claim to moral expertness. That might be the case if one were concerned with arriving at the solution of particular substantive normative questions, such as whether abortion is morally permissible. But what philosophers who do normative ethics have traditionally been concerned with is not so much the solution to particular moral questions, but, rather, the clarification and defense of basic moral principles, such as J. S. Mill's principle of Utility, or Kant's Categorical Imperative. And even when they have addressed themselves to particular moral questions, as for example Kant does in his essay "On the Alleged Right to Tell a Lie From Humanitarian Motives," they have been mainly concerned with the evaluation of arguments given in support of alternative answers, and with showing how certain answers follow from certain basic moral principles. It would seem that the kind of expertness required for moral philosophy as traditionally conceived, therefore, is not so much moral sensitivity or special factual knowledge, but rather skill in abstract thinking and argumentation, skills that philosophers may well claim to have to a special degree.

As regards the second argument, it is indeed a consequence of non-cognitivist meta-ethical theories that philosophy, assuming it to be a cognitive activity, should not as such concern itself with normative ethics. (No one denies that philosophers, who are also parents, husbands and wives, advisors, voters, etc., can and must in these latter capacities concern themselves with normative ethical questions). But it would be in a certain sense question-begging to assume at the outset that since moral judgments are non-cognitive, philosophers as such should not make them. On the contrary, the fact that philosophers have traditionally made normative ethical judgments could be taken as *prima facie* evidence that moral judgments *are* cognitive.

In general, the basic reason why Ayer and others restrict ethical philosophy to meta-ethics is that they tend to hold the view that all cognitively meaningful statements either are empirical hypotheses, and as such belong to science, or are statements which are true by virtue of the meanings of the words in the statement—definitional truths, as one may call them. The argument, in effect, is that since meta-ethical statements are definitional truths, or statements about definitional truths, they are cognitively meaningful, but since normative ethical judgments are neither definitional truths nor scientific truths, they are hence not cognitively meaningful and hence not the proper concern of philosophy. Obviously such an argument raises a host of basic philosophical problems. Hence, while one may well ultimately arrive at the conclusion that normative ethics is not properly the concern of philosophy, such a conclusion can only come at the end of inquiry, not at the beginning.

In the foregoing I have suggested that the view that philosophers should limit themselves to meta-ethics—at one time a widespread view stemming largely from Ayer's *Language, Truth, and Logic*—may not be well founded. (It should be noted that there seems to be a current reaction in favor of normative ethics, and there was no time at which Ayer's view achieved complete consensus). A more basic question raised by the meta-ethical/normative ethical distinction, however, concerns the extent to which the two can be separated. It appears to be a rather generally held assumption that the two are independent, in the sense that one can do meta-ethics without making any substantial normative commitment, and (this is less clear) can do normative ethics without committing oneself to any particular meta-ethical theory. But are they independent? One point sometimes made which suggests they may not be is the following. In order to get started in meta-ethics, one must somehow be able to make an initial distinction between ethical and non-ethical judgments. And it may be that this distinction, presupposed by meta-ethics, is itself normative or involves normative considerations.

Further, there are certain important statements which can be understood either as normative or meta-ethical, and the decision to treat them as one rather than as the other may involve an element of arbitrariness. Thus, consider the so-called "universalizability principle" emphasized by Hare, according to which my judgment that my action is right or wrong is not really a moral judgment unless I am prepared to judge the same action right or wrong when done by any relevantly similar person in relevantly similar circumstances. Hare regards this principle as meta-ethical: for him, part of what is meant by calling an action "right" is that I am prepared to universalize the judgment. Yet, essentially the same principle was put forth as a fundamental "axiom" by Sidgwick, who termed it the axiom of equity or justice and presumably regarded it as a normative ethical judgment, differing from other normative judgments only in its generality and self-evidence. Hare's decision to treat this principle as meta-ethical, an illustration of the general move from normative ethics to meta-ethics in twentieth century ethics, is not altogether easy to justify. It would be in a sense question-begging to argue that since Sidgwick's axiom of justice can be seen to be true by anyone who understands the meaning of the term "right," it must therefore be meta-ethical. For in effect, one would be arguing that all principles that have a good claim to be regarded as self-evident must belong to meta-ethics rather than to normative ethics, thereby making it a necessary truth that there are no self-evident normative ethical judgments, and thus begging a fundamental question concerning ethical knowledge. Similar considerations hold for another of Sidgwick's anxioms, namely the axiom of benevolence according to which one is morally obligated to treat another's good as equal in importance to one's own. Since acceptance of this principle in effect rules out egoism, a normative ethical theory, it would seem to be itself normative. Yet, one might claim that the principle of benevolence is really not normative at all but meta-ethical—true by virtue of the meanings of the terms "morally obligated" and "good." There seems no reason why, if the axiom of justice can be regarded as meta-ethical, the axiom of benevolence and indeed all of Sidgwick's axioms cannot likewise be so regarded.

There may, I have suggested, be an important sense in which meta-ethics and normative ethics are not independent: their possible interdependency might be illustrated in connection with definitions of ethical terms. As suggested above, what have been traditionally taken as basic normative principles could be regarded as definitional truths. Consider for example Mill's principle of Utility, according to which acts are right in proportion as they tend to increase happiness. This is usually taken as normative, and Utilitarianism is generally taken to be a normative ethical theory. Yet, Mill could be taken as answering the question "What is right?" in the sense of "What is the meaning of the term 'right'?" Taken in this way his principle of Utility would become a definition of the expression "right action," and as such would seem to belong to meta-ethics rather than to normative ethics. But it would then follow that meta-ethical statements have important implications for normative ethics: normative judgments of the form "A acted rightly in doing X" would follow directly from the definition of "acted rightly" plus the factual statement that the act in question maximized happiness. It might be argued that this consequence simply shows that Mill's principle cannot be taken as a definition. But one might equally well draw the conclusion that meta-ethics and normative ethics are intimately connected. This problem in connection with definitions of ethical terms such as "good," "right," "ought," etc. is perhaps what lies behind Stevenson's concept of the "persuasive definition." Stevenson would argue that Mill's principle, taken as a definition of "right action," is a persuasive definition, i.e. a process in which a term with a highly favorable connotation is made to designate certain things in order to create a favorable attitude toward those things—acts that promote happiness, in the case of Mill's definition. In general, Stevenson holds, definitions of ethical terms of the form " 'X is good (right, etc.)' means 'X has features A, B, C, etc.' " are persuasive and as such should be regarded as normative; they are really value-judgments disguised as definitions. In a sense, according to Stevenson, it is therefore not the task of meta-ethics to define ethical terms at all. But one could just as well conclude that meta-ethical statements can also be normative statements, that the categories "meta-ethical" and "normative" are not exclusive.

In sum, then, it is difficult to define the distinction between meta-ethics and normative ethics in a general way, it is not clear that there is any very good reason why philosophers should restrict themselves to meta-ethics, and, finally, it is far from clear that the two inquiries are independent in the way commonly assumed. In spite of these problems, however, it still seems clear that there is a useful and important distinction to be made between statements that are primarily answers to logical and epistemological questions about ethical judgments, and ethical judgments themselves which are primarily answers to practical questions about how to act. Further, while it may well be argued that English-speaking philosophers in the twentieth century have concerned themselves too exclusively with meta-ethical questions (an argument that has less force at present than it did ten or twenty years ago), this concern can be explained and even justified. To a certain extent it was forced on philosophers by general intellectual developments, such as the general scepticism concerning claims to possess truths not scientifically or empirically founded, and, in particular, the challenge to traditional assumptions about ethics stemming from Logical Positivism. In any case it is important to understand and appreciate any influential intellectual movement even when, or perhaps especially when, one wishes ultimately to reject it. It is in this spirit that the present book follows what has been, and to many philosophers still is, the main current of recent ethics in restricting itself largely to meta-ethics.

3 Types of Ethical Theory

In the course of the following chapters I shall consider the following theories in roughly historical order: (1) Moore's theory as stated primarily in *Principia Ethica,* sometimes called "Ideal Utilitarianism," (2) the theory of Prichard and Ross, anticipated by Sidgwick, which, following Sidgwick's own terminology, is generally called "Intuitionism," (3) the theories of Santayana, Perry, Dewey, and the so-called "Ideal Observer Theory" proposed by Brandt and Firth, commonly called "Naturalism," (4) the so-called "Emotive Theory of Ethics" held by A. J. Ayer and C. L. Stevenson, (5) the theory of R. M. Hare, which has been perhaps the most widely discussed theory advanced in the past thirty years, and finally (6) what is sometimes referred to as the "Good Reasons" theory advanced by a number of philosophers in recent years.

It will be at once apparent to anyone at all familiar with these theories that not all of them are exclusively or even primarily meta-ethical theories. Moore's theory and the opposing theories of Ross and Prichard certainly are not purely meta-ethical theories, for example. And it is not entirely clear that Perry's and Dewey's theories are to be regarded as exclusively meta-ethical. It is only with the last three theories that one is clearly dealing with philosophers who are consciously restricting themselves to meta-ethics. A systematic treatise on ethics would probably make a sharper distinction between meta-ethical and normative theories than the present work attempts to do. In the case of earlier writers in the period to be covered, such as Sidgwick, Moore and Prichard, the distinction in question is simply not made, at least not in an explicit and general way. A work that intends to be to some extent historical and to discuss the work of past philosophers in their own terms must in some sense recognize this fact. At the same time one can take advantage of hindsight. Philosophers now do attempt to make a rather sharp distinction between meta-ethics and normative ethics, and in discussing the work of Moore, for example, it is possible to distinguish his meta-ethical position from his normative ethical position far more sharply than he himself ever did. Accordingly, in the case of the earlier writers in the period the present work will be in the main concerned with their meta-ethical theories as meta-ethics is presently understood rather than with their positions in normative ethics. In the case of Moore, for example, the discussion will be largely limited to a discussion of his views about the meaning of "good" and his position concerning the status of judgments of the form "X is good" and our knowledge of such judgments.

In the light of the above it may be helpful to suggest here a possible classification of meta-ethical theories as a way of distinguishing the different theories to be discussed in the following chapters. I suggest the following scheme of classification. First, we may distinguish (I) *cognitive* theories from (II) *non-cognitive* theories. Roughly, cognitivists hold there is ethical knowledge; non-cognitivists deny it. Stated somewhat more precisely, the issue is whether normative ethical judgments such as "You acted wrongly in stealing that money" can be said to be known to be true in anything like the sense in which most people would say that "You stole that money" can be known to be true. Cognitivists say yes, non-cognitivists say no. More deeply, perhaps, the issue is whether normative ethical judgments can even be said to be true or false at all, in the same sense of "true" and "false" in which we ascribe truth or falsity to ordinary factual statements such as "It rained yesterday." Stating the issue in this way emphasizes the fact that what is at issue is not so much our cognitive powers as the status and meaning of ethical judgments themselves. Moore, for example, seems to have held that we can never be absolutely certain of the truth of any normative ethical statement; he certainly held this in the case of statements of the form "You ought to do X" or "It would not be wrong to do Y." Yet, Moore also certainly held that such statements are themselves either true or false, and he can therefore be classified as a cognitivist. Emotivists such as Ayer and Stevenson, on the other hand, and possibly Hare, hold that ethical judgments are not true or false in the same sense as ordinary factual statements. Emotivists compare ethical judgments with utterances such as "Shame on you" or "Hurrah for him," which serve primarily to express the speaker's feelings. Hare regards ethical judgments as imperatives comparable to utterances such as "Don't do X," or as at least containing imperatives. Neither of these types of utterances can be said to be literally true or false. The issue, in short, is not so much whether our knowledge claims in normative ethics are ever justified, but rather whether normative ethical judgments are to be regarded as knowledge claims at all.

Cognitivist theories, in turn, may be divided into (IA) *naturalistic* theories and (IB) *non-naturalistic* theories. This division, crucial in recent ethical theory, is not easy to explain in a precise way. Roughly, naturalists regard ethical judgments as empirical statements, verifiable by ordinary methods of observation and experiment used in everyday life and in science. For the non-naturalist, in contrast, ethical judgments cannot be known to be true by ordinary empirical methods, but, rather, are known or believed to be true by virtue of some kind of rational insight or intuition. Hence whereas naturalists tend to regard ethical judgments as empirical hypotheses, non-naturalists regard or tend to regard them as synthetic a priori truths. Moore, who introduced the term "naturalism" into recent ethical theory, characterized naturalism as the view that "good can be defined by reference to a natural object," understanding by "a natural object" something "of which the existence is admittedly an object of experience." As an example of a naturalistic ethical system in this sense, he cites Herbert Spencer's view that "good" in its ethical sense means "conducive to life, in self or others." Non-naturalism, in these terms, could be simply defined as the view that "good" and other basic ethical terms cannot be defined by reference to a natural object. (Strictly speaking Moore distinguished three types of theories: naturalistic theories, metaphysical theories according to which "good" is defined by reference to "an object which is only inferred to exist in a supersensible real world," and what might be termed non-naturalism proper according to which "good" cannot be defined by reference to anything else whatever.) It is not clear, however, that naturalism in ethics as presently understood, especially by those who regard themselves as naturalists, necessarily involves the thesis that "good" and other ethical terms are definable in terms of objects of experience. That thesis is stronger than the thesis that ethical judgments are empirically verifiable, in the sense that it entails but is not clearly entailed by the latter thesis. Many naturalists, it seems, want only to assert and defend the weaker thesis.

In general, one might distinguish two distinct issues in the controversy between naturalism and non-naturalism. One concerns what may be termed the *reducibility* of normative ethical judgments to purely factual statements; many naturalists tend to hold they can be so reduced, whereas non-naturalists deny it. Thus, Spencer held that "X is good" can simply be translated as "X is conducive to life, in self or others" without loss or change of meaning. The other issue concerns the *derivability* of normative ethical judgments from purely factual statements by ordinary inductive or deductive methods; naturalists hold they are so derivable whereas non-naturalists hold they are not. If ethical judgments can be reduced to factual statements, then it follows they can be derived from purely factual statements. But it is not clear that the converse holds true: one might hold that ethical judgments are derivable without holding that they are reducible. As suggested above it seems likely that many naturalists want only to defend the weaker thesis of the derivability of normative ethical judgments. Hence it seems better to characterize naturalism in terms of the weaker thesis that normative ethical judgments are derivable by ordinary methods from purely factual statements. In terms of the distinction stated in this way, Santayana, Perry, Dewey, and those who hold the Ideal Observer theory are naturalists; Moore and the Intuitionists are what may be termed Cognitivist Non-naturalists, as distinguished from the noncognitivists who are also in a sense non-naturalists but who deny that normative ethical judgments can be said to be known to be true at all.

Finally, naturalistic theories may be divided into (IAa) *subjectivist* theories and (IAb) *objectivist* theories. The distinction intended here is that for a subjectivist, as I am using the term, normative ethical judgments are statements about the speaker himself. An example might be the Personal Approval Theory, according to which the statement "X is good" means "I (the speaker) approve of X and desire others to approve of it." For the objectivist, in contrast, ethical judgments are not statements about the speaker, or not only statements about the speaker. They also assert, at least in part, some proposition which is true or false no matter what the speaker's own feelings, desires, attitudes, beliefs, etc. may be. Thus, Spencer was what may be termed an objective naturalist; the statement that something is conducive to life in self or others, while in a certain sense partly about the speaker, is not simply a statement about the speaker. In terms of this distinction, Santayana holds what may be termed a subjective naturalistic theory:

Perry, Dewey, and the Ideal Observer theorists are objective naturalists.

In terms of the above distinctions, Moore and the Intuitionists hold the same meta-ethical position, which may be termed "objective nonnaturalism." They both hold that normative ethical judgments such as "You acted wrongly in stealing that money" are true or false independently of the speaker's beliefs, desires, attitudes, etc., and also that such statements cannot be reduced to or derived inductively or deductively from purely factual statements. It might be argued, therefore, that the issue between Moore and the intuitionists is not meta-ethical at all, but normative. The issue between them is whether or not the rightness or obligatoriness of actions depends entirely on the goodness of the consequences of the action. Moore held that it does; the intuitionists held it does not. Yet, one could regard this issue too as meta-ethical. The issue, one might say, is whether terms such as "right," "wrong," "ought," and the like as applied to actions can be defined wholly in terms of "good" as applied to the consequences of actions. Moore, in *Principia Ethica,* held they are so definable, whereas Sidgwick, Prichard, and Ross hold they are not. Since the issue, stated this way, has to do with definitions of ethical terms, it might be regarded as an issue of analysis and, as such, meta-ethical. Accordingly, one might add a further distinction to the above scheme of classification, namely between (IBa) *teleological* theories and (IBb) *non-teleological* theories. Briefly, a teleological theory is one which holds that the rightness of acts is definable in terms of the goodness of the consequences of the act: a non-teleological theory holds it is not so definable. Moore, in these terms, was a teleological objective non-naturalist, as contrasted with the intuitionists, who are non-teleological objective non-naturalists.

It should be said that most books on ethics now treat the issue between Moore and the intuitionists—that is, the issue between teleological and non-teleological or "deontological" theories—as an issue in normative ethics. But it is not altogether clear why it must be so treated unless, following Stevenson, one were to regard Moore's definitions of "right" and "obligatory" (in terms of consequences) as persuasive definitions and, as such, disguised value judgments. But if one were to think along these lines, many naturalistic theories such as

Perry's, which provide naturalistic definitions of ethical terms, would also appear to be normative. Yet, naturalistic theories such as Perry's are generally treated as meta-ethical. (It should be said that Stevenson himself did draw the conclusion, in effect, that Perry's theory was to some extent normative. Speaking of Perry's remark that "An object which is loathed by L and M is worse, other things being equal, than an object which is loathed only by L, or only by M," Stevenson observes that "In effect, 'worse' has been persuasively defined in support of the majority".) In general, the difficulty of deciding whether the issue between Moore and the Intuitionists is meta-ethical or normative shows again the difficulty in regarding the latter distinction as an absolutely clear-cut one. There is a sense in which the classification of a theory as meta-ethical or normative depends on what one's own meta-ethical position is.

In conclusion, I want to say something about the classification of the two most recent theories to be discussed—Hare's theory and the Good Reasons theory. In the case of Hare's theory (similar considerations hold for Stevenson) I suggested he is a non-cognitivist on grounds that, for him, normative ethical judgments contain imperatives. If a judgment is even partly an imperative, it seems plausible to hold, the judgment as a whole cannot be said to be true or false; e.g. one would not ordinarily ascribe truth or falsity to "There's the door—open it." But on the other hand it may also seem plausible to hold that if a judgment contains as one of its parts a factual statement, then one can speak of evidence supporting the judgment as a whole. If one were to take the latter position, Hare and Stevenson too should be regarded as naturalists, since they hold that moral judgments do in some sense contain factual statements as well as having an imperative aspect. The classification of the Good Reasons approach is even more difficult. Insofar as this approach emphasizes the support of normative ethical judgments by purely factual considerations, it resembles naturalism. But insofar as it holds that the relation between purely factual premises and ethical conclusions is *sui generis,* not an ordinary inductive or deductive relation, it resembles objective non-naturalism. In general, the most recent ethical theories may be regarded as to some extent attempts to go beyond the classification I have suggested and find new alternatives. But while the issues and positions discussed in the earlier chapters of this book have thus in a sense been superseded by later work, a survey of the entire period such as the present work attempts may contribute something to the understanding and appreciation of present trends. For one way of understanding these trends is to see them as attempts to resolve past controversies.

I

MOORE AND THE REFUTATION OF NATURALISM

1 Three Assumptions of Moore's Ethical Theory

MY AIM IN THE PRESENT CHAPTER is to discuss critically G. E. Moore's ethical theory, and in particular what is probably the most influential and widely accepted part of Moore's ethical theory, his refutation of naturalistic ethics in *Principia Ethica*. I want to begin this discussion, however, by considering three basic assumptions Moore makes in *Principia Ethica*—assumptions which, as it turns out, are involved in Moore's very characterization of naturalism. I shall try to show that these assumptions are not in fact universally held by philosophers who regard themselves as naturalists, and, perhaps more important, that these assumptions are controversial in the sense that they have in fact beeen challenged by many philosophers in the course of the development of recent ethical theory.

Moore, as stated in the previous chapter, characterizes naturalism in ethics as the thesis that "good" in its ethical sense may be defined with reference to a natural object, understanding by a "natural object" something that is observed or inferred from what is observed by ordinary inductive methods. This characterization of naturalism involves three assumptions which are fundamental in *Principia Ethica*—so fundamental in fact that Moore does not really argue for them. He tends to take them for granted as not needing serious argument. The three assumptions in question may be stated in the following way. First, Moore assumes that the fundamental concept in ethics is the concept of goodness, in a sense of "goodness" in which it applies to the consequences of actions as well as to actions themselves—as opposed to the view that the fundamental concept of ethics is the concept of rightness, or obligatoriness, as applied to actions themselves. In his characterization of naturalism, Moore seems to assume that the naturalist accepts this assumption, and that the issue between Moore and the naturalist must therefore concern the analysis of goodness in a generic sense, as applying to things other than conduct. Second, and more important, Moore assumes there is a clear and generally understood concept of what he terms "intrinsic goodness" (as opposed to extrinsic goodness, or instrumental goodness), a concept which does not really need serious explanation and defense. And, third, Moore seems to assume that the term "good" in its ethical sense must, if it has any meaning at all, designate a property or set of properties, and that to define the term "good" is to mention such a property or set of properties.

It is perhaps not quite true to say that Moore simply made these assumptions without any argument whatever. He did offer certain arguments, especially for what I have called the first assumption. But it would be not far wrong to say that he considered them all as so obvious that they needed no extended and serious argument, especially as regards the second and third assumptions, and perhaps most especially as regards the third. Yet, as I shall argue, all three assumptions raise certain basic problems in ethics, and have in fact been questioned by many recent ethicists following Moore. Thus, Moore's ethical writings illustrate what may be a common phenomenon in the history of ideas. A thinker's ideas often owe their influence to the fact that he brought to light certain assumptions which the thinker himself took to be self-evident, but which thinkers following him, in the light of the consequences implied by these assumptions, questioned and indeed rejected in favor of alternative assumptions. In any event, Moore's three assumptions, as stated above, have in fact become main topics of controversy in recent ethical theory. In the following paragraphs I want to suggest some of the problems attending each of the three assumptions.

Ethics, Moore argues, is concerned with the question "What is good conduct?" But, he maintains, it is concerned with much more: in fact it is concerned with the general question "What is good?" And in the part of *Principia Ethica* in which Moore sought to answer the question "What is good?" in the sense of "What things are good?" as opposed to the question of how good is to be defined, Moore took the position that the most important goods are not kinds of conduct at all, but rather certain kinds of experiences, in particular the enjoyment of beautiful objects and the pleasures involved in human relationships such as love and friendship. Moore thus consciously broadened the scope of ethics to make it a general theory of value, rather than confining it to what may be termed specifically moral questions—questions concerning good and bad conduct. Moore was aware that this was a departure from the way ethics had generally been treated. And he did give an argument for his position. "Ethics," Moore argued,

> is undoubtedly concerned with the question what good conduct is; but, being concerned with this, it obviously does not start at the beginning, unless it is prepared to tell us what is good as well as what is conduct. For "good conduct" is a complex notion: all conduct is not good; for some is certainly bad and some may be indifferent. And on the other hand, other things, beside conduct, may be good; and if they are so, then "good" denotes some property that is common to them and conduct; and if we examine good conduct alone of all good things, then we shall be in danger of mistaking for this property some property which is not shared by those other things: and thus we shall have made a mistake about Ethics even in this limited sense; for we shall not know what good conduct really is. (*Principia Ethica*, p. 2)

But this argument itself makes an important assumption whose truth is not obvious. For, granting that there are other things besides conduct which we call "good," it certainly does not *follow* that when we call these other things "good," we are using the word "good" to designate the same property it designates when applied to conduct—assuming indeed that it designates a property at all. It certainly seems to be the case that "good" is used in a wide variety of senses: we speak of "good roads," "good weather," "good health," for example, and it is far from clear that "good" in such uses means the same thing it means in "good conduct." In a certain sense it might be held that Moore did not broaden the scope of ethics enough: had he considered all the different ordinary uses of "good," we would have seen the difficulty in holding that "good" in all these uses designates the same property. And, assuming there is some sense in which "good" in all these uses has the same meaning, he might have been led to question the assumption that the meaning of "good" is to be identified with some property the term denotes—considerations which led Hare in *The Language of Morals* to stress the commendatory meaning of "good" as opposed to its descriptive meaning. In any event, it is at least possible that "good" when applied to aesthetic experiences, for example, does *not* denote the same property it denotes when applied to good conduct. If it does not, Moore has given no good reason for concerning oneself with goods other than good conduct in a treatise on ethics.

The above remarks concern Moore's assumption that ethics should be concerned with "good" in a sense in which it applies to more than good conduct. Perhaps the more fundamental assumption, however, is that ethics is concerned primarily with goodness as applied to consequences of actions, as opposed to right and wrong as applied to acts themselves. Moore himself points out the distinction involved at the very beginning of *Principia Ethica*. He argues that writers on ethics have in fact dealt with two questions which they do not usually clearly distinguish, namely, "What kind of things ought to exist for their own sakes?" and "What kind of actions ought we to perform?" The first question, Moore says, amounts to the question of what is good in itself or has intrinsic value; the second is the question "What is it that we ask about an action when we ask whether we ought to do it, whether it is a right action or a duty?" Moore's first assumption is that the first question is the fundamental question in ethics, in the sense that once one has the answer to it, one can answer the second question. For, Moore held, "right" and "duty" when applied to actions can be defined in terms of "good." Roughly, a right action for Moore is one that is at least as productive of good as any other action one might have done in the circumstances: an action is a duty when any other action would produce less good, all things considered. Moore himself in

Principia Ethica and in his later book *Ethics* did not, it seems, regard this assumption as requiring serious argument. But it became the center of controversy between Moore and the so-called Intuitionists such as Prichard and Ross. For the Intuitionists, right and duty cannot be defined in terms of good: they argue that the notions of rightness and obligatoriness are primitive notions, not reducible to anything else—in much the same way that Moore himself argued in connection with "good." Clearly basic issues, both meta-ethical and normative, are involved here, issues I want to discuss later in connection with Intuitionism.

The second assumption Moore makes is that there is a relatively clear and unproblematic concept of intrinsic goodness, as opposed to extrinsic or instrumental goodness—a concept, Moore appears to have held, which is employed in all ethical theories that need to be taken seriously, including the theories that Moore terms "naturalistic." Moore himself asserted that "everybody is constantly aware of this notion." Yet, the expressions "intrinsic goodness" or "intrinsic value," as employed by Moore and by most writers on normative ethics since Moore, designate rather clearly a technical notion. The expression "intrinsic value" and synonyms such as "intrinsically desirable" or "intrinsically good" do have an ordinary use. But in their ordinary use they do not mean what Moore meant by "intrinsic value." For Moore, intrinsic value contrasts with extrinsic value: it is the value a thing has because of its inherent nature as opposed to value which depends on a thing's relations, or accompaniments, or consequences. In ordinary speech, in contrast, intrinsic value seems to contrast with such things as sentimental value (as when we say the jewelry has little intrinsic value but great value to its owner), or with the actual market value (as when we say the property is intrinsically worth much more than the price one can get for it in existing economic circumstances), or with historical value, or military value, or symbolic value, and so on. Insofar as there is a general notion of intrinsic value in ordinary speech, it seems to be roughly the value a thing has to most people in ordinary circumstances, as contrasted with its value to exceptionally situated persons or under exceptional circumstances. It does not necessarily contrast with extrinsic or instrumental value at all: we speak of a diamond as having intrinsic value, for example, although its value depends largely on its scarcity, and Sidgwick, who did not use "intrinsic value" as a technical term, speaks of the intrinsic value of services (as opposed to the price actually paid for them). Clearly services have value primarily as means, not as ends in themselves.

The fact that the concept of intrinsic value is a technical notion that needs careful explanation emerges clearly in some of Moore's later writings, in which he tried to define the notion in various ways. The problem is that Moore gave several definitions, and it is not at all clear that the same concept is involved. Thus, first, in his book *Ethics*, written in 1912, Moore defined the notion of intrinsic value as follows:

> Saying that a thing is intrinsically good . . . means that it would be a good thing that the thing in question should exist, even if it existed quite alone, without any further accompaniments or consequences whatever. (*Ethics*, p. 42)

Second, in his essay "The Conception of Intrinsic Value," written in 1917, Moore gives this account of intrinsic value:

> To say that a kind of value is "intrinsic" means merely that the question whether a thing possesses it, and in what degree it possesses it, depends solely on the intrinsic nature of the thing in question. (*Philosophical Studies*, p. 260)

And third, in his essay "Is Goodness a Quality?," written in 1932, Moore suggests that "intrinsically good" may be defined as "worth having for its own sake" in a sense of "having" in which only experiences may be said to be "had." Perhaps Moore regarded these as simply verbally different characterizations of the same concept. But it seems clear that the third definition, at least, involves a different concept than the first two, a point Moore himself later made. In "A Reply to My Critics" in *The Philosophy of G. E. Moore*, Moore remarked that the concept of intrinsic value as defined in "Is Goodness A Quality?" would preclude ascribing intrinsic value to a state of affairs in which two or more persons are having experiences that are worth having for their own sakes, whereas the first two accounts would not: hence, Moore concluded, the account in "Is Goodness A Quality?" introduces a new sense of "good."

More generally, the third account differs from the first two in that, according to the third, it would be contradictory to ascribe intrinsic value to anything that is not an experience, whereas it would not be on the first two accounts. As for the first two accounts, it is less clear that they involve different concepts. But it might be argued that they do, for the following reason. A thing could have a value which depends entirely on its intrinsic properties—hence intrinsic value according to the second account—and yet be such that it is logically or conceptually impossible for it to exist "quite alone." Thus, one might want to ascribe an intrinsic value to certain actions, such as an act of compassion. But it seems clear that in general it is impossible to conceive an action as existing "quite alone," if that means apart from an agent. And an act such as an act of compassion presupposes another person who is the object of the action. Since something might therefore have intrinsic value in the second sense, and yet be such that it is meaningless to ascribe intrinsic value to it in the first sense, different concepts of intrinsic value are involved.

In the above paragraph I have argued that there are differences in the concept of intrinsic value as variously defined by Moore. But even if there were no important differences, there are difficulties in Moore's concept of intrinsic value, difficulties which could and in fact have inclined some philosophers to give up the notion altogether. One of these difficulties, emphasized by William Frankena in his essay "Value and Obligation in the Ethics of G. E. Moore" in *The Philosophy of G. E. Moore,* is that Moore separates questions of value from questions of obligation. For Moore, it is not part of the meaning of "X is intrinsically valuable" that one has an obligation to try to produce X, or to prevent it from being destroyed. Moore held that "X has intrinsic value" entails "One ought to try to produce X." But for him, the relation is synthetic, not analytic. This position, however, poses problems. Apart from the generally problematic status of synthetic a priori knowledge, Moore's position is that obligation statements are never, strictly speaking, part of what is asserted in an assertion of intrinsic value. It would not therefore be a logical contradiction in the strict sense, on Moore's view, to assert that something is intrinsically good but that no one has any obligation to produce it, or that something is intrinsically bad but that everyone has an obligation to produce it. But if that is the case, there is a question whether Moore's notion of intrinsic goodness is a moral or ethical notion at all: if "good" means "morally good," it would seem contradictory in the strict sense to say that we have an obligation to destroy what is intrinsically good, since that would be equivalent to saying that we morally ought to destroy what is morally good.

Again, to make the same point somewhat differently, Moore's view appears to be that a statement of the form "You ought to destroy what is intrinsically good" or "You ought to produce what is intrinsically bad" is intelligible, in the same sense that "All cubes have twelve corners" is presumably perfectly intelligible although false and known a priori to be false. But it might be argued that a statement such as "You ought to produce what is intrinsically bad" is not even intelligible: we should say that a person who makes it shows thereby his failure to understand the meanings of "bad" and "ought." Hence, the connection between value statements and obligation statements seems closer than Moore was willing to admit. Moore, it is true, was willing to go a considerable way in connecting value statements and obligation statements. He was even prepared to say that in some instances such statements are logically equivalent, e.g. the statement that X is intrinsically valuable, and the statement that it would be one's duty to create a world with nothing in it but X rather than creating no world at all. But he was never prepared to say that obligation statements are part of the meaning of value statements: he contrasted his view with the view that value and obligation statements are "identical," presumably meaning by "identical" something like "having the same meaning, as a whole or in part." The problem is difficult to handle in that the very distinction between analytic and synthetic judgments has itself become problematic, whereas Moore never questioned the distinction. But insofar as a clear analytic-synthetic distinction can be made, Moore, it can be argued, was mistaken in wanting to regard all statements connecting value with obligation as synthetic.

In general, Moore's concept of intrinsic value includes no reference whatever to the actions, choices, preferences, desires, etc. of human agents who make ascriptions of intrinsic value. For Moore, statements of the form "X has intrinsic value" are simply statements about X and about nothing else. One might say that, for Moore, value statements are purely objective, in the sense that they are in no way statements about the speaker himself. That intrinsic value statements are in this sense purely objective probably seemed to Moore to be too trivially true to need defense. If by "intrinsic value" one means a value that is in some sense "in" the thing which has it, as Moore doubtlessly assumed, it appears to follow that to ascribe intrinsic value to a thing is simply to say something about that thing and nothing else. But it could be held that intrinsic value need not be understood in this purely objective way: it could be held that to say that a thing has intrinsic value is to say, among other things, that we ought to prefer its existence to its non-existence, to choose its presence rather than its absence, and to approve of it ourselves and commend it to others. Moore, I should argue, confused the *grounds* for ascribing intrinsic value to a thing with the *meaning* of such ascriptions. The grounds for ascribing an intrinsic value to a thing may well be simply the properties of the thing itself and nothing else. (Even this may be argued: it seems at least plausible to hold, as H. J. Paton suggested in his essay "The Alleged Independence of Good" in the Moore volume, that the intrinsic value of an action such as sharing water with a companion depends to an extent on the surrounding circumstances. Sharing my water with my companion has much more intrinsic value when it is the last water we will have for several days than it would if water were plentiful). But granting this, it does not follow that the meaning of an intrinsic value statement is purely objective; as suggested above it could be held that what such an ascription means is that we as subjects ought to have certain desires, attitudes, preferences, etc. in regard to the thing in question.

But in any case, Moore's view that ascriptions of intrinsic value are purely objective has been taken by some philosophers since Moore as grounds for concluding that nothing has intrinsic value, or, more radically, that the notion of intrinsic value is meaningless for ethics, on grounds that it is meaningless to ascribe value to anything except as an object of someone's desire and choice. Naturalists in particular, such as Dewey and Perry, would reject the notion of intrinsic value as value residing simply in the thing said to have such value. Dewey in particular, for reasons I will discuss later, rejected the notion of intrinsic value altogether. Hence there is a sense in which Moore's characterization of naturalism is in terms of a concept of value which some naturalists were to abandon.

The third assumption Moore made is that "good" in its ethical sense designates a property, or else has no meaning at all. And the further assumption seems to be that the meaning of "good" is to be identified with the property, or set of properties, which it designates. This assumption, more than any other, appears to be one which Moore took to be so obviously true that it needed no argument nor even an explicit statement. Yet, the assumption is far from being self-evident. Noncognitivists such as Stevenson and Hare in fact reject the assumption: they hold that while expressions such as "good" and "right" are certainly meaningful, they do not have, or at least do not primarily have, what they term "descriptive meaning"; that is, such terms are not primarily property-designating terms at all. And even if one were to hold that ethical terms do designate properties, it does not follow that the meaning of such terms is to be identified with the properties which they designate. The latter assumption, indeed, can easily be shown to be mistaken. For it seems to make no sense, for example, to say that I am now observing the meaning of "good," even though one might hold that "good" designates an observable property. Moore, one might say, confused the meaning of a term with its reference. But apart from this confusion, Moore in effect, as indicated above, simply assumed what Hare has called "Descriptivism," i.e. the thesis that if ethical terms are meaningful at all, they designate a property of the thing to which they are applied. A major development in recent ethical theory has been the rejection of the assumption that ethical terms, if they are meaningful, must designate a property. More recent philosophers have sought new kinds of meaning which will allow one to say that ethical terms, while certainly meaningful, are not primarily descriptive. Here again Moore's influence was profound; not in the sense that later philosophers agreed with him, but that his work brought to light assumptions which Moore himself tended to take for granted but which later philosophers questioned and in many cases rejected.

2   Moore's Refutation of Naturalism

In the preceding section I have emphasized the fact that in his very statement of naturalism, Moore makes certain assumptions which many later naturalists do not accept. In the present section I want to consider critically Moore's argument against naturalism as Moore himself understood naturalism—the so-called "open question" argument. Naturalism as Moore himself understood it might be phrased somewhat more generally than Moore did, as follows: it is the view that ethical expressions such as "good" or "right" used in an ethical sense are synonymous with expressions which designate natural properties. Thus, to use again one of Moore's own examples, Spencer was a naturalist in that he held that the predicate "good" is synonymous with "conducive to life in self or others": he held that the latter expression can be substituted for the former in all ordinary contexts without loss or change of meaning. A question at once arises— namely, what is a natural property? It might be suggested that a natural property is one that can be observed. But Moore himself held that in some sense goodness is an observable property. And many properties Moore considered natural, such as conduciveness to life, are certainly not directly observable. Moore himself raised this question in *Principia Ethica,* but failed to give what he later considered a satisfactory answer. In *Principia Ethica,* section 26, Moore suggests that a natural property is one that can be conceived of as existing in time all by itself and not simply as a property of another thing. But this characterization is problematic (Moore later called it "utterly silly and preposterous") since, while properties such as brownness or squareness are certainly ones Moore would want to call "natural," it seems clear that they cannot be conceived of as existing "all by themselves." And there seem to be properties which are not in time at all, e.g. oddness, or evenness, as ascribed to numbers, which again Moore would almost certainly want to call "natural." It might be best, then, to abandon the notion of a natural property in characterizing naturalism, and simply characterize it as the view that ethical terms are synonymous with non-ethical terms. This too is not entirely satisfactory, since there seems to be no clear way of picking out ethical from non-ethical terms. Until a criterion is given, the decision to treat a given theory as naturalistic is therefore to a degree arbitrary. In practice, however, there has not been much serious disagreement on this matter: Moore and others following him are agreed that expressions such as "pleasant" or "conducive to life" or "forbidden by the ruler of our state" are non-ethical, as contrasted with expressions such as "worthy of desire," "obligatory," and similar expressions.

Moore's famous argument against naturalism, the open-question argument, might be phrased as follows in terms of the above definition of naturalism. Moore argued that if naturalism were true, there is some non-ethical expression "F" such that the question "Are F's good?"

would be equivalent to the question "Are F's F?" But, Moore argued, questions of the form "Are F's good?" where "F" is a non-ethical expression are always significant, whereas the question "Are F's F?" is not a significant question. Hence, he concluded, naturalism must be false. The argument may be stated in a slightly different and perhaps slightly more precise way as follows:

1. If naturalism is true, then some sentence of the form "Whatever is F is good" is analytic, where "F" is replaceable by a non-ethical expression.
2. If ethical sentences of the form "Whatever is F is good" are analytic, then we cannot significantly ask "Are F's good?"
3. But we can always significantly ask "Are F's good?"
4. Hence no sentence of the form "Whatever is F is good" is analytic, and hence naturalism is false.

Formally the argument is valid, and superficially at least it is clear. But there are difficulties, especially in the notion of "significance." The term "significant" has a number of meanings, and it seems clear that in one of its common meanings, the sense in which "significant" means "important," the question "Is X an F?" can be significant even though it is analytic. Thus, the question "Is a rhombus a parallelogram?" could certainly be an important question even though "A rhombus is a parallelogram" is presumably analytic. One can even imagine contexts in which "Are bachelors unmarried?" might be a significant (i.e. important) question, but surely "Bachelors are unmarried" is analytic if any statement is. And, on the other hand, many questions could be asked which lack significance in this sense even though their answers are not analytic: e.g. "How many words are there in *Principia Ethica?*" Moore, of course, was concerned with ethical generalizations such as "Pleasure is good." And he certainly wanted to say that a question such as "Are all pleasures good?" is an important question. But that cannot, it seems, be the sense in which he argues that analytic statements cannot be significantly questioned.

Moore suggests two clues as to what he means by saying that a statement can or cannot be significantly questioned. The first is contained in the following passage:

Moreover, anyone can easily convince himself by inspection that the predicate of this proposition [whatever we desire to desire is good]—"good"—is positively different from the notion of "de-siring to desire" which enters into the subject. "That we should desire to desire A is good" is not merely equivalent to "That A should be good is good." It may indeed be true that what we desire to desire is always also good; perhaps even the converse may be true; but it is very doubtful whether this is the case, and the mere fact that we understand very well what is meant by doubting it shows clearly that we have two different notions be-fore our minds. (*Principia Ethica*, p. 16)

Moore is arguing that no non-ethical expression is synonymous with the ethical predicate "good." His argument is that if this were so, then, for some non-ethical expression "F," the sentence "Whatever is F is good" would be equivalent to the tautology "Whatever is F is F," which, Moore holds, it is not. And such sentences are never equivalent because while the former can always be doubted, the latter cannot be doubted. By saying that sentences of the form "Whatever is F is F" cannot be doubted, Moore presumably means that their denials are self-contradictory. This suggests the possibility that when Moore says we can always significantly ask "Are F's good?" he means that "F's are not good" is never a self-contradiction. Moore's argument might, then, be restated in the following way:

1. If naturalism is true, then, for some non-ethical expression "F," the sentence "F's are not good" is self-contradictory.
2. But sentences of the form "F's are not good" are never self-contradictory.
3. Hence naturalism is false.

How does Moore know that it is never self-contradictory to deny sentences of the form "Whatever is F is good"? To say this is, after all, only another way of saying that "F's are good" is not analytic. And that is precisely what the naturalists affirm, as Moore conceives naturalism. The hedonist, for example, will surely have no trouble with Moore's argument: having defined "good" as "pleasant," and hence holding that "Whatever is pleasant is good" is analytic, he will simply reply that in point of fact it is self-contradictory to say that something is pleasant but not good. Moore would have no answer; at the very most his argument only pushes the dispute back a step with-out doing anything to settle it. I conclude that the above interpretation is not a satisfactory explanation of what Moore means by "significant question"; if it is, then Moore's open-question argument is unconvincing.

A second clue to what Moore might have meant by "significant question" is contained in the following passage:

> But whoever will attentively consider with himself what is actually before his mind when he asks the question "Is pleasure (or whatever it may be) after all good?" can easily satisfy himself that he is not merely wondering whether pleasure is pleasant. And if he will try this experiment with each suggested definition in succession he may become expert enough to recognize that in every case he has before his mind a unique object, with regard to the connection of which with any other object, a distinct question may be asked. (*Principia Ethica,* p. 16)

Again Moore is attacking the view that ethical words are synonymous with non-ethical expressions. And his argument is that when we ask "Are F's good?" we can recognize on reflection that there are two distinct things before our mind, and we are asking about the connection between them. The question "Is S P?" is significant, then, if S and P designate two distinct things; it is not significant if they designate only one thing. Moore's argument, interpreted in this way, can be paraphrased as follows:

1. If naturalism is true, there are sentences of the form "Whatever is F is good" in which "F" and "good" designate the same properties.
2. But whenever we ask "Are F's good?" we can see, on reflection, that "F" and "good" designate two distinct properties.
3. Hence naturalism is false.

Understood in this way, the dispute between Moore and naturalism reduces to the question of what is "before our minds" when we ask questions such as "Are all pleasures good?" And it is not easy to see how such a dispute can be settled. As Frankena has pointed out in his article "The Naturalistic Fallacy," the error of the naturalist, on Moore's view, would be a certain kind of blindness which prevents him from noting what in fact is before his mind. But the naturalist could make the rejoinder that Moore suffers from a kind of hallucination which makes him see two things where there is in fact only one.

Viewing the question as an empirical one, the issue would become one of accurately describing what we observe to be before our minds when we make certain statements or ask certain questions. Moore has not, it seems, given any empirical evidence for saying that we always have two distinct things before our minds when we ask, e.g. "Are all pleasures good?" It might well be that some do and others do not, with the result that naturalism is false for some and true for others. Or, it might be that at some times we do and at other times we do not have two distinct things before our minds, with the absurd result that naturalism is sometimes false and sometimes true. In fact, however, it is doubtful whether the issue is an empirical one at all. What sort of evidence would be required to show that we do or do not have two distinct things before our minds? Many naturalists would question the very notion of properties, in the sense of abstract entities which are designated by the words we use—a notion Moore seems to presuppose in the way he formulates the issue. To conclude, then, it is far from clear that Moore's open-question argument is a conclusive refutation of naturalism as Moore himself understood naturalism. Neither of the two interpretations discussed above seem to yield an argument which would appear convincing to naturalists. Moore may have been right in rejecting all naturalistic ethical theories. And in a latter chapter I will consider Hare's attempt to restate Moore's open-question argument, an attempt which many would consider more successful than Moore's own statement of the argument. But as far as Moore's own statement of the argument is concerned, it cannot be regarded as laying naturalism to rest once and for all.

3   Moore and the Problem of Ethical Knowledge

In the preceding sections of this chapter I have discussed, first, the assumptions Moore makes in his characterization of naturalism and, second, Moore's argument against naturalism: in connection with the latter, I have argued that Moore's refutation of naturalism is less conclusive than Moore himself and others have thought. In the present section I want to deal at least briefly with certain fundamental problems about ethical knowledge, problems which result more or less directly from Moore's own answer to the question of how good is to be defined. My purpose here is to suggest that even if one accepts

Moore's refutation of naturalism, his own ethical theory leads to certain important difficulties concerning ethical knowledge, difficulties which cannot be easily answered within the frameworth of Moore's theory, including the basic assumptions discussed in the first section.

Moore's own answer to the question "How is good to be defined?" is, as is generally known, that "good" in its ethical sense cannot be defined. Moore's thesis of the indefinability of good has to be understood however in the light of a rather special sense of "define." The sense in which good cannot be defined, according to Moore, is that it cannot be given what he terms an "analytic definition," which is roughly a definition mentioning the parts of the thing to be defined and their interrelationships. (Moore did not of course deny that "good" could be defined by what he termed an "arbitrary verbal definition"; he did not deny that one could simply stipulate a certain meaning of "good." And he also appears to have held that in some sense one could describe the meaning of "good" as ordinarily used—what he terms a "verbal definition proper." Indeed, the definitions of intrinsic value discussed above are in a sense definitions of "good" by Moore himself.) Good—what Moore terms the concept or object designated by "good"—cannot be defined, Moore held, because it is without parts. Hence Moore's thesis of the indefinability of good is essentially the thesis that good is "simple," i.e. has no parts. Adding this thesis to the thesis that good is not a natural property (Moore's conclusion from his refutation of naturalism), he reached the conclusion that good is a simple, non-natural property, a property whose presence in a thing can only be known by some kind of direct inspection or intuition.

Moore himself, it seems safe to say, took his thesis that "good" designates a simple non-natural property as his most important and also most conclusively established contribution to ethics. Yet, there are basic difficulties growing out of this thesis. First, it should perhaps be stressed that the theses of the non-naturalness and of the simplicity of good are logically independent. A naturalist might agree that good is simple in Moore's sense: presumably a hedonist who identifies good with pleasant would in fact accept it. And, on the other hand, one could agree with Moore in rejecting naturalism and disagree with him about the simplicity of good. One might, e.g., define good as that which we ought to desire, thereby making "good" designate a complex property but not in Moore's sense a natural property. But while

Moore does argue at some length that good is not a natural property, there is no real argument at all that good is simple. Moore, it may be said, never considered the possibility that "good" designates a complex non-natural property. Second, there are serious epistemological problems arising from Moore's thesis. As Moore himself points out, the consequence of his view that good is a simple non-natural property is that statements of the form "X is good" are synthetic (except for the limiting case of "What is good is good") and non-empirical—the former following from the simplicity thesis, and the latter from the non-naturalness thesis. This leads more or less directly to Moore's view that all statements of the form "X is good" cannot be in any usual sense proved to be true, but must rather be known to be true, if they can be known, by a process of direct inspection or intuition. That X is good, on Moore's account, could not be derived from some other proposition of the form "X is F" where "F" designates a complex property, either natural or non-natural (assuming that goodness is not itself part of F-ness). Hence propositions of the form "X is good" cannot, it seems, be established or supported by either of the ways in which propositions are ordinarily considered to be established: not by induction from experience, because that would be to make good a natural property, nor by deduction, except in the trivial sense in which "X is A" can be deduced from "X is A and B." For Moore, propositions of the form "X is good" must, it seems, each one separately be taken as self-evident, if taken as true at all. And this position involves serious epistemological problems. One such problem is that the notion of synthetic truths that are non-empirical has become increasingly problematic in recent philosophy. For presumably such truths are alleged to be necessary truths. And the notion of necessity involved is far from easy to explain. In the case of synthetic non-empirical truths, necessity does not mean logical necessity, as it does in the case of analytic statements. Nor does it mean causal necessity—the sort of necessity involved in saying that unsupported bodies "must" fall. Some other kind of necessity is involved, but Moore leaves it obscure just what this necessity amounts to.

One might well agree with Moore that certain statements of the form "X's are good" are true and even in a certain sense self-evident, meaning by self-evidence simply that no reasonable person with the relevant knowledge and experience would deny them. But Moore seems to be committed to more: that the enjoyment of beautiful objects is good is, for him, not simply a fact of experience, not even a truth about what ideal judges would prefer, but is rather a necessary truth. And it is unclear in Moore how such a judgment could be supported or even what it is supposed to mean. (In section 3 of the Conclusion I will, however, suggest that there can be a necessary connection between two statements A and B, where B is not included in the meaning of A. If this is right, there is a sense of "necessity" which is distinct from both causality and from analyticity, as "analyticity" is most commonly characterized.) But, further, Moore's position seems to reach an impasse in the following way. Moore held that statements of the form "X is good" are intuitive. But he says that all he really means by calling them "intuitive" is that they cannot be proved true in any way. "Intuitive," he says, means simply accepted as true without evidence or proof, simply on the grounds that the proposition in question seems self-evident. But the fact that a proposition seems self-evident, Moore holds, does not guarantee its truth. There is no such guarantee. For Moore, then, there seems to be lacking any criterion of truth for ethical judgments. If there were a cognitive faculty involved in intuition which we had some independent reason to think infallible or even generally reliable, then we would have reason for thinking that the ethical propositions which seem to us self-evident are in fact true. But Moore holds there is no such faculty of intuition as traditionally conceived by philosophers such as Descartes, for example; there is no cognitive faculty, he holds, which is such that we can be certain that the propositions accepted as true on the basis of an exercise of that faculty are bound to be true. (Moore may have had in mind the problem that even if there were such a faculty, we could not be sure that its employment in ethics would lead to correct results unless there were some independent test for the truth of ethical propositions—which according to Moore there is not.) But the result of Moore's position could easily be viewed as a kind of scepticism in ethics. One could conclude that we never have adequate grounds for asserting the truth of any ethical judgment.

Even further, one might draw the conclusion that since there is no way of knowing whether an ethical judgment is true or not, on Moore's account, the very notion of truth and falsity have no meaning in connection with ethical judgments. For in general, one might argue, it only makes sense to raise the question whether a given proposition is true if there is some criterion or test of truth in regard to propositions of that kind. Considerations of this kind, in fact, have led philosophers to the conclusion that since ethical judgments are completely unverifiable, they do not really express propositions at all and, as A. J. Ayer expresses it, they "say nothing."

The problem raised above, the seeming unverifiability of ethical judgments on Moore's account, presents an especially serious problem when one considers the fact of ethical disagreement. As long as there is no disagreement about the truth of an ethical proposition, then one might say there is no practical problem resulting from the unverifiability of such propositions, although even then one would not be justified, on Moore's account, in taking general agreement as a test or criterion of the truth of ethical propositions. But when there is disagreement, Moore's account seems to lead to a final impasse. And there certainly is such disagreement: normative ethics would not have the importance generally ascribed to it unless it offered some hope of providing methods for settling ethical disagreement. There is, for one thing, a certain sense in which the very fact of ethical disagreement is hard to explain on Moore's account. His view is that ethical judgments of the form "X is good" are a priori, not empirical. But if they are a priori, it would seem that their truth ought to be generally accepted by all who understand them. Indeed that might be one way of characterizing an a priori truth. Hence the claim that ethical judgments are a priori would seem to conflict with the fact of widespread ethical disagreement, assuming there is in fact such disagreement.

More important, however, Moore's account seems to provide no way whatever for resolving ethical disagreement. Each party to the disagreement can only appeal to his own intuitions, without having any way of showing that his intuitions are right and the other person's are wrong—a situation that, as suggested above, has led positivistically-minded philosophers to draw the conclusion that there is no sense in speaking of "right" and "wrong" in this connection. One might almost say that Moore's position, then, commits him to a denial in some sense of ethical disagreement. Yet, Moore's own normative views are far from universally accepted. And even within Moore's own normative system serious disagreement could arise; Moore's view is that there are several things which are independently intrinsically good, such as aesthetic experiences, love, and virtues such as courage and compassion. Disagreement might well arise as to what the order of priorities among these should be. In sum, then, Moore's view that ethical judgments are in his sense intuitive leads to the conclusion that they are unverifiable, and that conclusion suggests that Moore's meta-ethics makes normative ethics either unnecessary or impossible, assuming that at least one main aim of normative ethics is to provide ways of resolving existing ethical disagreements.

It should be said that Moore was aware of the problem of the verification of ethical judgments, and did provide a kind of method for verifying them. This is the so-called method of isolation. Consider, Moore says, whether the thing you are inclined to consider good would still be considered good if it were the only thing that existed in the entire universe. If it would be so considered, then you are justified in ascribing intrinsic value to it; if not, then you are not so justified. Much of the ethical disagreement that exists, Moore suggests, results from failure to use this method: failure to agree results from not really considering the same question. If everyone used the method of isolation, their results would tend to converge much more than they in fact do. There is, moreover, a principle which Moore states in his essay "The Conception of Intrinsic Value" which could also be viewed as providing a kind of test of ethical judgments. The principle in question is that if two things have the same natural intrinsic properties, then they must have the same intrinsic value. As Moore himself states the principle: "A kind of value is intrinsic if and only if when anything possesses it, that same thing or anything exactly like it would necessarily or must always, under the same circumstances, possess it to exactly the same degree." According to this principle, if one were to ascribe goodness to a thing on one occasion and not do so on another similar occasion, or if one were to ascribe intrinsic value to a certain thing, say a thing owned by oneself, and not ascribe value, or ascribe less value, to another exactly similar thing, say a thing owned by another, then on Moore's principle one would have to conclude that one or the other of the two ascriptions must be mistaken. It is not quite true, then, that Moore provides absolutely no way of verifying ethical judgments. But problems still remain. Unless Moore can provide a way of settling disagreements between persons who have used the method of isolation, and who are consistent in their value judgments, it is not clear that his methods take one very far toward settling ethical disagreements. And there do seem to be such disagreements, e.g. between Moore himself and W. D. Ross on the intrinsic value of knowledge.

Further, the methods available in Moore's account themselves involve difficulties. The method of isolation, as suggested previously, cannot be used in the case of things which cannot be conceived of as existing all alone. Yet, many of the things which have commonly been regarded as having intrinsic value seem incapable of so existing, e.g. actions, intentions, motives, and traits of character such as courage or compassion. In general, actions, for example, cannot be conceived of apart from some agent. And many particular actions presuppose persons other than the agent toward whom the action is directed, e.g. just or compassionate actions. Moore himself, it seems, regarded such things as courage and compassion as "states of consciousness" and was only prepared to ascribe intrinsic value to them when so regarded. But it seems doubtful whether one can really separate even in thought the state of consciousness from the actions which display it: the alleged mental state of courage, for example, seems to be a disposition to feel and act in certain ways. And in any case, a state of consciousness would seem to imply a subject which has it. Moore's method of isolation is thus itself somewhat problematic; Moore's own use of the method has been criticized on grounds that he tried to separate things that are conceptually inseparable such as pleasure and consciousness.

The other method, based on the assumption that things with the same intrinsic nature must have the same intrinsic value—itself a somewhat doubtful assumption—also does little to help settle value disagreements. The notion of "intrinsic nature" is not entirely clear, and certain disputes in normative ethics could be viewed as involving different conceptions of the intrinsic nature of an action; e.g. whether the agent's intention is part of the intrinsic nature of the action, or whether the fact that others are doing the same action is to be viewed as part of the act itself. In any case the second method really only asserts that one's value judgments must be in a certain sense consistent, and it seems highly likely that there are many equally consistent sets of valuations which nevertheless conflict. Consistency in the relevant sense is at most a necessary condition for arriving at an acceptable normative system; it is hardly sufficient. In sum, then, while it is not quite true that Moore provides no way of testing statements of the form "X is good," it is very nearly true. The methods available on Moore's account take us only a little way toward verifying such claims, and hence do not help a great deal to meet the demand for a method of settling ethical disagreements.

So far in this section I have been concerned with the problem of our knowledge of what things are good—the fundamental problem in ethics according to Moore himself. By way of concluding this chapter I want to say something about the problem, in Moore's theory, of our knowledge of what actions are right and wrong. Since Moore defines the notions of rightness and obligatoriness in terms of the notion of goodness, it follows that to the extent that there are difficulties in knowing what is good, there are also to the same degree difficulties in knowing which actions are right and wrong. But it is readily apparent, given Moore's definition of "right action," that the difficulty in knowing which actions are right is far greater than the difficulty in knowing what is good. For Moore, a right action is one that produces at least as much good as any other action that could have been done in the circumstances. Hence, as Moore himself points out, to claim to know for certain that an act is right, one would have to claim to know all the future consequences of the action. But it seems clear that one would never in practice be able to justify a claim to know all the future consequences of any action. And if there are an infinite number of consequences then in a certain sense the notion of "all the future consequences," and hence the notion of right itself, lose their meaning. Hence it follows on Moore's theory that we are never justified in claiming to know that an action is right or wrong, a result that appears paradoxical. Nor, even, is it clear that we are ever justified in claiming that an action is probably right, or more probably right than wrong, on Moore's account. For to speak of probability seems to imply that we can make some rough estimate of the frequency with which actions of that sort have good consequences on the whole. And if we can never know in any individual case whether an act does have good consequences on the whole, it is hard to see how we could be in a position to make even rough estimates of the sort required. The best one could do, on Moore's account, is to claim that relative to the evidence available to us at the time, it is probable that an action is right. But we must always be prepared to revise our judgment in the light of new evidence. We could know, in other words, that A *seems* right—i.e. has the greatest probability of producing good consequences on the basis of the evidence available to us at the time—but not that A *is* right.

In summary, I have tried in this chapter to suggest problems in Moore's ethical theory primarily as stated in *Principia Ethica*. In particular I have tried to show that Moore's refutation of naturalism—itself characterized by Moore in a way that would by no means be acceptable to all those philosophers who regard themselves as naturalists in ethics—is inconclusive. And in the last section I have tried to show that even accepting Moore's refutation of naturalism, the view he advances as an alternative presents problems of its own, problems in particular about the very possibility of ethical knowledge. In later chapters I want to explore some of the further alternatives put forth in recent ethical theories, alternatives which their supporters would consider more acceptable than either naturalism or Moore's theory itself.

II

INTUITIONISM

IN THE PRESENT CHAPTER I want to consider the ethical theory commonly called "intuitionism," especially as held by Henry Sidgwick in his book *The Methods of Ethics;* by H. A. Prichard in his 1912 article "Does Moral Philosophy Rest on a Mistake?"; and by W. D. Ross in his book *The Right and the Good.* I will conclude with a discussion of some of the more important difficulties in intuitionism, difficulties which to some extent are shared with Moore's theory. Indeed, since the issues between Moore and the intuitionists are not clearly fundamentally meta-ethical issues at all, less time need perhaps be spent on the latter than was spent on the former. Still, there are differences. And in any case in view of the importance generally attached to the intuitionists, and a certain contemporary interest in their views in connection with their attack on utilitarianism, a discussion of their theories as distinct from Moore's seems warranted.

1 Sidgwick and the Irreducibility of "Ought"

The term "intuitionism" was first used in more or less its present sense in ethics by Sidgwick in his *Methods of Ethics;* intuitionism is one of the three main types of ethical theory Sidgwick discusses, the other two being utilitarianism and egoism. It would seem, then, that since utilitarianism and egoism are clearly normative theories, intuitionism should also be. Yet, it is not clear that this is so. Sidgwick regards it as basically a thesis concerning ethical knowledge, as indeed the name implies. And there seems no reason why it could not be combined with any normative ethical theory, and in particular with utilitarianism. Indeed, Sidgwick himself wanted to combine in some sense intuitionism with utilitarianism. Why, then, did he treat them as contrasting theories? The answer lies in a distinction Sidgwick made between intuitionism in a broader sense and intuitionism in a narrower and stricter sense. In the broader sense, intuitionism is simply the view that some ethical propositions are known to be true immediately and without proof—the traditional philosophical conception of intuitive as opposed to discursive or inferential knowledge. In this sense, it seems clear, any normative ethical theory is consistent with intuitionism. And, it may be noted, Moore was an intuitionist in this broader sense, insofar as he held that judgments of intrinsic goodness can only be known to be true directly and without proof. In the narrower sense, however, intuitionism is defined by Sidgwick as the view that we can know that certain *actions* are morally right directly and immediately, and without consideration of their consequences. It is of course in this sense that Moore was not an intuitionist, whereas men such as Prichard and Ross were—with qualifications to be discussed later.

Sidgwick's own position is not entirely clear, but on the whole it appears he was an intuitionist in the narrower sense as well as in the wider sense. He held that there are certain ethical principles which are known to be true directly, without regard in a sense to consequences. In particular, he held this view concerning what he terms the axiom of justice or equity, according to which if an action is wrong when done by one person, A, to another, B, then it must also be wrong when done by B to A. Or, more generally, if it is right or wrong for a certain person to do an action in certain circumstances, it must be likewise right or wrong for all similarly situated persons to do the action. He likewise held there are self-evident "axioms" concerning the distribution of good: e.g. that I ought to aim at the greatest good regardless of whose good it is—that I ought not to aim at my own good at the expense of someone else's, if his good is greater than mine. This "axiom of benevolence" clearly seems a principle concerning what is right or obligatory and yet which, Sidgwick holds, is known directly to be true and cannot be derived from any kind of ulterior consideration (or at least need not be so derived since it can be known directly; Sidgwick seems not to be entirely clear on this point).

In the light of his view concerning these axioms, Sidgwick can reasonably be considered an intuitionist in the strict sense in which Prichard and Ross are intuitionists. Still, there are differences which might be stated in terms of a distinction between (a) moral principles, (b) moral rules, and (c) the moral rightness or wrongness of particular actions. Sidgwick held that certain principles concerning what is right or obligatory are known intuitively, understanding a principle to be a generalization which applies to all cases and which has no exception. It is less clear whether he held that any moral rules are known intuitively, understanding a moral rule to be a generalization such as "Promises ought to be kept" or "Debts ought to be paid" (favorite examples of later intuitionists), which do not apply in all morally significant cases and which do, it can be argued, have exceptions. And it is still less clear whether he held that one can intuit what is right or obligatory in particular cases of actions without reference to rules or principles. Probably he held that one cannot intuit what is right or wrong in particular cases. In this respect he differs from the later intuitionists who did apparently wish to hold that one could know intuitively what was right or obligatory in particular cases as distinct from knowing intuitively the truth of general moral rules or principles.

What makes it even more correct to associate Sidgwick with the later intuitionists is that he shares with them the view that the term "right" in the sense of "morally right" designates a unique unanalyzable concept which cannot be reduced to or defined in terms of any other concept. In this connection Sidgwick laid the basis for later intuitionism by arguing that statements of the form "X is right" cannot be reduced to other kinds of statements, in particular to some empirical statement, without some important loss or change of meaning. Thus, he argued (a) against the classical utilitarian theory as held by

Bentham, according to which "X is right" means that X is conducive to the greatest happiness of the greatest number, (b) against subjectivist theories, according to which statements of the form "X is right" mean that the speaker himself has a certain attitude or feeling toward X, (c) against the social approval theory, as it may be termed, according to which "X is right" means that society takes a certain attitude or acts in certain ways toward those who do or fail to do X, and finally (d) against the theological theory according to which "X is right" means that God commands or enjoins us to do X.

As against the classical utilitarian theory, Sidgwick argued, first, that it runs counter to the common belief that certain actions such as justice and truth-telling are right regardless of ulterior consequences, and, second, that it is meaningful to say, as indeed Bentham himself did, that it is right to aim at the general happiness, whereas if "right" simply meant "is conducive to the general happiness," the statement in question would reduce to "It is conducive to the general happiness to aim at the general happiness"—not exactly a tautology, as Sidgwick says, but a sociological rather than an ethical statement. It is not clear that Sidgwick himself accepts the alleged common belief that the rightness of certain kinds of actions such as justice and veracity are independent of ulterior consequences; the important argument against utilitarianism is the second argument. It anticipates Moore's open question argument, with the difference that Moore stressed the fact that naturalistic definitions of ethical terms transform significant ethical statements into tautologies, whereas Sidgwick only makes the claim that such substitutions yield non-ethical statements in place of ethical ones. The suggestiveness of Sidgwick's argument is that it shows how something very like Moore's argument concerning the indefinability of good can be used to show the indefinability of right as well: if it can be, Moore was on somewhat unsafe ground in using this kind of argument insofar as he himself held that right in its moral sense is definable.

As against subjectivism, Sidgwick used an argument later used by Moore, namely that contradictory ethical statements both turn out to be true. If by saying "X is right" one person, A, means "I, A, approve of X" and another person, B, means by "X is not right" that "I, B, disapprove of X," then both A's and B's statements could be true: yet, they appear to be contradictory. In a certain sense the argument is question-begging: the subjectivist can always say that the apparent contradiction is only verbal and that A and B are not in reality contradicting one another at all. But Sidgwick's argument does have the merit of pointing out the relativistic consequences of subjectivism, understanding "relativism" as the view that moral judgments which verbally contradict one another can both be true.

As against the social approval theory, Sidgwick argued that it would make nonsense of the idea of the moral rebel or reformer—the man who is prepared to reject the moral judgments of his society as mistaken. (He also argued, acutely, against the suggestion that "X is right" means that society disapproves of those who fail to do X: it makes sense to say that society ought to disapprove of some things, and that does not mean that society will disapprove of society's failing to disapprove of those things.) Finally, against the theological theory he argues that it makes sense to ascribe rightness to God's own actions, and that does not reduce to saying that God commands or enjoins himself to act as he does.

In general, Sidgwick's arguments represent acute criticisms of a variety of theories—the main reason why *The Methods of Ethics* remains one of the great works in ethical theory. At the same time it cannot be said that his arguments strictly prove the conclusion that "right" is the name of a primitive unanalyzable concept, although they may strongly suggest that conclusion. And, perhaps more important in the light of later intuitionism, Sidgwick seems not to recognize that his arguments could be used to make a far-reaching attack on utilitarianism. He seemed to think that the thesis of the indefinability of "right" and "ought" is perfectly consistent with utilitarianism as well as with intuitionism in the narrower and stricter sense. Possibly he was right in thinking this, but the point is not altogether clear. Certainly some versions of utilitarianism are incompatible with the unanalyzability of the concept of the morally right—Bentham's version, for example, or Moore's view in *Principia Ethica* that rightness can be defined in terms of goodness. Also, as Sidgwick himself remarks, to say X is right because it conduces to some ulterior result, Y, e.g. to the preservation of society, appears to entail that Y itself is something that ought to be aimed at. But the statement that one ought to aim at Y, e.g. the preservation of society, cannot itself be justified by the consequences of doing so—otherwise one would be embarked on an infinite regress.

If Sidgwick is right in holding that the idea that X is good as an end entails that one ought to aim at X, there are thus "ought" statements that cannot in a sense be justified in terms of ulterior consequences. It might be said that "One ought to aim at X" is justified by the fact that X is intrinsically good, thus making the notion of good prior to the notion of right or ought. But one might also say that "One ought to aim at X" is prior and that "X is intrinsically good" is to be explained in part in terms of the obligation to aim at X. The latter would seem to be Sidgwick's position: it is not the fact that aiming at the general good has some feature independent of the obligation to aim at it which makes it obligatory to do so, since part of the meaning of regarding something as ultimately good is that one ought to aim at it. Hence there is a certain sense in which utilitarianism is not compatible with the indefinability of the notions of "right" and "ought." Hence Sidgwick's arguments for the primitiveness of the concepts of right and ought at least raise the question whether any form of utilitarianism, or indeed any theory which attempts to derive the rightness of acts from any sort of ulterior consideration, is tenable. In the following section I will discuss Prichard's essay "Does Moral Philosophy Rest on a Mistake?" in which precisely this conclusion is drawn.

2   Prichard: The Attack on Utilitarianism

Prichard's central thesis in his essay "Does Moral Philosophy Rest on a Mistake?" is that the rightness or obligatoriness of an action is "absolutely underivative or immediate" and, in particular, in no way depends on or results from either the goodness of the consequences of the action (the utilitarian view) or on the motives of the agent (the Kantian view). The mistake in moral philosophy, alluded to in the title of the essay, is the attempt to establish the rightness or obligatoriness of actions by what might be termed ulterior considerations, i.e. considerations other than simply giving a fuller description of the action itself. For Prichard, putting his thesis in another way, the question "Why ought I to do X?"—when X describes an act generally considered obligatory such as keeping a promise or being truthful or showing gratitude for another's help—simply has no answer beyond the tautological answer that doing X is obligatory or right. Thus, in particular, he argues that all attempts to show I ought to do X because it would be in my interest, or in the interest of others, necessarily fail: they can only succeed at most in making us want to do the action in question, not that we ought to do so. In general, he argues, an "ought," if it is to be derived at all, can only be derived from another "ought." Thus, Prichard aims at undercutting the vast majority of traditional ethical theories, such as all interest theories, traditional utilitarianism, Kantian ethics, and such popular views as that I ought to do X because God commands doing X. Hence the importance of the essay: if Prichard is right, most of traditional ethics does indeed rest on a mistaken presupposition, namely the presupposition that it is possible to derive the rightness or obligatoriness of an action from considerations other than the nature of the action itself.

What are Prichard's arguments? Against the Kantian theory or what in general may be called an ethics of motive, he presents the following dilemma. Either the motive in question which makes the act right is what he terms a "sense of obligation," or it is some other motive commonly considered good such as love or gratitude or humanitarian feeling or the like. If it is the latter, then we are regarding the act not as obligatory at all, but simply as something we desire to do. Hence the rightness of actions cannot be derived from the fact that they are done from motives other than the sense of duty or obligation. But the view which Kant suggests, that right acts are acts done from a sense of duty, leads to an infinite regress: the sense that the act is obligatory cannot be sufficient to make the act obligatory, since if it were, the sense that an act is obligatory would be a sense that the act is done from a sense that the act is obligatory, and so on ad infinitum. Prichard's point here is that the sense that an act is obligatory presupposes that the act has been already conceived to be one which is obligatory independently of the motive by which it is done: otherwise a circle occurs. To a certain extent, perhaps, this is not an entirely fair criticism of Kant: Kant seems to have held that there is some test of the rightness of actions independently of the motive with which they are done. And it is not entirely clear that any important moral philosopher ever actually held that what makes actions right is the motive of the agent in doing the action. Yet, one does sometimes hear it said that a person is acting rightly when he does what he thinks or feels is right—a view that seems decisively refuted by Prichard's argument. And in any event Prichard here makes a contribution of some importance to moral philosophy by showing why it would be a mistake to seek to derive the rightness of actions from the agent's motive, whether anyone has actually sought to do so or not.

The more important and arguable part of Prichard's thesis is that the rightness or obligatoriness of an action cannot be derived from its consequences. Of course if one accepts his principle that an "ought" statement can only be derived from another "ought" statement, one could not derive a statement of the form "One ought to do X" from any statement of the form "X has consequences C." But, one might ask, why accept this principle? As is often the case with Prichard he seems to offer this principle as if it were self-evident and in need of no argument. Yet, the principle in question is by no means obvious. Sidgwick, as remarked earlier, seems to have held that "X is good in itself" entails "One ought to aim at X," an instance of deriving an "ought" statement, one could say, from a statement that is not at least on the surface an "ought" statement. And in a certain sense Prichard himself seems committed to the derivability of an "ought" from an "is." His position seems to be that given a certain description of an action, it in some sense follows that the act is obligatory: given that so and so has helped me in the past, so that my act of helping him is an act of showing gratitude, it in some sense follows that I ought to do it. It is not entirely clear in just what sense, according to Prichard, it would follow. Very likely Prichard's view was that there is a necessary but synthetic connection between "X is an action of sort F" and "X is obligatory," a connection which we apprehend by what might be termed an exercise of moral perception or intuition. But the fact remains that in some not clearly defined sense, Prichard's own view commits him to the derivability of an "ought" from an "is."

Prichard, I have suggested, gives no completely convincing reason for his rejection of utilitarianism. It is also the case that he did not completely deny what the utilitarian maintains, namely, that the rightness or obligatoriness of actions is a function of their consequences. First, he does not deny that in many cases we only know that a given act is right or obligatory by considering its consequences: e.g. we know it would be wrong to tell a certain story by knowing that it will cause someone pain. To an extent, then, the difference between Prichard and the utilitarian is less than might at first sight appear. Both agree that in many cases, at least, one cannot apprehend the rightness or wrongness of an action apart from its consequences. But further, Prichard did not deny that in general the fact that an action has good or bad consequences is a necessary condition of its rightness or wrongness. He held that "there is this element of truth in Utilitarianism," namely, that "unless we recognized that something which an act will originate is good, we should not recognize that we ought to do the action": e.g. "unless we thought pain a bad thing, we should not think the infliction of it without special reason wrong." But, he argued, even though having good consequences may thus be a necessary condition of the actions being wrong, it is never the reason why the act is right or wrong: the badness of pain, for example, is not the reason why we ought not to inflict it without special cause.

Prichard's position is somewhat puzzling. For surely if A is a necessary condition of B, it makes sense ordinarily to say A is at least *one* reason for B: if there can be no life without air, it seems reasonable to say that a reason or even the reason for loss of life is lack of air. One wonders, then, if the issue between Prichard and the utilitarian view may not be to a large degree merely verbal: Prichard does not deny that in some sense consequences make an action right or wrong, but still insists that the reason the act is right or wrong is simply the nature of the action itself apart from its consequences. Perhaps what he has in mind is that while the occurrence of certain consequences may be a necessary condition of the rightness or wrongness of actions, it is not sufficient: this is suggested by his argument that the fact that an act causes pain is not the reason it would be wrong, because if it were, then the infliction of pain by a person on himself would be wrong— which, Prichard maintains, it is not. But while it does seem plausible to say that the infliction of pain on oneself is not wrong in a moral sense, it could be held that in the case of infliction of pain on another, it is the fact that pain rather than pleasure is produced that in that context is sufficient to make the action wrong. And in any event it is clear, as Prichard himself remarks, that he is not denying altogether the utilitarian point that the consequences of an action make a crucial difference to the action's rightness or wrongness; whether one chooses to regard an act's having certain consequences as an answer to the question "Why, in the sense of for what reason, is the action wrong?" seems a relatively minor point.

In general, Prichard's discussion displays an extraordinary confidence that our doubts about what our obligations are can be settled by simply reflecting on the situation, as opposed to either seeking to derive a judgment concerning our obligation from some general test or procedure such as Kant's test of asking whether the maxim of our action can be universalized, or seeking factual knowledge concerning the consequences of actions as the utilitarian would do. If, Prichard maintains at the end of his essay, I am in doubt as to whether I should, e.g., pay a debt, "the only remedy lies in actually getting into a situation which occasions the obligation, or—if our imagination be strong enough—in imagining ourselves in that situation and then letting our moral capacities of thinking do their work." Of course, in one sense everyone would agree with this. But most traditional theories of normative ethics have been based on the assumption that our unaided capacity of moral thinking needs help from some general theory or method which it is the philosopher's task to state, explain, and defend in a general way. Prichard, it would seem, holds that no such theory or method is of the least use. It seems fair to say that for Prichard, ethical theory as traditionally conceived is at best redundant and at worst a harmful way of obscuring and distorting the immediate deliverances of an unaided faculty of moral appreciation.

3   Ross: The Meaning of "Right"

In some respects W. D. Ross's discussion of the meaning of "right" and of the question "What makes right actions right?" in his book *The Right and the Good* is a fuller and perhaps more precise statement of the themes considered in connection with Sidgwick and Prichard: the indefinability of the notion of right as applied to actions, and in particular its indefinability in terms of the good consequences of the action; the appeal to immediate intuition as the warrant for judgments concerning what is right or obligatory; the rejection of the agent's motives as part of what is meant by asserting an act to be right or obligatory, and the rejection of either hedonistic utilitarianism or what Ross terms "ideal utilitarianism" in referring to Moore's theory, as acceptable theories of normative ethics. In regard to the last point, Ross does not, as perhaps Prichard did, deny that there is an obligation to do acts that have good results. Ross holds that the tendency of an action to promote general good is one of the main factors in determin-

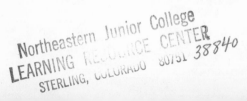

ing whether they are right. And in the absence of any other obligation, Ross holds, we are obligated to do the action that will produce the most good to all concerned. But, he argues, it is very often the case that other obligations are involved. And in such cases, he suggests, it may very well not be obligatory to do what produces the most good: e.g. if I have promised to confer a certain benefit on one person, A, and not to another, B, then I ought to benefit A even though doing so might produce somewhat less good than if I were to benefit B.

There is, however, at least one respect in which Ross modifies Prichard's theory in an important respect. This involves Ross's distinction between what is right all things considered, or absolutely, and what is only right *prima facie*. An act is *prima facie* right or obligatory, for Ross, when it is such that, as falling under a certain description or being of a "morally significant kind," say an act of fulfilling a promise, it actually would be right or a duty if it were not also at the same time an act of another morally significant kind, say an act of harming a close friend. What we intuit, according to Ross, is not that acts are right or obligatory all things considered or absolutely: we only intuit the fact that insofar as they are acts of a certain kind they are *prima facie* right. This is, of course, consistent with also intuiting that as acts of some other kind, they are at the same time also *prima facie* wrong. When an act is both *prima facie* right and *prima facie* wrong, as a result of having different and in a sense conflicting characteristics, then Ross holds we can never be sure whether it is right or wrong on the whole or all things considered. Indeed, since according to Ross we can never be sure that any particular act is not in this way both *prima facie* right and *prima facie* wrong, it follows that on Ross's view we are never sure what the "actual" duty, as he sometimes terms it—the duty all things considered—really is. Hence there is no suggestion in Ross as there is in Prichard's essay that our faculty of moral perception can be relied on to give certainty as to what is right or wrong in particular cases.

The meaning and importance of Ross's distinction between absolute and merely *prima facie* obligations can perhaps be brought out by viewing it as a solution to a problem which inevitably arises in a view such as Prichard's, namely the problem of a conflict of duties. Certainly there do frequently occur what may be termed "moral dilemmas" where we are morally pulled, as it were, in opposite directions, e.g. a case where telling the truth will involve breaking a promise to someone else to remain silent, or where returning something I have borrowed may result in serious injury to someone. In such cases it seems implausible to say with Prichard that all we need do to discover our obligation is to imagine ourselves actually being in such a situation. We seem to need some theory or method for resolving the conflict. Ross, to be sure, no more than Prichard provides such a theory. His only solution is to say we must consider which *prima facie* obligation is the more pressing, and to remark that our judgment on this kind of question is never infallible. Yet, it does seem an advance to explicitly recognize the fact of conflicts of duty and to at least provide a vocabulary for describing what is involved morally. In this sense Ross's statement of the intuitionist position seems a definite advance over Prichard.

4   Some Problems for Intuitionists

Plausible as intuitionism is, viewed as a criticism of utilitarianism as a normative ethical theory, it raises a number of difficult questions at the meta-ethical level. There is, first, the general difficulty discussed in connection with Moore in appealing to intuition. Presumably the claim that something is right or wrong for the intuitionist is a cognitive claim, one that can be said to be true or false. But insofar as the claim is said to be made on the basis of intuition, doubts may well be raised about the cognitive status of such claims. Presumably a part of what is usually involved in regarding a claim made on the basis of a certain cognitive faculty, or generally by the use of a certain procedure, is that we have some way of knowing how reliable that faculty or method is, either by comparing its results with results arrived at by some other method (as one might check by direct observations the results of inferences employing some kinds of inductive procedures in science), or, if not by some other method, by the same method employed in other instances (as when we judge the reliability of sense perception by comparing the results of one sense against the results of another—checking sight by touch, for example). But in the case of our alleged faculty of moral intuition, no such test or check seems available: there seems absolutely no way in which one can test the reliability of this faculty. How, then, can we make any statements about the reliability of the faculty at all: how can we even say, as Ross does, that it is "fallible," since that implies there are cases where we know for certain that it has produced mistaken results? Can we, then, make any kind of cognitive claim at all on the basis of such a method—if indeed it can be called a "method"? It would seem that a judgment based on intuition should be considered more as a report of one's own impression or feeling, not a truth claim in any objective sense.

Of course if there were some independent test of what the intuitionist claims to know by intuition, such as the agreement of all men—or of all men of a certain description such as all informed, impartial men—then the difficulty raised here could perhaps be dealt with. But this kind of reply would run counter to the intuitionist view, going back to Sidgwick, that there is no necessary connection between what is right or wrong and what is judged right or wrong by persons described in any non-moral empirical fashion. One cannot adduce the approval of all persons of some empirically describable kind as a criterion of an action's being right, for example; there simply are no such criteria for the intuitionist. And in the absence of any criteria for the correctness or incorrectness of our intuitions, the claim that the deliverances of our intuitions are modes of cognition seems open to doubt.

The above objection is as much an objection to Moore's theory as to the theories of Prichard and Ross: it is an objection to intuitionism in what Sidgwick terms the broader sense, not especially to intuitionism in the narrow and strict sense. But there are also special difficulties involved in intuitionism in the narrower sense. One such difficulty concerns the proper selection of the description of an action. It is clear, as Ross points out, that a given action can be described in a perhaps indefinitely large number of ways, not all of which are, in Ross's phrase, "morally significant." Thus, we would not ordinarily consider the fact that the action was done on Tuesday, or was done by someone with red hair, as morally relevant descriptions of an action. But it is not altogether easy to say just how we pick out the morally relevant descriptions from those that are not. And there might be disagreement on this matter: is, for example, the fact that the action was done on Sunday to be considered morally relevant or not? Further, it would seem that in many cases the descriptions we give to actions are themselves not morally neutral. We describe actions, often, in such a way as to imply or suggest evaluations which would not be made if the ac-

tion were described differently: as, for example, when American inter-
vention in World War I was described as "making the world safe for
democracy."

Insofar as this is the case, the question of whether an action is properly described in a certain way may itself involve a moral issue. To a
considerable extent, one's willingness to accept certain descriptions of
actions depends on one's prior moral appraisal of the action: hence,
rather than the appraisal depending on the description, as the intuitionists seem to hold, it may be that the description depends on the antecedent evaluation. Abortion could be described as "deliberately killing unborn children," but probably only one who is already
committed to an anti-abortionist stand would be prepared to accept
that description.

The problem of picking out the correct description of an action
could also be raised as a problem of distinguishing an action from its
accompaniments and consequences. In regard to the accompaniments
of an action, the distinction between an act and its accompaniments,
while perhaps not too problematic in many or most ordinary contexts,
does raise questions. Is, for example, the fact that others are doing the
same as I am doing, walking on the grass for example, to be considered a part of my action, so that the action should be described as
walking-on-the-grass-while-others-are-doing-the-same? Or is this only
an accompanying circumstance? It is not easy to say; yet, the act
might be evaluated differently if one included the circumstances in the
description than if one did not. Here again seems a case where the
decision to give a certain description of an action may reflect a prior
evaluation of the action: the evaluation itself could not therefore without circularity be said to rest simply on the description. Or, in regard
to the consequences, it is not always easy to draw the line between
what may be called "the consequences of the act" and the act itself.
The question whether the rightness and wrongness of an action is intrinsic to the action itself, or results from the goodness or badness of
the consequences of the action, seems to presuppose that the act can
be clearly and sharply distinguished from its consequences. But this
presupposition could be challenged. Just as we sometimes describe an
event or state in terms of its cause, as in "bugbite" or "pinprick," so
an action could be described in terms of its effects, as we seem to do
in speaking of "killing" or "converting." If so, no very clear distinc-

tion can always be made between an act and its consequences, and the very issue between the intuitionist and the utilitarian becomes hard to formulate.

In addition to the above difficulties, there are difficulties involved in Ross's notion of *prima facie* rightness and wrongness. One difficulty raised by Peter Strawson in his essay "Intuitionism" is that "X is *prima facie* wrong" is to be interpreted as "X tends to be wrong," and that the only clear meaning of the latter is that X is wrong in the majority of cases. But if that is what is meant by *"prima facie* wrong," it makes no sense to say, as Ross apparently wants to do, that an individual action is *prima facie* wrong. This is not, perhaps, a very strong objection to Ross, who could reply that "tends to be wrong" does not mean "is wrong in a majority of cases," but means rather that the action in question has a wrong-making characteristic—i.e. a characteristic which would result in the actions being wrong unless counteracted by some stronger right-making characteristic. Strawson also argues, however, that there cannot be a necessary connection between having characteristic C and being wrong (or right) if having characteristic C only shows the *prima facie* wrongness of the action. This objection, too, is perhaps not conclusive. It is true, Ross might concede, that if there is a necessary connection between X and Y in any one instance, there is a necessary connection always, so that whenever X is the case, Y is the case. But in the case of *prima facie* wrongness, he might say, it is not that having characteristic C ever entails simply being wrong: what is entailed by having characteristic C is that in the absence of any other feature, the action is wrong—and this entailment does hold in all cases. The necessity, in short, is not of the form if X then Y, but of the form if X, and if not W, X, Z, etc., then Y. (Strawson acknowledges this possible reply in a footnote, but argues that since we cannot enumerate all the other characteristics in the absence of which the action would be wrong but which, if present, might make the action not wrong, therefore we can never say just what the connection is. It is not clear, however, just why Strawson holds this. There seems no reason why one could not simply say that if an act has characeristic C then, if that were its only characteristic, it would be wrong: it is not clear why, in order to claim to know this, one must claim to know all the other characteristics which, if present, would make the action not wrong.)

At the same time, Strawson may be right in his suspicion of alleged intuitions concerning what may be termed right-making or wrong-making characteristics. Is it really self-evident, for example, that the fact that an action would be an act of lying goes to show just by itself that the action would be wrong? Surely there is something to be said for the utilitarian here: it seems that wrongness, even *prima facie* wrongness of lying is somehow tied to the consequences of lying and would be unintelligible if completely separated from consequences. One might consider this to be Kant's essential insight: that the wrongness of acts we generally consider wrong does not lie in the particular act at all, but in the difficulty of making that kind of action a general practice. But to make such a suggestion is to return to the view that our intuitions about what is right or wrong need some general principles or theory to support them, a view which leads away from the whole intuitionist approach to ethics.

In concluding this discussion of intuitionism, something should perhaps be said about the view that the concepts of right and wrong are simple and undefinable. No one would deny, presumably, that "right" has a variety of meanings, some of which at least can be characterized in empirical terms. Thus, we speak of the "right road," the "right answer" to a mathematical problem, the "right way" of, e.g. hammering a nail in, and so on, in addition to "right" in the sense of "morally right." Why could not "right" in the sense of "morally right" be empirically characterizable too? I cited earlier some of Sidgwick's arguments to the effect that "right" in its moral sense cannot be defined in certain ways. But it hardly seems to follow that it is in no way definable. Surely, one might suggest, "right" in the moral sense is at least partly characterizable in empirical terms: it seems in some sense a logical absurdity, for example, to say that actions which make people happier without any other morally significant effects are not right. For the intuitionist, this represents a synthetic a priori truth, not a definitional necessity. But why could it not be regarded as, in some sense, part of the meaning of "right"? In the following chapter I will consider the naturalist rejoinder to both Moore and the intuitionists, which does consist fundamentally in rejecting claims of a priori synthetic moral truths, and searching for empirical characterizations of fundamental ethical terms such as "right," "good," and "obligatory." Like the intuitionists, the naturalists reject Moore's thesis that "right" is definable in terms of a non-natural property of goodness. But the naturalist attack on Moore is far more radical: they give up the notion of non-natural properties altogether, and seek to identify ethical statements about both the right and the good with empirically testable statements of fact.

III

NATURALISM

IN THE PREVIOUS CHAPTER I discussed the intuitionist response to Moore, which was primarily a response to Moore's normative ethical theory; the intuitionists were not fundamentally opposed to Moore's meta-ethical views. In the present chapter I shall discuss the naturalistic rejoinder to both Moore and the intuitionists, a rejoinder which does involve a direct conflict between fundamentally opposed meta-ethical positions. In the first section of this chapter I shall discuss the question, already discussed briefly in connection with Moore, of the meaning of "naturalism" as a meta-ethical theory. My primary purpose here is to criticize some recent conceptions of naturalism, especially the conception of naturalism presented in R. M. Hare's *Freedom and Reason*. In the following sections I will discuss some main examples of naturalistic theories that have been set forth since the publication of Moore's *Principia Ethica*. These are George Santayana's theory as set forth in *Winds of Doctrine* (1913), Ralph Barton Perry's theory of value as set forth in his *General Theory of Value* (1926), John Dewey's theory as set forth in Chapter 10 of *The Quest for Cer-*

tainty (1929) and in *Theory of Valuation* (1939), and the so-called "Ideal Observer Theory" as set forth in Roderick Firth's 1952 article "Ethical Absolutism and the Ideal Observer." I shall conclude with a brief discussion of some of the general problems facing naturalistic ethical theories.

1   The Meaning of "Naturalism"

Moore, as stated earlier, characterized naturalism as the view that "good" in its ethical sense can be defined in terms of some natural object, understanding by a "natural object" a characteristic that is observed or whose existence can be inferred inductively from what is observed. This way of characterizing naturalism, I have suggested, while not altogether misleading as a statement of what is held in common by all those who have been prepared to call themselves "naturalists" in ethical theory, cannot altogether serve as an accurate characterization of naturalism since Moore either. Moore's characterization applies to what may be termed "analytic" or "definitional" naturalism: the position that "good," and ethical terms generally, can be replaced by some non-ethical empirical expression without loss or change or meaning. Some naturalists, perhaps Santanyana and almost certainly Perry, for example, do seem to take this position. But in the case of others, Dewey for example, it is less clear that this is an accurate characterization. Dewey's naturalism is primarily an argument for the empirical character of ethical statements, and it is not obvious that if a statement of the form "X is good" or "Y is right" is empirical, then it must be the case that the terms "good" and "right" can be replaced with some non-ethical empirical expression without loss or change of meaning. Dewey, in fact, does not really address himself to this latter question. And in the case of the Ideal Observer Theory, it is arguable whether ethical statements are even to be regarded as empirical, in any usual sense of "empirical."

In the light of these considerations, naturalism in ethics is sometimes characterized simply as the view that ethical statements are merely one kind of factual statement. But this characterization seems obviously too broad; the intuitionists and Moore himself held that ethical statements are a kind of factual statement, if "factual statement" means a statement that something is the case whose truth or fal-

sity is independent of the speaker's beliefs and attitudes. All naturalists, one can safely say, are committed to the view that ethical
statements can be supported deductively or inductively by non-ethical
statements of empirical fact; it is not clear that anything more precise
than this can be given as an accurate general characterization of naturalism.

In his book *Freedom and Reason,* R. M. Hare characterizes naturalism as a form of what he terms "descriptivism." Naturalists, he asserts, think that the meanings of value words are completely determined by "descriptive meaning rules," understanding by a "descriptive meaning rule" a rule that "lays it down that we may
apply an expression to objects which are similar to each other in certain respects" :

> Naturalists hold that the rules which determine to what we can
> apply value-words are simply descriptive meaning-rules, and that
> these rules determine the meaning of these words completely, just
> as in the case of descriptive expressions. For him, a value-word is
> just one kind of descriptive expression. (*Freedom and Reason,*
> p. 16)

Hare appears to be saying that for naturalists, the application of a
value word such as "good" or "right" to something is entirely determined by empirically observed similarities and differences of these objects. Thus, naturalism as he understands it implies that we cannot attach a value predicate to a certain object and refuse to attach it to an
empirically similar object without changing the meaning of the predicate in question. For

> a person who admitted that two things were exactly similar, but
> applied some descriptive term to one while refusing to apply it to
> the other, though he claimed to be using the term unambiguously,
> would be showing that he either did not understand that the ex-
> pression was a descriptive term, or did not understand what a
> descriptive term was. (*Freedom and Reason,* p. 13)

In general, Hare appears to attribute to naturalists the view that all
those who agree on the meaning of a value word will apply it to the
same objects, so that any serious disagreement about the application of
a value word may be regarded as merely a verbal dispute. And,
against this, Hare wants to stress the fact that serious disagreements

about the application of value words often represent not just ambiguous usage, but, rather, differences of moral principle.

I believe Hare's characterization of naturalism as a form of descriptivism, taken literally, is far too narrow. There may be naturalistic definitions of value words which do make the application of such words determinate, in the way Hare appears to have in mind. But not all naturalistic definitions appear to do so. The utilitarian definition of "right act" as an "act that tends to promote happiness," for example (construing utilitarianism as a meta-ethical theory about the meaning of "right"), treats the application of "right" to an action as equivalent to making a certain prediction about the action. And it is most implausible to call a prediction about an action a "description," taking "description" to mean, as Hare seems to, simply noting a "feature which has to be present in a thing." On the contrary, a utilitarian would strongly deny that rightness is a feature of actions themselves, holding, rather, that the rightness of an act depends entirely on consequences, and stressing the fact that a particular action may have very different sorts of consequences depending on circumstances. Hence a utilitarian would certainly question what Hare regards as a consequence of any naturalistic definition of a value-word, namely, that one cannot without ambiguity apply the word to an object and refuse to apply it to another, admittedly exactly similar, object. There are many practices, a utilitarian will say, which were once called "wrong" but which we should not now call "wrong"—buying on credit, for example; but this is not, he will say, because the words "right" and "wrong" have changed their meanings. It is because the practice in question is no longer thought to have the kind of result it was once thought to have and perhaps actually did have in a different economic context. It appears misleading, then, to say that all naturalists regard value words as just one kind of descriptive expression. For that suggests that all naturalists regard value words as names of features of the objects to which they are applied. And many naturalists would certainly deny this. Thus Dewey, who stressed the predictive character of *all* value judgments, would almost certainly have denied that value words are just one kind of descriptive expression. He held that

to declare something satisfactory [in contrast to merely declaring that it satisfies] is to assert that it meets specifiable conditions.
. . . It involves a prediction. . . . It asserts a consequence the

thing will actively institute. . . . That it is satisfactory is a judgment, an estimate, an appraisal. . . . *Judgments about values are judgments about the conditions and the results of experienced objects.* (*The Quest For Certainty*, pp. 260–61; 265)

It is even doubtful whether the most straightforward identifications of value words with descriptive expressions, such as Hobbes's definition of "just" (person) as "He that observes in his actions the laws of his country" or the hedonists' identification of "good" with "pleasant," are descriptivist in the sense Hare appears to have in mind. To say that someone is law-abiding is no doubt to describe him. But we do not apply the term "law-abiding" to persons on the basis of any particular empirical feature or set of features. It is true that when we describe a person as law-abiding, we are committed to saying that any other person who acts in exactly the same way is also law-abiding; if we refused to admit this then, as Hare points out, we would show either that we are using "law-abiding" ambiguously, or that we are using the expression without any descriptive meaning, or that we do not know how a descriptive term is used. But Hare himself admits that when we apply a value-word to an object we are thereby committed to applying it to any other exactly similar object. Hence, the fact that when we call a person "law-abiding" we commit ourselves to calling everyone else "law-abiding" who acts in exactly the same way does not by itself show that "law-abiding" is descriptive in Hare's narrowly defined sense. Hare understands the naturalist to hold that a value word is descriptive in the sense that its application is wholly determined, given the empirically observed features of objects, so that to know how to use the word "we should have to know to what kind of things it was properly applied, and no more" (p. 22). But it is not obviously true that "law-abiding" is descriptive in that sense. There are, for example, situations where to obey a state law is to disobey a federal law and vice versa; in these situations there well may be serious disagreement as to which course of action a law-abiding person will take, and we should not regard this as merely a verbal dispute.

In general, it does not seem true, as Hare appears to suppose, that naturalistic definitions of value words in effect settle all important questions about the application of the word, so that any serious disputes about the application of the word become mere cases of ambiguous usage. Nor have naturalist intended their definitions to have that consequence. Even the hedonist, for example, is not likely to admit that the application of "good" to an object is determinate in the way Hare appears to have in mind; nor does the fact that "pleasant" is a descriptive expression entail that its application is thus determinate. For we do not apply the word "pleasant" to an object on the basis of some particular feature or set of features possessed by it, any more than we do the expression "tends to promote happiness." It appears, then, that Hare has altogether too narrow a conception of naturalism. Naturalists do not regard value words as just one kind of descriptive expression, if we understand "descriptive expression" to mean an expression designating an empirically observed feature of the object to which the word is applied.

Hare may have arrived at his characterization of naturalism as a form of descriptivism by way of a suggestion Moore made in his essay, "The Conception of Intrinsic Value." Moore there maintains that ethical predicates ascribing intrinsic value to objects are like some non-ethical predicates, such as "yellow," in that they "depend only on the intrinsic nature of what possesses them," so that "it is impossible that, of two exactly similar things, one should possess it and the other not, or that one should possess it in one degree and the other in a different one." The difference between "good" and predicates such as "yellow," Moore held, is that predicates such as "yellow" "seem to describe the intrinsic nature of what possesses them in a sense in which predicates of value never do." For if, Moore argued, "you could enumerate all the intrinsic properties a given thing possessed, you would have a complete description of it, and would not need to mention any predicates of value it possessed" whereas "no description of a given thing could be complete which omitted any intrinsic property." Moore has been criticized in this connection for having too narrow a conception of a description. But in any case Moore did not hold, as Hare appears to, that *all* naturalistic definitions of value words treat value words as just one kind of descriptive expression. In the passage cited above, Moore was trying to distinguish intrinsic value from what he called "natural intrinsic properties," such as yellow. His argument was that, whereas the latter sort of property has to be mentioned in any complete description, the former does not. Hence, Moore was in effect arguing that a naturalist must hold that ethical predicates are descriptive *if* he holds that they designate intrinsic properties, that is, properties whose possession by an object depends entirely on the intrinsic nature of the object. But Moore clearly recognized that many naturalistic definitions of value words do not treat the value word in question as the name of an intrinsic property at all. Thus, Moore discusses a naturalistic analysis of "better than" according to which to which the statement "One type of human being, A, is better than another type, B," means the same as the statement "The course of evolution tends to increase the numbers of type A and to decrease those of type B." Moore plainly regards this analysis as naturalistic. But he points out that it does not treat the predicate "better than" as intrinsic in his sense, since although at present A may be more favored than B, under other circumstances or with different natural laws, the same type B might be more favored than A," so that the very same type which, under one set of circumstances, is better than B would, under another set, be worse." In general, then, it is not true that as Moore understood naturalism, all naturalists believe that value words are descriptive. Hare's characterization of naturalism as a form of descriptivism does not therefore appear to characterize what Moore understood by naturalism, and what has generally been understood by "naturalism" since Moore.

2 Santayana and Subjectivism

One of the earliest naturalistic replies to Moore is Santayana's criticism, in his 1913 book *Winds of Doctrine,* of Bertrand Russell's 1910 essay, "The Elements of Ethics," an essay Russell acknowledged to be "largely based on" Moore's *Principia Ethica.* (Russell later wrote that he gave up his Moorean views partly as a result of Santayana's criticism.) Santayana does not take issue with Russell's (and Moore's) thesis that ethics is primarily concerned with what is good, in a sense of "good" which applies to things generally and not just to conduct. Santayana, indeed, approves of the idea that ethics should concern itself with goodness in its most extended meaning. Nor, he says, does he take issue with the thesis that "good" in its generic sense is indefinable. What Santayana takes issue with is the thesis that "good" is the name of a non-natural property; his basic objection is, as he puts it, to the "hypostatizing" of goodness. The precise meaning Santayana attaches to the "hypostatization" of good, and his objections to this alleged hypostatization by Russell and Moore, are not easy to follow. Nor is it altogether clear what theory Santayana himself wants to propose. (Santayana himself concedes that his argument is not "very accurate or subtle.") In part, Santayana's objection to what he terms the "hypostatization" of good is normative rather than meta-ethical. He suggests that Moore's conception of "good" as the name of an objective non-natural property may lead to moral intolerance and even fanaticism, whereas a view making "good" in some sense a description of individual human feelings and attitudes would encourage tolerance; "a consciousness of the relativity of values," he asserts, "if it became prevalent, would tend to render people more truly social than would a belief that things have intrinsic and unchangeable values, no matter what the attitude of any one to them may be."

Santayana's criticism here seems not entirely fair; Moore, as I have indicated, certainly did not think we are ever entitled to claim absolute certainty for our judgments of intrinsic value. The reasoning which led Santayana to make this charge is not clear. Perhaps it was something like the following. If goodness is in Moore's sense an objective non-natural property, whose presence in a thing is independent of our interests, attitudes, and beliefs, then in making a statement of the form "X is good" one is in effect claiming that everyone else must likewise judge that X is good. But if "X is good" merely expresses in some sense the speaker's own attitudes and feelings, one can say "X is good" without claiming that everyone else must likewise judge X to be good. But granted that Moore's thesis that goodness is an objective non-natural property does involve the claim that judgments of the form "X is good" must be accepted as true by everyone, regardless of their attitudes and beliefs, it hardly seems to follow that one must be intolerant and fanatical in one's ethical convictions—any more than it follows that because scientists claim objective truth for their theories, they must be intolerant or fanatical in holding these theories. It might indeed be argued that what appears to be Santayana's own view (according to which ethical statements of the form "X is good" are reports by the speaker of his own attitudes and preferences, roughly equivalent to "I approve of X") is equally if not more conducive to intolerance than Moore's view. It would seem that my statement "I approve of X" is one which others are not in a position to correct me about, any more than my statement "I am hungry" or "I have a head-ache." If, then, "X is good" is equivalent to "I approve of X," my statement "X is good" is one which I will not admit as a topic of rational discussion and debate with others: for I cannot admit I might be mistaken in saying "X is good" any more than I could be mistaken in saying "I am hungry." I do not think this would be a particularly good objection to the view that ethical statements are first-person reports of the speaker's attitudes and preferences. I should say that what might lead to intolerance is neither that view nor Moore's view, but the view that one's own ethical statements are incorrigible combined with the view that they are objectively true, independent of one's own attitudes and preferences. But it can, I think, be argued that Santayana's appeal to the virtue of tolerance can be used against Santayana himself with at least as much validity as it can be used against Moore. As Santayana himself acknowledges, we can assert our preferences "fiercely" as well as with "sweet reasonableness."

I have argued that insofar as Santayana's objection to Moore's "hypostatization" of good is based on the argument that Moore's view leads to ethical intolerance, he is not on firm ground. But Santayana does have some not entirely unconvincing things to say in support of what may be termed a subjectivist theory of ethical statements, understanding a subjectivist theory of ethical statements as a theory which regards such statements as assertions by the speaker of his own attitudes. For Santayana appears to be pointing out that certain objections to subjectivism in this sense are themselves not entirely convincing. In particular, he appears to be pointing out that the argument that subjectivism entails relativism, in some sense of "relativism" in which relativism is necessarily a defect in an ethical theory, is a bad argument. It would clearly be a defect in an ethical theory to entail relativism if "relativism" is understood as the view that contradictory ethical statements can both be true. But does subjectivism really have that consequence? Santayana appears to be pointing out that it does not. An ethical statement of the form "X is good" is, on the view Santayana seems to be suggesting, roughly equivalent to the statement "I, the speaker, approve of X." It is, then, true that A's statement "X is good" is compatible with B's statement "X is not good." For A is asserting, roughly, "I approve of X," and B is asserting, roughly, "I don't approve of X." But as Santayana points out, this is not really to say that contradictory ethical statements are both true. For the subjectivist, an ethical statement of the form "X is good" is really an incompletely stated relational statement: it is comparable to "John is the tallest" or "The table is on your left." Clearly "John is the tallest" could be both true and false depending on the basis of comparison: he might be the tallest person in his philosophy class, and the shortest person on the basketball team. So, on the subjectivist view, ethical statements are disguised relational statements: my statement "X is good" is not really the contradictory of your statement "X is not good," any more than the statement "The table is on my left" is the contradictory of your statement "The table is on my right." Conflicting ethical statements, on a subjectivist view, are only verbally in conflict: the contradiction between A's statement "X is good" and B's statement "X is not good" is only apparent, not real. If this is Santayana's point, it seems sound enough: A's statement "X is good" and B's statement "X is not good" are not contradictories unless one assumes that the statements purport to be true statements of what is the case independently of the speaker's attitudes and beliefs—the very assumption that is at issue.

At the same time, the argument that seemingly contradictory ethical statements can, on a subjectivist view, both be true raises a further difficulty, a difficulty which Moore himself pointed out and which is acknowledged by later non-cognitivists such as C. L. Stevenson. The difficulty is that it would seem that on a pure subjectivist view, when A says "X is good" he is not at all disagreeing with B who says "X is evil," any more than I would be disagreeing with someone who says "I'm hungry" when I say "I'm not hungry." But this consequence seems implausible: surely there is some sense in which there is a real disagreement between A and B when one says "X is good" and the other says "X is evil." Any satisfactory theory, it would seem, must explain how it is that the two parties are thought to be in disagreement in such a case. This consideration led Stevenson to distinguish two kinds of disagreement: *disagreement in belief,* where persons hold beliefs not all of which can be true, and *disagreement in attitude,* where persons hold attitudes not all of which can be satisfied. Stevenson's view is that ethical disagreement is primarily of the latter sort: when one person says "X is good" and the other says "X is evil," they are not really stating incompatible beliefs at all; it is more like

one person saying "Let's eat" and the other saying "Let's not eat."
But this account of ethical disagreement involves an account of ethical
statements which is not naturalistic at all, as "naturalism" is generally
understood; it involves an account according to which ethical statements (if indeed they can be called "statements" on this view) do not
simply state the fact that the speaker has certain attitudes, but also and
more importantly express or evince the speaker's attitudes and recommend to the listener that he share these attitudes. Santayana, it should
be said, while calling himself a naturalist, does at one point in his discussion seem to take some such non-cognitivist view. "To speak of
the truth of an ultimate good would be a false collocation of terms,"
he suggests, since "an ultimate good is chosen, found, or aimed at; it
is not opined. The ultimate intuitions on which ethics rests are not
debatable, for they are not opinions we hazard but preferences we feel,
and it can be neither correct nor incorrect to feel them." This passage
can be read in several ways. But one way of reading it is that Santayana is abandoning both intuitionism and naturalism as generally understood, and, although not altogether clearly, is anticipating later
non-cognitivist theories.

3 Perry's Theory of Value

Ralph Barton Perry's theory of value, whatever one may think of it
in the end, has the virtue of being a relatively clear and explicit statement and defense of a naturalistic ethical theory in the sense of "naturalistic" introduced and made popular by Moore. The basic concept of
ethics, Perry holds—and in a sense follows Moore in holding—is the
concept of goodness in the most generic sense, or "value." To have
value, according to Perry's theory, is simply to be the object of someone's interest, understanding by "interest" a "state, act, attitude, or
disposition of favor or disfavor toward something." "Good," one
might say, means "object of positive interest" and "bad" means
"object of negative interest." "Good" in its specifically ethical sense,
the sense in which we speak of a "good person" or "good conduct,"
is defined by Perry in terms of the generic notion of goodness: to
ascribe goodness in an ethical sense to a person or course of action is,
roughly, to say that his interests satisfy the requirement of "harmony," i.e. are such that the person has considered possible conflicts

of interest between his interests, or between his interests and the interests of others, and has freely and rationally decided on a scheme of
satisfaction of interests which minimizes conflict. An act is "right"
according to Perry when no other act possible in the situation would
provide more mutual satisfaction of interests, i.e. no other act would
produce more harmonious satisfaction of the interests of the persons
whose interests are affected by the action. An act is "morally obligatory" if it would result in more harmonious satisfaction of the interests
of persons affected by the action than any other action that might be
done in the circumstances.

Perry's definition of value as any object of any interest is in one
clear sense relativistic. It is relativistic in the sense that value is not inherent in the thing to which value is ascribed, but consists rather in a
relation between the object which has value and some subject. Perhaps
"relational" would be a less misleading term to use than "relativistic," however, since as Perry himself points out his theory is clearly
not relativistic in certain senses which are frequently considered objectionable. It is not, for example, relativistic in the sense in which Santayana's subjectivist theory, according to which ethical judgments are
statements by the speaker about his own attitudes and feelings, is relativistic—relativistic in the sense that verbally contradictory ethical
statements could both be true. On Perry's theory, it could not be the
case that my statement "X has value" is true whereas someone else's
statement "X does not have value" is likewise true: if X has value, it
has it by virtue of a fact (someone's taking an interest in X) which is
independent of the speaker's own attitudes and preferences. I may take
no interest whatever in, e.g. modern abstract art, but on Perry's theory
I must concede that it has considerable value in that I must grant it to
be a fact that many people do take an interest in it. There is, to be
sure, a certain sense in which Perry's theory might be said to have
relativistic implications. It would seem to follow from his definitions
that one and the same thing could be both good and bad, in that some
might take a positive interest in it by favoring it, while others at the
same time take a negative interest in it by disfavoring it. If, for example, I enjoy a certain food and positively seek it, while you detest it
and avoid it, one would have to say the food has positive value and
negative value at the same time—i.e. is both good and bad. Or, a similar situation would seem to occur in competitive situations: my being

elected for an office which we are both seeking would be good as an object of my positive interest but bad as something you consider to be opposed to your interests.

Perry does not, it would seem, try to deny that, in the sense that one and the same thing can at the same time be both good and bad, his theory is relativistic. But he regards this as a harmless rather than a vicious relativism. He holds that the seeming paradox that a thing can be both good and bad at the same time is not really a paradox given the relational character of goodness and badness on his theory—any more than it would be a paradox to say that the same trip might be both long and short: a long drive, say, but a short airplane trip. And while a thing could, on Perry's theory, be both good and bad at the same time in the generic sense of "good" and "bad," it would not be the case that something is at the same time both morally good and morally bad. A thing is morally good if it is an object of an interest which satisfies the requirement of harmony, and it would seem that interests cannot at the same time be both harmonious and non-harmonious. Torture, for example, could not on Perry's theory be morally good, since the satisfaction of the desire to inflict torture on another must in the nature of the case conflict with the strong desire of the victim to avoid it.

There is, I have suggested, a sense in which Perry's theory could be called "relativistic." But, I have argued, it is not clear that there is a paradox (as W. D. Ross maintains in a discussion of Perry in his book *The Right and the Good*) in Perry's relativism. Similarly, Ross's argument that Perry's theory "denies the existence of intrinsic value" is not, I should say, a serious objection to Perry's theory. It is, of course, quite true that in one sense of "intrinsic value," Perry's theory does deny the existence of intrinsic value. If by "X has intrinsic value" one means that X has value independently of anything else, so that X would have value even though it were the only thing that existed, then there seems a clear sense in which nothing has intrinsic value on Perry's theory. Things cannot have value independently of subjects who take an interest in them. (Perry himself tried to meet this objection by pointing out that whether a property is internal to the thing to which the property is ascribed depends on the description of the thing: if a thing is described as "An object which someone takes an interest in," then that thing's value would be an internal property of it in the sense that the thing would, on Perry's theory, have value even though nothing else existed. But this way of arguing could show that any property whatever is internal: if, e.g., I described the moon as "The first extra-terrestrial body explored by man" then it would follow that "Being explored by man" is an internal property of the moon. But most of us would not want to say that an intrinsic property of the moon is that it is the first extra-terrestrial body to be explored by man.)

The proper response Perry might have made is simply to reject the characterization of "intrinsic value" on which the objection rests. If one regards "X has intrinsic value" as a way of saying that X is an object of interest for its own sake, as opposed to saying that X is an object of interest because it leads to Y, then there is no difficulty whatever on Perry's theory in saying that many things have intrinsic value. Surely Perry need not deny that, e.g. the experience of listening to and enjoying a concert is something some persons take an interest in for its own sake, i.e. is something they would take an interest in even though it had no accompaniments or consequences, as opposed to, e.g. driving to the concert, which few would regard as having value regardless of its consequences. But if this distinction can be made, Perry's theory allows a distinction between intrinsic value and extrinsic or instrumental value. Here again the objection seems to beg the question, by assuming that the only meaningful sense of "intrinsic value" is the Moorean sense in which a value is only intrinsic if it in some sense inheres in the thing to which value is ascribed, independently of any interest or desire on the part of human subjects.

The objection most likely to be raised against his theory, according to Perry himself, is also, I should say, the most serious objection to it. This objection is that there are desires or interests which are bad and ought not to be satisfied, whereas on Perry's theory it would seem to be meaningless to evaluate desires or interests themselves as either good or bad. Perry's reply to this objection is plausible up to a point. He simply remarks that while in his theory a desire or interest could of course be judged *morally* bad, as conflicting with the satisfaction of other interests by the person himself or by others, its satisfaction still has some value in the generic sense of value: e.g. a person's ambition to rule the state might be bad in the sense that undesirable consequences might result if it were satisfied, i.e. consequences harmful to the interests of others and, perhaps, to the person himself, but we should not say that the desire to rule the state is in itself bad apart from the effect of satisfying it on the satisfaction of other and perhaps stronger desires. But while this line of reply seems plausible in some instances, it does not appear to meet the difficulty altogether. We seem to want to rank interests in terms of their intrinsic worth—that is, apart from the effect of satisfying them on the satisfaction of other interests. Thus, we seem inclined to regard an interest in art or music or science as in some sense superior to an interest in football or horse racing. This may be said to be mere snobbery. Perhaps Bentham was right when he asserted that quantity of pleasure being equal, pushpin is as good as poetry. But it does seem a little odd that an ethical theory should make it meaningless, as Perry's seems to do, to rank interests in terms of their intrinsic goodness, apart from their conduciveness or non-conduciveness to the satisfaction of other interests. There seem, further, to be interests which we feel are in some sense unworthy to have, where their unworthiness is not clearly a matter of their frustrating other interests, or the interests of others: e.g. a person who takes pleasure in imagining ways of torturing others may not be interfering with any other interest in doing so, but we seem to regard this as in some sense inherently bad. There seems to be an ethical difference between the person who amuses himself by imagining himself committing sadistic acts on others, and the person who amuses himself by imagining ways in which he might make others happier, and it is not altogether obvious that Perry's theory can account for the difference we feel in this matter. In general, we do seem to evaluate interests themselves in a way that is not clearly accounted for by Perry's theory.

Perry might argue that interests *can* be evaluated on his theory, in at least two ways. The first way might be in terms of intensity: the more intense interest a person takes in something, then, other things being equal, the more value the thing has. And, secondly, interest might be evaluated in terms of the numbers of people who take an interest in the thing in question, so that a thing in which many people take an interest has more value, other things being equal, than a thing in which few take an interest. But this does not seem to entirely account for the way in which we evaluate interests: we do not, it would seem, regard an interest in serious music as better than an interest in football on grounds of the intensity of the former interest as opposed to the latter, or on grounds of numbers. By these tests, the interest in football would probably have to be rated as better than an interest in serious music. In general, it can be argued against Perry that if his theory does imply that things of more intense and widespread interest are better, other things being equal, than things of less intense and widespread interest, then his theory entails unacceptable normative conclusions. One would have to say that, e.g. violent or pornographic movies are better, as objects of more widespread and intense interest, then, say, performances of serious music. Or, that the mud puddle in which the two-year-old takes an intense interest is better than the painting in which his parents take a less intense interest. Do we really want to say that Sunday football on TV is better than the Sunday concert, on grounds that the former is an object of a more intense and general interest than the latter? Perhaps we do want to say this. But it would seem that Perry's theory might run into conflict with some person's normative ethical judgments. And if, as Perry's discussion seems to imply, his definitions of "value," "good," "right," etc. report what we actually mean by these words, it is strange that his definitions seem to have implications which, at first sight at least, seem to be considerably different from the evaluations many people would make.

I have argued that Perry's definitions of "value," "good," "right," etc. may lead to unacceptable normative ethical conclusions, and that this is odd if his definitions simply report what we mean by these evaluative terms. Perry could, of course, claim that his definitions are not just reports of usage, but are to be taken as redefinitions of ethical terms—recommendations, as it were, as to how we should use these words rather than reports of how we actually do use them. But then Perry's theory would be open to the charge, mentioned previously, of giving persuasive definitions: making value judgments in disguise, as it were. Perhaps Perry's meaning is that words such as "value," "good," etc. have no clear, generally accepted, descriptive meaning, and that his theory does not so much change the meanings of these words as give them the clear meaning which they do not ordinarily have. If this is his intention, it would be somewhat hard to refute his theory. But he would still seem to be faced with the problem, mentioned above, that the employment of his definitions together with indisputable matters of fact entail value judgments which many might not want to accept. Hence, to a considerable degree the extent to which one finds Perry's definitions of ethical terms plausible—something which seems a purely meta-ethical issue—is not really separable from the normative implications of his definitions.

4 Dewey's Theory of Valuation

Dewey wrote extensively on ethics, and a full treatment of his ethical theory could be a book in itself. I shall restrict myself here to some remarks on Chapter Ten, "The Construction of Good," of his 1929 book *The Quest For Certainty,* and, more briefly, to his 1939 essay, *Theory of Valuation.* Dewey's chapter "The Construction of Good" in part repeats the attack on ethical non-naturalism made by earlier naturalists. In particular, Dewey attacks the view of Moore and the intuitionists that ethical terms name unique non-empirical properties which in some sense inhere in things independently of human desires, feelings, and attitudes: he attacks what he calls variously an appeal to "eternal values," "immutable and transcendent values," "transcendental absolutism," or "values eternally in Being," expressions which, insofar as they have a clear meaning, suggest that Dewey rejected non-naturalism largely because of a belief that it implies that values are unchanging. (It may be noted that it is not entirely obvious that this belief is true: it seems at least logically possible to hold that while values are non-natural, they are not unchanging in all respects. Certainly an intuitionist, for example, could admit that the rightness of an act is dependent on circumstances, so that the same act which would be right under one set of circumstances might not be right under different circumstances.) But more importantly, perhaps, Dewey's discussion is a criticism of earlier naturalists such as Santayana and Perry; he is not so much concerned with defending naturalism against non-naturalism as he is in correcting what he takes to be inadequacies in previous statements of ethical naturalism.

The earlier naturalists, Dewey suggests (he does not cite particular authors or passages, so that it is to a degree a matter of conjecture who he is criticizing), made the mistake of going to an opposite extreme, as it were, from Moore and the intuitionists. Seeking to relate values to experience, they regarded value judgments as immediate unreflective reports of personal feeling or desire—a view, Dewey suggests, that fails to account for the practical role played by value judgments in organizing and directing conduct. Hence, he suggests, non-naturalism and naturalism as so far presented amount to equally unsatisfactory extreme positions which in a sense give rise to each other: "we oscillate between a theory that, in order to save the objectivity of judgments of values, isolates them from experience and nature, and a theory that, in order to save their concrete human significance, reduces them to mere statements about our own feelings." The solution, Dewey implies, is a theory which will be naturalistic in the sense that it preserves the empirical status of value judgments, without making them "mere statements about our feelings," whether it be statements about the speaker's own feelings, as seems to be the case in Santayana's subjectivist theory, or statements about the feelings and desires of a "someone," as in Perry's theory. Dewey, one could say, is calling for a theory which regards value judgments as in some important sense "objective," and yet still empirically verifiable.

The theory Dewey suggests, which he terms "experimental empiricism in the field of ideas of good and bad," is far less easy to characterize in any precise way than the intuitionist and naturalistic theories he rejects as equally, although in opposite ways, defective. He can be interpreted in a number of different ways. One interpretation, suggested by Morton White in an article entitled "Obligation and Value in Dewey and Lewis," is that Dewey is saying in effect that judgments of immediate liking or interest are to value judgments as judgments of immediate sensory impressions are to statements ascribing some objective property to an object. "Someone takes an interest in X" is to "X is valuable" as "X appears red" is to "X is (objectively) red," on this interpretation. Dewey, so understood, is making the point that the difference between the first and second statements in each pair is roughly the same; just as what is meant by saying that something is objectively red is, roughly, that it appears red under certain standard conditions, or satisfies certain standard experimental conditions for being red, so in a similar way having value means being an object of an interest that, in some sense, is subject to experimental test.

This interpretation is plausible: it accounts for Dewey's stress on the predictive aspect of value judgments. Just as "X is red" could be said to involve a prediction to the effect that X will appear red to normal observers under standard test conditions, so "X is valuable" could be said to involve a prediction that X will be an object of interest or desire to suitably qualified persons under normal conditions. Further, certain passages in Dewey's discussion strongly suggest this interpretation; e.g. his suggestion that the difference between "X is desired (or admired)" and "X is desirable (or admirable)" is comparable to the difference between "That thing has been eaten" and "That thing is edible," where the latter is understood as involving empirically verifiable predictions about the consequences of eating the thing in question. Yet, while this interpretation undoubtedly expresses an important part of what Dewey is saying, it is not clear that it exhausts his theory. If this were all Dewey were saying, it could be objected against him, as indeed White does in the above mentioned article, that Dewey does not really account for the normative or *de jure* character of value judgments. For, as White argues, it certainly does not seem that "X is (objectively) red" is normative: it does not say "X ought to be red." But "X is desirable" seems to imply that X ought to be desired as opposed to the merely factual statement that X is desired. Or, to use Dewey's own example, surely "X is edible" does not imply that X ought to be eaten: hence if "X is desirable (or admirable)" were strictly analogous to "X is edible," one would have to say that "X is desirable" does not imply that X ought to be desired, which in its ordinary use it seems to do. (It could perhaps be argued that "X is objectively red" *does* imply "X ought to appear red." But this would seem to be a non-moral sense of "ought": it is the sense of "ought" used in "The bus ought to be coming any minute now" or "This medicine ought to relieve your pain.") Thus Dewey's theory, understood in the above way, seems to miss the normative character of value judgments altogether.

The objection sketched above is that, insofar as Dewey's theory is that judgments of the form "X is desirable" are to "X is desired" as judgments of the form "X appears red" are to "X is (objectively) red," he does not account for the normative character of "X is desirable." There are, however, passages in which Dewey appears to be fully aware of the normative character of value judgments, and to acknowledge an important distinction between value judgments and merely factional statements, even when those factual statements involve predictions about the future. Thus, in a passage in "The Construction of Good'' Dewey seems to acknowledge that value judgments have an essentially prescriptive role (to use R. M. Hare's term) rather than a mere fact-stating role:

> Not stern moralists alone but everyday experience informs us that finding satisfaction in a thing may be a warning, a summons to be on the lookout for consequences. To declare something *satisfactory* is to assert that it meets specifiable conditions. It is, in effect, a judgment that the thing 'will do.' It involves a prediction; it contemplates a future in which the thing will continue to serve; it *will* do. It asserts a consequence the thing will actively institute; it will *do*. That it is satisfying is the content of a proposition of fact; that it is satisfactory is a judgment, an estimate, an appraisal. It denotes an attitude *to be* taken, that of striving to perpetuate and to make secure. (*The Quest for Certainty*, pp. 260–261).

Here Dewey is again clearly stressing the predictive character of value judgments, as opposed to the views of Santayana and Perry that the judgment that X has value is a non-predictive statement (as it would seem) to the effect that I the speaker (Santayana) like X or that someone takes an interest in X (Perry). But it would seem that Dewey here is asserting more than that a value judgment is not a mere statement of fact in the sense in which "statement of fact" contrasts with "making a prediction." There are, of course, many predictions which we should not regard as value judgments but, rather, as factual statements: e.g. "If you turn the oven on to high, the bread will burn." What Dewey seems to be asserting here is that in addition to their predictive role, value judgments have prescriptive force: they urge, advise, recommend, encourage, etc. the listener to undertake some course of action, as opposed to simply predicting what the probable consequences will be of his undertaking some proposed course of action. There is a further passage in the chapter "The Construction of Good" which appears to make this point even more explicitly:

> It is worth noting that besides the instances given, there are many other recognitions in ordinary speech of the distinction. The endings "able," "worthy," and "ful" are cases in point. Noted and notable, noteworthy; remarked and remarkable; advised and advisable; wondered at and wonderful; pleasing and beautiful; loved and lovable; blamed and blameworthy; objected to and objec-

tionable; esteemed and estimable; admired and admirable; shamed and shameful; honored and honorable; approved and approvable, worthy of approbation, etc. The multiplication of words adds nothing to the force of the distinction. But it aids in conveying a sense of the fundamental character of the distinction; of the difference between mere report of an already existent fact, and judgment as to the importance and need of bringing a fact into existence. The latter is a genuine practical judgment, and marks the only type of judgment that has to do with the direction of action. (*The Quest for Certainty*, p. 261).

It might be argued that insofar as Dewey is stressing the action-guiding or controlling function of value judgments, he is abandoning naturalism and, without clearly realizing it, is suggesting a non-cognitivist position similar to Hare's, according to which value judgments, although somewhat misleadingly stated as declarative sentences of the form "X is good" or "Y is right," are really to be regarded as imperatives of the form "Choose X" or "Let Y be done." This argument, however, would depend on an assumption which I shall question in the Conclusion, namely, that insofar as a statement has prescriptive force, it cannot be regarded as a statement of empirical fact. Dewey, I should say, appears not to make this assumption: he appears to hold that value judgments, while in a certain sense not factual, i.e. not "reports of an already existent fact," are still factual in the sense in which a prediction is factual. And he seems to hold that they have the function of guiding or directing action. In section 2 of the Conclusion I shall argue that this is not clearly an impossible or mistaken view.

I have suggested above that while Dewey agrees with non-cognitivists such as Hare in recognizing the prescriptive character of ethical judgments, he is unlike them in continuing to stress their empirical status. There is a further aspect of Dewey's theory, more clearly in evidence in his essay *Theory of Valuation*, which may throw some further light on the difference between Dewey's ethical theory and non-cognitivism as it is usually presented. In "The Construction of Good," and more particularly in *Theory of Valuation*, Dewey criticizes the whole notion of "good" or "right" in the sense of "intrinsically good" or "intrinsically right," and suggests instead that value judgments should be regarded as judgments about the suitability of actions to attain ends which in a given context are not themselves questioned—a view which might be termed "contextualism." Thus, in *Theory of Valuation* he asserts that "propositions which lay down rules for procedures as being fit and good, as distinct from those that are inept or bad, are different in form from the scientific propositions upon which they rest. For they are rules for the use, in and by human activity, of scientific generalizations as means for accomplishing certain desired and intended ends." Here again Dewey contrasts value judgments with what might be termed merely factual statements, in that value judgments guide human conduct in a way in which purely factual statements do not. "You ought to quit smoking" directs action in a sense in which "Statistics show that heavy smokers have a high incidence of heart disease" does not, although the former statement may well be made on the basis of the latter statement.

It may be argued that "you ought to quit smoking" is only a judgment of prudence, not a moral judgment: it says, in effect, "If you want to preserve your health, you ought to quit smoking." But Dewey's point seems to be that all meaningful value judgments are in this sense judgments of prudence. They all have the basic form "If you want Y, you ought to do X," where the statement as a whole is one that can be empirically tested. Indeed, Dewey's main motive in questioning the notion of "intrinsic value" as he understands it seems to be to make value judgments empirically testable. Critics of Dewey, of course, will argue that he confuses genuine moral judgments of the form "X is good" or "Y is right" with merely prudential judgments: he fails to account for the difference between, e.g. "You ought to return the money you borrowed" and "You ought to lose weight." But Dewey argues at some length that while he does not wish to deny the difference between what we ordinarily term "moral judgments" and merely prudential judgments, it is still the case that moral judgments do not in a Moorean or intuitionist sense assert something to be intrinsically good or right, but only assert a thing to be good or right conditionally on acceptance of a further thing as good or right—an acceptance which is not in that situation practically disputed. The question Moore and intuitionists would of course raise is precisely about the goodness or rightness of the end which, in the situation, is assumed. And it must be said that Dewey's answer is not entirely clear. Perhaps he is not fundamentally in disagreement with Perry's view that a thing's moral goodness is a matter of harmonizing the various interests of the persons affected by the action. If that is so, the difference between Dewey and Perry is perhaps less than Dewey would seem to want to indicate. Whatever may be the case, however, it seems clear that Dewey, unlike Perry, avoids giving simple empirical definitions of ethical terms, and for this reason it may be misleading to call Dewey's theory "naturalistic" in the sense in which Moore used the term "naturalism." But in the broader sense in which "naturalism" is the position that ethical judgments are empirical propositions, tested by experience, it seems clear that Dewey's ethical theory is an impressive statement of a naturalistic theory of ethics.

5 The Ideal Observer Theory

A recent formulation of a theory which could be called "naturalistic" in a somewhat broader sense than Moore's or Hare's sense of "naturalism" is the so-called "ideal observer theory." I shall comment briefly on this theory as set forth by Roderick Firth in his article, "Ethical Absolutism and the Ideal Observer." In brief, the ideal observer theory is that ethical terms such as "better (morally) than" are definable in terms of the attitudes that would be felt by an observer or judge of the act or thing in question who is "fully informed," "vividly imaginative," "impartial," "in a calm frame of mind," and "otherwise normal." "X is better than Y" means that such an observer would prefer X to Y; "X is wrong" means that X would be disapproved by such an observer, and similarly for other ethical terms. It may be questioned, as suggested earlier, whether this is really a naturalistic theory in Moore's sense of "naturalism." It could be argued that it is not, since it could be questioned whether the attitudes taken by an ideal observer are really natural objects as Moore understood "natural object." The ideal observer theory certainly does not assert that there are any ideal observers, and it might be questioned whether there even could be an ideal observer in any but a purely logical sense of "could." It is not clear, for example, that it is possible for anyone to be *fully* informed about an action if that is taken to mean that one knows *all* the consequences, antecedents, and accompaniments of the action.

Yet, in some broad sense of "naturalism" the ideal observer theory does seem to be a form of naturalism. For it does, one might say, seek to provide definitions of ethical terms such as "right" or "better than" according to which such terms are synonymous with expressions that are not themselves explicitly ethical. And if naturalism is understood in its broadest sense, as the thesis that ethical judgments can be supported inductively or deductively by non-ethical statements of fact, it seems fairly clear that the ideal observer theory is naturalistic. Presumably there are degrees of being informed, impartial, imaginative, etc. and it would seem that according to the ideal observer theory, an actual observer's judgments have a greater or lesser probability of being correct depending on the degree to which he possesses these features. But if that is so, one can on the basis of observed fact ascribe a degree of probability to a person's ethical judgments. The theory thus can reasonably be termed "naturalistic" although certainly in a rather extended sense of "naturalism."

Without attempting anything like a thorough examination of the ideal observer theory, a few general remarks may be made concerning it. It is not, as critics have remarked, entirely free from difficulties even if one is willing to accept the consequence that it is a mere tautology to say that what is approved by ideal observers as defined by the theory is right or good. Moore, of course, would insist this is a synthetic although presumably true statement, but as argued previously Moore's view is itself open to some question, and one might of course raise the question whether the distinction between analytic and synthetic statements is as clear as Moore assumes. But apart from this issue there are other problems in the theory. One frequently raised question is whether one is entitled to assume, as the theory seems to do, that all ideal observers agree in their attitudes. If they do not agree, it would appear one would have to say that one and the same action could be both right and wrong at the same time.

One could, of course, make it part of the meaning of terms such as "right" or "good" that the things to which these terms apply are approved by all ideal observers: one could, that is, make unanimity among ideal observers a part of what is meant by calling things "right" or "good." But in that case it would seem that if there were any things on which there is not unanimity, the terms "good" and "right" and their opposites would simply not apply, which seems contrary to the way we use these terms. Again, what, it might be asked, is the nature of the attitude held by ideal observers which defines the rightness or goodness of the thing toward which that attitude is felt? Is it a specifically moral approval? If that were the case, it would seem that the notion of "moral" is itself being employed in the definition of "morally right," so that the definition appears circular. If, on the other hand, the attitude felt by the ideal observer is not specifically moral approval, it would seem that ideal observers could approve of many things without actually judging them to be morally right; the definition would then be too broad. And, finally, it is perhaps a bit odd to say that what we commonly mean by calling something "right" or "good" is that an ideal observer, described in a more or less elaborate way, would approve of it. Certainly the claim that this is what we are actually thinking of when we judge something to be right or wrong is rather difficult to maintain. In sum, then, there seem to be difficulties in the theory that have not been entirely answered by those who hold it. That is not to say the theory has been refuted. But it does not seem entirely satisfactory as so far formulated.

6   Some Problems for Naturalists

Insofar as this book is an argument for a particular meta-ethical theory, it is intended as a defense of naturalism, to the extent at least of arguing that the difficulties in naturalism are less decisive than the difficulties in the main alternative theories advanced by and since G. E. Moore. And in the final chapter I shall attempt a more systematic defense of certain positions which are more clearly associated with naturalism than with any other meta-ethical theory. At the same time, in accordance with the general aim of providing a critical survey of the main types of meta-ethical theory, some critical remarks may be made of naturalism as has been done already in the case of Moore and the intuitionists. My purpose here is not to refute naturalism, but simply to present problems that are suggested by the types of naturalistic theories discussed in the course of this chapter, and which an acceptable formulation of naturalism will have to deal with in some way or other. In this concluding section I shall only list and discuss a few of the main difficulties of this sort, without trying to arrive at a conclusion as to whether naturalism in general is a tenable theory; my own belief is that it can be made so, but that no naturalistic theory yet formulated is free from certain objections.

(1) If naturalism takes what I have termed a "definitional" or "analytic" form, according to which ethical terms such as "good," "right," "ought," etc. are viewed as replaceable without loss or change of meaning by non-ethical empirical expressions—the form it appears to take in Perry's theory—then an obvious problem arises in regard to the status of the definitions put forth. Are they simply stipulative definitions, in which the definer is simply explaining how he himself proposes to use the ethical terms in question? If this were all that is involved, then it is not clear that the naturalistic definitions in question would have any particular philosophic interest. No one would deny that a philosopher can, if he chooses, assign in a more or less arbitrary way empirical meanings to ethical terms, but it is not clear what the point of doing so would be, or why anyone else should take these definitions seriously. But if naturalistic definitions are not simply stipulative, they must, if would seem, be understood either as reports of what is actually meant by the ethical terms in question, or, if the definitions depart from ordinary usage, as recommendations as to how these terms ought to be used. The real issue concerning the status of naturalistic definitions, then, is whether the naturalist is basically *describing* the meanings of ethical terms as actually used, or is basically *prescribing* certain meanings to be given to these terms.

The naturalist, faced with these alternatives, seems caught in a dilemma. If he is giving descriptive definitions, then, it would seem his definitions should be obviously true and there should be no particular argument about them. For presumably the ethical terms in question are commonly used and as such, one would suppose, are in some sense already well understood. But it seems that in fact, naturalistic definitions are not generally accepted: the fact that there are various alternative naturalistic definitions gives rise to doubt here, not to mention the fact that Moore and the intuitionists, for example, simply find no naturalistic definitions of ethical terms satisfactory accounts of what *they* mean by these terms. If, on the other hand, the naturalist is prescribing rather than describing in giving his definitions of ethical terms, one wonders what the justification of his prescription is. Probably most naturalists would argue that giving empirical meanings to ethical terms makes it possible to resolve ethical disagreement in some objective rational way, whereas it is not possible as long as ethical terms have no relatively clear and precise empirical meaning. But this is a very general argument: it does not serve to support one set of naturalistic definitions as opposed to some alternative set. And, further, one might wonder whether the goal of resolving ethical disagreement can really be achieved by way of naturalistic definitions. If may well be that acceptance of a certain set D of naturalistic definitions supports normative position A rather than B, whereas another set of definitions D_1 supports B rather than A. But then the argument over A versus B, originally a normative argument, is simply shifted to the meta-ethical level: it now appears as an argument over D versus D_1. And, one might ask, is anything really gained by this procedure? It hardly seems likely that normative ethical issues can be resolved by restating them as meta-ethical issues: if anything, this procedure would seem to disguise them rather than help to resolve them. In sum, there are problems for the naturalist on any of the obvious positions he may take concerning the status of his naturalistic definitions of ethical terms.

(2) Naturalism may take the form of suggesting that statements containing such terms as "good," "right," "ought," etc. are empirical statements, without holding that these terms themselves are simply synonymous with some empirical expression. This would seem to be Dewey's position, insofar as he appears to hold that statements of the form "X is good" or "Y is right" are conditional statements, asserting that X or Y are appropriate means to attain an end which itself is assumed as desired or intended. The difficulty Moore and the intuitionists would raise concerning this view is, of course, that while statements asserting something to be good or right as a means are doubtless empirically verifiable, this is not the sense of "good" and "right" and related terms which is at issue in ethical theory. What is in question is the meanings of "good," "right," etc. as ascribed to ends themselves. This does seem a plausible objection: there is a sense in which statements about the goodness or rightness of something as a means is not a moral sense of "good" and "right" at all. The murderer can say "This poison would be better than that" and one might in a sense agree that his statement is true, without in any way subscribing to the morality of murder: one could also say that in the moral sense of "right" or "ought," one ought not to give anyone poison.

Dewey might maintain that the moral judgment that murder is

wrong is itself to be construed as a statement to the effect that it is not conducive to the ends we actually have. But to argue along these lines seems to be to take, in effect, a version of utilitarian ethics in which conduct is judged good or right in terms of its conduciveness to human welfare, broadly conceived. If this is so, then it would appear that Dewey's meta-ethical theory is only plausible if one assumes that human welfare in some sense is what we ought to promote in all our actions, that is, a normative ethical theory. And there are many ethical theorists, the intuitionists for example, who would question utilitarianism as an acceptable normative theory. Further, insofar as Dewey's meta-ethical theory rests on an unexamined normative theory, it would seem to be, in an important sense, incomplete. What, one would want to ask, is the correct analysis of the basic normative principle itself, namely that it is right to aim at promoting human welfare? If Sidgwick is right, the statement "It is right to aim at human welfare" cannot itself be interpreted as a statement to the effect that it is conducive to human welfare to aim at human welfare, since the former has normative force whereas the latter seems not to have. Hence, in sum, while there is considerable force in Dewey's criticisms of earlier forms of naturalism such as Santayana's and Perry's, it is not clear that his version of naturalism is entirely free from difficulties either.

(3) Naturalism, I have suggested, might be understood most generally as simply the view that ethical judgments can be confirmed or disconfirmed by non-ethical statements of empirical fact by the use of ordinary methods of deduction and induction. So understood, naturalism is basically a certain position on the so-called "Is-Ought" question, namely, that "Ought" statement can be deduced from "Is" statements or, as the position might be more carefully stated, there are logical connections (in a non-special sense of "logical") between empirical statements of fact and ethical judgments. So understood, naturalism seems free from most if not all of the most common objections raised against naturalism, in particular from the objections Moore and the intuitionists raise against it. And in the course of this work I shall present some arguments in favor of naturalism understood in this sense. At the same time, certain problems may be mentioned which naturalism, even in this broader sense, must face. One such problem which any form of naturalism faces is that it follows from a naturalis-

tic theory that ethical disagreement would seem impossible between persons who are agreed on all the relevant facts involved in a given moral issue. The naturalist, that is, seems committed to the view that in the case of all ethical disagreement, if it is genuine disagreement and not just verbal misunderstanding, there is some set of facts such that if everyone agrees to these facts, they will necessarily take the same ethical position.

As indicated earlier in the case of Hare's account of naturalism, I do not think the naturalist wants in any way to deny or minimize the importance of ethical disagreement. But he does seem committed to the view that at least in principle it is always possible to resolve such disagreement by securing agreement on non-ethical matters of fact. Perhaps the naturalist is right in taking this view, but it is far from clear that the truth lies on the side of the naturalist on this question. There would seem to be ethical disagreements which, although perhaps in some sense resolvable if all could agree on certain relevant facts, are not clearly resolvable by securing agreement on empirical facts alone: e.g. the abortion issue which would seem to involve disagreement concerning the metaphysical nature of a person. And in other cases there would seem to be ethical disagreement which does not clearly involve any disagreement on matters of fact at all, e.g. over whether it is wrong to hunt and kill animals for the fun of it. Perhaps it can be shown that all such disagreements really do involve disagreement on matters of empirical fact, but this is not in all cases easy to do, and in any case it seems difficult to show by any general argument that such is always the case. Perhaps there are ultimate ethical disagreements which simply cannot be settled by securing agreement on any set of non-ethical facts. It is perhaps this possibility, as much as anything else, which makes the non-cognitivist views I shall discuss in the next two chapters seem plausible as an alternative to both intuitionism and to the naturalistic theories discussed in the present chapter.

IV

NON-COGNITIVISM:
THE EMOTIVE THEORY

1 Ayer's Pure Emotive Theory

IN THE INTRODUCTORY CHAPTER I have already mentioned briefly the
nature of the emotive theory of ethics and some of the philosophical
presuppositions underlying it. In the present section of this chapter my
purpose is to examine this theory and its presuppositions in somewhat
more detail: I shall restrict my discussion here to A. J. Ayer's presentation of the emotive theory of ethics in Chapter 6 of his 1936 book
Language, Truth, and Logic. In the two remaining sections of this
chapter I shall discuss the somewhat more complex version of the
emotive theory set forth by C. L. Stevenson in his 1937 article "The
Emotive Meaning of Ethical Terms" and subsequently developed in
his book *Ethics and Language* and in his more recent book *Facts and
Values*.

The emotive theory of ethics as presented in Chapter 6 of Ayer's
Language, Truth, and Logic is what might be called a "pure emotive

theory,'' meaning that for Ayer, ethical judgments, insofar as they are ethical judgments and not statements of non-ethical scientific fact, are nothing but an expression of the speaker's feelings. ''Statements of value,'' Ayer asserts, ''in so far as they are not scientific, . . . are not in the literal sense significant, but are simply expressions of emotion which can be neither true nor false.'' Thus, Ayer holds,

> if I say to someone, ''You acted wrongly in stealing that money,'' I am not stating anything more than if I had simply said ''You stole that money.'' In adding that this action is wrong I am not making any further statement about it. I am simply evincing my moral disapproval of it. It is as if I had said ''You stole that money,'' in a peculiar tone of horror, or written it with the addition of some special exclamation marks. The tone, or the exclamation marks, adds nothing to the literal meaning of the sentence. It merely serves to show that the expression of it is attended by certain feelings in the speaker. (*Language, Truth, and Logic,* p. 107)

Ethical statements, for Ayer, are thus not in a sense statements at all, if ''statement'' is taken to mean the utterance of a sentence in order to say something which is true or false. In this respect Ayer's theory, as he himself goes on to point out, differs from what are frequently called ''subjectivist'' theories, such as the theory Santayana seems to have held. There is a sense in which, as Ayer says, his theory is ''radically subjectivist.'' It is subjectivist in the sense that the utterance of an ethical judgment by a speaker gives information, and only information, about the feelings or attitudes of the speaker himself. But that is not to say that in making the ethical statement, on Ayer's theory, the speaker is asserting that he has certain feelings or attitudes. Ayer would not deny there is a difference between, e.g. ''I feel horrified by people who steal money'' and ''Stealing money is morally wrong.'' But the difference, as the above quoted passage indicates, is not that the second statement asserts something not asserted by the first. The first simply says what the speaker's emotions are, while the second is an actual expression of that emotion. It is roughly comparable to the difference between saying ''I detest asparagus'' and ''Asparagus— ugh! '' The information content, one might say, of the two statements is the same. But the first is a presumably true report of the speaker's feelings, whereas the second has no truth value at all. It is comparable to a plea, a request, a prayer, a command, etc. in simply not asserting something to be the case, and hence in not having either truth or falsity. For Ayer, it would make no more sense to ask "Is it true that stealing money is wrong?" than it would to ask "Is it true that please shut the door"? or "Is it true that look out below?" Perhaps, Ayer might concede, when we make an ethical statement of the form "X is wrong" we *think* we are saying something which is true. But this belief, Ayer would have to say, is a mistake, perhaps engendered by the grammatical form of the sentence. Truth and falsity in their literal sense, Ayer holds, no more apply to ethical statements than they do to cries of pain or joy. They are indeed strictly comparable to such cries ("ejaculations" Ayer terms them) rather than to statements of fact.

What considerations led Ayer to take this position? And how compelling are these considerations? One consideration, certainly, is Ayer's general theory of knowledge, mentioned in the introductory chapter, to the effect that all meaningful statements that can be termed "true" or false" are either (a) definitional truths, such as "All bachelors are unmarried," or (b) statements which can be empirically verified or falsified, by at least possible sensory reports, e.g. "There is no indigenous life on the moon." The argument would then be that since ethical statements such as "Stealing money is wrong" are neither definitional truths nor empirically verified, they must therefore lack significance: "say nothing" as Ayer at one point puts it. But it is far from clear that Ayer's general position on knowledge commits him to the ethical theory he holds. As he himself points out in the Introduction to the 1946 edition of *Language, Truth, and Logic.* the position he takes on knowledge generally is consistent with other ethical theories. Notably, it would be consistent with some form of naturalism, according to which ethical statements *are* to be regarded as statements of empirical fact, verifiable by sensory observation. And, on the other hand, one could maintain that Ayer's general theory of knowledge is mistaken, and yet contend he is right in holding that ethical statements "say nothing" but merely evince the speaker's emotions. Ayer's general theory of knowledge is thus neither a necessary nor a sufficient condition for holding the emotive theory of ethics. Not necessary, because one could hold the ethical theory without holding the theory of knowledge: not sufficient because one could hold the theory of knowledge, and not the ethical theory. At the same time, one feels that

Ayer's theory of knowledge does play an important role in inclining him to adopt the ethical theory he does. One obvious consideration here is that Ayer could not, given his general theory of knowledge, accept the view of Moore and the intuitionists to the effect that moral judgments are a priori synthetic truths. For Ayer on general philosophical grounds denies there are any a priori synthetic truths. Ayer himself concedes this point. "Considering the use which we have made of the principle that a synthetic proposition is significant only if it is empirically verifiable," he asserts, "it is clear that the acceptance of an 'absolutist' [i.e. an intuitonist] theory of ethics would undermine the whole of our main argument."

Does Ayer then in an important sense beg the question as between himself and the intuitionist? Perhaps he does, to the extent that his rejection of intuitionism is based on the fact that intuitionism conflicts with the verification principle. The intuitionist might argue that one cannot decide the question whether there is a priori synthetic knowledge apart from a prior examination of the status of ethical judgments: yet Ayer appears to argue that since on non-ethical grounds there is reason to think there is no a priori synthetic knowledge, therefore ethical statements cannot be a priori synthetic truths. Probably this does represent Ayer's line of thought in arriving at the conclusion that the intuitionist theory of ethical judgments is unacceptable. And, insofar as it does seem to a degree question begging, intuitionists in particular have some justification for directing their attack on Ayer against the verificationist assumption. At the same time it would be a mistake, as argued above, to think that if one can refute the general principle that a proposition, in order to be a genuine factual statement, must be empirically verifiable, then one would have refuted Ayer's emotive analysis of ethical judgments. It is perfectly possible to hold that Ayer's general principle is mistaken, and yet hold that Ayer is right in holding the emotive theory of ethics.

Apart from his verificationism, then, what argument does Ayer give for his theory? As often seems the case in philosophy, his argument is essentially an argument by elimination: no other theory is tenable, so the emotive theory remains as the only possible alternative Thus, against the theory which he himself calls "subjectivist," according to which "to call an action right, or a thing good, is to say that it is generally approved of," Ayer argues that it is not self-contradictory to assert that some actions which are generally approved of are not right, or that some things which are generally approved of are not good.'' And against what has been called ''subjectivism'' in the previous chapters of this work, according to which to call an action right is to assert that the speaker himself approves of it, Ayer argues similarly that it is not self-contradictory to assert that I sometimes approve of what is bad or wrong. Against utilitarianism, according to which right actions are (if we interpret utilitarianism as a meta-ethical theory defining ''right'' and ''wrong'' as Ayer evidently does here) actions that maximize pleasure, he argues likewise that it is not self-contradictory to say it is sometimes wrong to perform the action which would cause the greatest balance of pleasure over pain, or that some pleasant things are not good. And in regard to what he terms ''absolutism,'' meaning by this intuitionism as discussed earlier, understood in the wider sense in which Moore could be called an intuitionist, Ayer argues that ''unless it is possible to provide some criterion by which one may decide between conflicting intuitions, a mere appeal to intuition is worthless as a test of a proposition's validity.''

If the argument against Moore and the intuitionist suggested earlier in this work is correct, then Ayer is justified in rejecting what he terms ''absolutism'' and in looking for some alternative ethical theory. It does seem that the claim that in an ethical dispute one person is right and the other mistaken implies there is some test or criterion by which to decide who is right, although it need not necessarily be an empirical test. But what about subjectivism and utilitarianism: how compelling are Ayer's arguments against these theories? His arguments against subjectivism and utilitarianism, it might be noted, are suprisingly unoriginal. In effect, they are mere brief statements of Moore's open question argument against naturalism. (As J. O. Urmson has pointed out, Ayer's argument against what is called ''subjectivism'' in this work, which in at least one formulation says that ''X is good'' means ''I [the speaker] approve of X,'' is not quite the Moorean argument. The Moorean argument would be that it is not self-contradictory to say ''X is good but I don't approve of it,'' whereas Ayer's argument is that it is not self-contradictory to say ''I *sometimes* don't approve of things that are good.'' I shall comment below on this argument as an argument against subjectivism.) If the preceding discussion of Moore's open question argument is sound, however, this is not a very conclusive kind of argument to use. Thus, surely a hedonist who maintains that "good" simply means "pleasant" could reply to Ayer (and Moore) by maintaining that in point of fact it is contradictory to say that something is good but not pleasant, and it is not altogether easy to see how the disagreement could be resolved.

The truth is that arguments over whether given assertions are or are not self-contradictory are by no means easy to decide, at least in philosophical contexts: consider the issue over whether the proposition "God exists" is such that to deny it would be in some sense to contradict oneself. It almost seems as if Ayer himself, having rejected the appeal to intuition at the normative level on grounds that there is no way of telling who is right in cases of conflicting intuitions, resorts to mere intuition at the meta-ethical level as a means of telling what is or is not self-contradictory. And just as Ayer rejects intuitionism because it provides no test for resolving cases of conflicting intuitions about what is right or wrong, so one might question the validity of appealing to meta-ethical intuitions concerning the self-contradictoriness or non-self-contradictoriness of ethical sentences.

Further, in connection with subjectivism, while it may seem difficult to deny Ayer's point that it is not self-contradictory to say that I sometimes approve of what is bad or wrong—apparently just a way of saying that I am sometimes mistaken in my moral judgments—this is not really a telling objection against the subjectivist. The subjectivist who says that "X is bad" means "I, the speaker, disapprove of X" could point out that there are several senses in which, on his theory, a person could admit that he sometimes approves of what is bad or wrong. "Bad" or "wrong," he might say, have a conventional sense in which they mean "is generally called 'bad' " or "is generally called 'wrong.' " There is no problem for the subjectivist in conceding that I can say without contradiction "I sometimes approve of what is generally called 'bad.' " Or he could say, "What it means to say that I sometimes approve of things that are bad or wrong is that I have in the past and perhaps will again in the future approve of things that I now disapprove of." Or, again, he might agree that it sounds paradoxical to say that he cannot conceivably approve of something that is bad or wrong, but explain that this implies no superior ethical knowledge on his part, since on the subjectivist theory no one else can approve of something that is bad or wrong either, including those he should normally take as disagreeing with him. And while there are doubtless paradoxes in subjectivism, perhaps one cannot rule out a theory on these grounds alone. Accepted scientific theories too, one might say, sometimes have their paradoxes from a common sense point of view. My purpose here is not to defend subjectivism. I am simply trying to make the point that Ayer's dismissal of it, and more generally his dismissal of any naturalistic theory, is too quick and easy.

I have been concerned so far with the considerations that led Ayer to adopt the emotive theory, and have suggested they are not entirely compelling. I shall turn now to a critical discussion of the theory itself as Ayer presents it. What is to be said about the thesis that ethical judgments "are simply expressions of emotion which can be neither true nor false" ? Surely, to take the second part of the thesis first, there is something paradoxical about saying that ethical judgments can be neither true nor false. We often do speak of ethical statements as true or false, and there is nothing odd in speaking this way: e.g. when we say "It may be true that he acted wrongly in stealing that money, but he shouldn't be punished for it now," or "It may be true that abortion is wrong, but it shouldn't be made illegal." Ayer might reply that we àre misled here by the form of the statement: since "X is good" or "Y is right" have the same grammatical form as "X is red" or "Y weighs 200 pounds," we suppose that we can characterize the first kind of statement as true or false in the same way as the second. But what evidence is there that we *are* misled in this way? It does sometimes happen that statements which are really commands, or requests, and as such neither true nor false, are stated in a way which is grammatically like a true or false statement of fact, e.g. the Army practice of stating commands in the form of predictions ("All men will wear class A uniforms tomorrow"), or the teacher's admonishment, "We all like to be neat." But no one is misled by such practices into thinking that the Army command, for example, is really just a prediction, whereas Ayer's position would have to be that we have all been seriously misled by our practice of making ethical statements with the same grammatical form as true or false statements of fact.

Further, the problem is not simply whether truth or falsity can be ascribed to ethical statements. It is whether a whole variety of what may be called epistemic terms can be ascribed, such as "know," "believe," "doubt," "wonder whether," and so on. As far as "true" and "false" themselves are concerned, Ayer could escape the objection. He could appeal to the theory of truth according to which to say of a statement that it is true adds nothing to the act of making the statement itself: that when a person asserts "p" he is asserting nothing further by asserting "p is true" except perhaps to make his assertion more emphatic. Ayer himself, in his discussion of truth in Chapter 5 of *Language, Truth, and Logic,* does, as a matter of fact, hold this theory of truth, sometimes called the redundancy theory of truth. "When, for example," he asserts," one says that the proposition 'Queen Anne is dead' is true, all one is saying is that Queen Anne is dead." Similarly, Ayer might explain, to say "It is true that you acted wrongly in stealing that money" says nothing more than "You acted wrongly in stealing that money," and that nothing about the cognitive status of ethical judgments can be inferred from the fact that we can speak of them as true or false. But then, one wonders, why does Ayer think it important to stress the claim that ethical judgments are neither true nor false? And in any case, the problem as suggested above is not simply that we do in common speech ascribe truth and falsity to ethical judgments. The problem is that we ascribe the same epistemic terms to ethical judgments as to non-ethical statements of fact. Thus, we speak of "believing that," "doubting that," "having evidence that," "knowing that," "learning that," "remembering that," etc. X is bad or Y is wrong. And it is hard to see how any of these forms of speech could be preserved on Ayer's account. It is hard to see what could be meant by e.g. "remembering P" if P were understood merely as the expression of an emotion of approval or disapproval. These considerations do not exactly disprove Ayer's thesis: he could simply reply that we radically misconceive what we are actually doing when we make ethical judgments of the form "X is bad" or "Y is wrong." But the burden of proof is on Ayer here. He has to give more convincing reasons than he gives to show that it is not, rather, his theory that radically misconceives the meaning of ethical judgments.

Turning now, finally, to the thesis that ethical statements are simply expressions of emotion, a great many objections can be and have been raised against this. I shall simply indicate here those that seem to me to have, at least taken together, considerable force. First, it simply is not the case that an ethical judgment need be attended with any particular emotion in the sense that the speaker must, when he makes the judgment, be in any particular emotional state. I could say "You acted wrongly in stealing that money" in a tone of horror, or anger, or grief, or in general in a tone indicating any of a variety of emotional states. Yet, in all these cases I am in some important sense making the same judgment. Moreover, it is perfectly possible to make an ethical judgment in what we should ordinarily regard as a calm, unemotional state, as when a parent is teaching moral rules to his child, or in cases such as the one cited above where one says, e.g. "It is true that abortion is wrong, but it ought not to be made illegal." The emotion one would probably feel, if any, in making such a statement is a negative feeling toward making abortion illegal, not a negative feeling toward abortion itself, even though one is asserting it to be wrong. If Ayer's theory were true, it would be impossible to make an ethical assertion in anything but a highly charged emotional tone, and that clearly is not the case.

Second, even granting that when a person makes a statement of the form "X is bad" or "Y is wrong" he always feels some negative emotion toward X and Y, it is not the case that the degree of badness or wrongness he is prepared to ascribe to the action corresponds in any particular way to the strength of his emotion, as it presumably would on Ayer's theory. Thus, if I simply learn that a person has stolen someone's money sometime in the past, and I say to him "You acted wrongly in stealing that money," the negative emotion I would feel, if any, is likely to be very slight, whereas if I am speaking to someone who has just stolen money that belongs to me, I might well feel a very strong emotion when I say "You acted wrongly in stealing that money." Yet I may not wish to ascribe a greater wrongness to the theft in the second case than in the first: indeed, the reverse might be true. In general, the degree of emotion does not correspond at all closely with the degree of rightness or wrongness: I think that someone's stealing my wallet is trivial compared with, e.g., the confiscation of the property of the Jews by the Nazis, and yet at the present time I should very likely feel more strongly in the sense of actually having a stronger introspectable surge of emotion at the thought of the theft of my wallet than at the thought of the confiscation of the property of the Jews.

Third, again granting that when we make a judgment of the form

"X is bad" or "Y is wrong" we are experiencing some kind of negative feeling toward X, it does not follow that the judgment is *simply* the expression of the emotion, as Ayer holds. And there is reason to think it is not. Consider, for example, a crowd booing the visiting team at a football game. They are certainly expressing a strong negative emotion, but they are hardly making any ethical judgment. Expressing an emotion may be a necessary condition of making a moral judgment (although I have argued above it is not even that): it certainly is not a sufficient condition. Fourth, while expressions of emotion such as cries of joy or shouts of anger are neither true nor false, we do speak of them as fitting or unfitting, appropriate or inappropriate, called for or uncalled for, etc. in a way that Ayer appears not to account for. Perhaps he could account for this way of evaluating expressions of emotion themselves. He might say that what I mean when I say, e.g., it is fitting that a person feel a strong emotion of moral disapproval at wanton killing is that I feel a strong emotion of moral approval of persons who feel a strong emotion of moral disapproval at wanton killing. But then how, on Ayer's theory, are we to analyze the further claim that this second emotion is itself fitting or appropriate? In general, the judgment that a certain emotion is fitting or not involves a value judgment about what we ought and ought not to feel under certain circumstances, and that value judgment itself cannot, without danger of an infinite regress, be analyzed as itself merely the expression of a certain further feeling.

In sum, I have argued that Ayer's positive thesis—that ethical judgments are simply the expression of emotions and as such are neither true nor false—does not stand up at all well under critical scrutiny, quite apart from what one may think of the general philosophical position Ayer maintains in *Language, Truth, and Logic*. As a final comment, it might be worth remarking that perhaps Ayer adopted the emotive theory in its present form not so much because of its intrinsic merits as a meta-ethical theory, but as the only way out of what Ayer perceived as an impasse in ethical theory. On the one hand, Ayer accepts the view originating with Moore that the only real alternatives in ethical theory are either (a) that ethical terms such as "good" and "right," insofar as they are not definable with reference to other ethical terms, designate empirical properties ("naturalism") or (b) that they designate non-natural properties, or (c) that they designate nothing at all and that, hence, ethical judgments say nothing and are without literal significance in the sense of having cognitive meaning. Further, Ayer agrees witth Moore that naturalism is untenable for essentially the reason Moore gave. But because of his empiricism, Ayer rejects the theory that ethical terms designate non-natural properties in the sense of properties whose presence or absence in a thing cannot in principle be detected directly or indirectly by any empirical test. That leaves (c) which is the position Ayer adopted. Perhaps one should feel a certain admiration at Ayer's philosophical courage in adopting this position, uninviting and paradoxical as it is. But one might also wonder whether, had he pursued the argument even further, Ayer might not have been led to question whether the above listed alternatives really are the only available alternatives in ethical theory.

2 Stevenson: The Meaning of "Meaning" and the Concept of Emotive Meaning

Since the publication of his article "The Emotive Meaning of Ethical Terms" in 1937, Stevenson has greatly expanded and modified his version of the emotive theory of ethics, principally in *Ethics and Language* (1944) and in *Facts and Values* (a selection of previously published articles published in 1963). It would therefore be grossly unfair to discuss the 1937 article as if it were all one needed to read in order to understand Stevenson's ethical theory. At the same time it seems not unfair to say that the 1937 article is still in many respects the best introduction to Stevenson's ethical theory. Accordingly, my discussion in this and the following sections will be centered on this article, with references to the later work when necessary to indicate ways in which Stevenson has changed or modified his position to meet subsequent problems and objections. A more adequate study of Stevenson's ethical theory would doubtless concentrate on *Ethics and Language* and the subsequent articles: this has, to a degree, already been done in J. O. Urmson's book, *The Emotive Theory of Ethics* (1968).

Ayer's version of the emotive theory is, as was indicated above, a purely emotive theory: for Ayer an ethical judgment of the form "X is bad" or "Y is wrong" asserts nothing whatever about X or Y but only evinces the speaker's feelings concerning X and Y. Stevenson, in contrast, does not deny that ethical judgments of this form are frequently, even always, in some sense partly descriptive or factual. "Doubt-less," he asserts, "there is always *some* element of description in ethical judgments." Stevenson even concedes that judgments of the form "X is good" are sometimes used to make a purely factual state-ment. Thus, discussing Hobbes's view that "good" means "desired by me" and Hume's theory that "good" means "approved by most people," Stevenson asserts that it is pointless to deny that "good" is ever used in these senses. What Stevenson does appear to hold, how-ever, is that the main or primary meaning of "good" in its most typi-cal use in ethical contexts is not descriptive but emotive. And it is in fact his central aim in the essay to call attention to the emotive mean-ing of "good" (.and of ethical terms generally) and to show how the emotive meaning of ethical terms enables them to play what Stevenson takes to be their characteristic role or function in ethical discourse.

There is a further difference between Ayer and Stevenson which is indicated by Stevenson's very use of the expression "emotive mean-ing," a difference related to Stevenson's general conception of the meaning of "meaning." Ayer is quite commonly said to hold that ethical statements are meaningless, and while he perhaps never quite says this, he does say things which strongly suggest it, e.g. that "statements of value . . . are not in the literal sense significant." Stevenson, in contrast, distinguishes two kinds of meaning; descriptive (or cognitive, as he terms it in *Ethics and Language*) meaning, and emotive meaning. His thesis, in these terms, is that the meaning of ethical terms is primarily emotive, not descriptive: no one could ac-cuse Stevenson of saying that ethical terms or judgments are meaning-less. Stevenson can take this position because he adopts what he has sometimes himself called a pragmatic or psychological theory of meaning. In general, for Stevenson, the meaning of a word or expres-sion is its *tendency,* in the sense of its causal or dispositional property, to be connected with some set of psychological causes and effects that attend the word's utterance, including under the psychological re-sponses which the words tend to produce "not only immediately in-trospectable experiences but *dispositions* to react in a given way with appropriate stimuli." (It may be worth noting that although in the 1937 article Stevenson can be easily read as saying that the meaning of an expression is identical with the psychological states which cause or are caused by its utterance, that is not quite his view. He identifies meaning, rather, with the tendency of a word to be causally connected with certain psychological states rather than with the psychological states themselves.)

His general conception of meaning as developed in *Ethics and Language*, as summarized by Stevenson himself in a footnote added to the 1937 article as reprinted in the 1970 edition of Sellars' and Hospers' *Readings in Ethical Theory*, is as follows: "When used in a generic sense that emphasizes what C. W. Morris calls the *pragmatic* aspects of language, the term 'meaning' designates a tendency of words to express or evoke states of mind in the people who use the words. The tendency is of a special kind, however, and many qualifications are needed [including some that bear on syntax] to specify its nature.") This notion of meaning permits Stevenson to regard the tendency of a word to express certain emotions felt by the speaker who utters the word and (more important for Stevenson) its tendency to have certain effects on the feelings and attitudes of the listener—to regard these tendencies as part of the meaning of a word, at least when these tendencies to have certain causes and effects are more or less constant and stable in the language. Ayer would not deny that in this sense of "meaning," ethical sentences are (emotively) meaningful. But in his discussion of the meaning of "meaning" in chapter 3 of *Language, Truth, and Logic,* he rejects a psychological theory of meaning in the light of a somewhat austere conception of philosophy typical of early Logical Positivism, Philosophy in general, he holds, is concerned with the analysis of meanings, but not with "meanings" in the ordinary sense in which the meaning of a sentence is its psychological effect on the listener—since philosophical analysis would then become confused with empirical psychology. Stevenson, with no reason to keep philosophical analysis and psychology so strictly apart, and also wishing to avoid the unfavorable connotations of calling ethical statements "meaningless," finds it possible to employ a psychological theory of meaning generally, and hence to stress the (emotive) meaningfulness of ethical terms.

A still further difference between Ayer and Stevenson is that whereas Ayer emphasizes the use of ethical judgments to evince or express the speaker's own feelings, Stevenson emphasizes their use to affect the feelings or "interests" (in *Ethics and Language* Stevenson speaks of "attitudes" rather than "interests") of the listener. Ayer acknowledges this role of ethical judgments: he says "they are calculated also to arouse feeling, and so to stimulate action." But he mentions it as something of an afterthought. For Stevenson, in contrast, it is strongly emphasized. In part, Stevenson is here simply laying stress on an aspect of ethical language which Ayer, while having no reason to deny, did not happen to emphasize. But it also reflects Stevenson's primary concern with what may be termed the interpersonal aspect of ethical language generally, an interest which appears most strongly in his analysis of ethical disagreement to be considered in the next section.

A final difference between Ayer's version of the emotive theory and Stevenson's statement of it in the 1937 article is that Stevenson brings a pragmatic dimension into his discussion by distinguishing *meaning* and *use*. The meaning of an expression, as indicated above, is the tendency of a word to result causally from certain psychological states or dispositions in the speaker and to affect causally certain states or dispositions in the listener. The use of an expression, in contrast, is given by describing the purpose of the speaker in making the statement. And just as he distinguished between descriptive and emotive meaning, Stevenson distinguishes what he terms the descriptive and the dynamic use of expressions. An expression or statement is used descriptively for Stevenson insofar as it is used to record, clarify, communicate, etc. a belief. A statement is used dynamically, in contrast, when it is used to "give vent to our feelings (interjections), or to create moods (poetry), or to incite people to actions or attitudes (oratory)." The point Stevenson is getting at in making these distinctions is that ethical judgments are most frequently and typically used dynamically, not descriptively, at least not primarily descriptively, and that this is a natural consequence of their primarily emotive meaning. The emotive meaning of ethical terms, he suggests, "assists" the dynamic purpose of the speaker in using such terms, this purpose being primarily to influence and affect the listener's feelings and attitudes.

Stevenson does not deny that words or sentences which have no emotive meaning can also be used dynamically, to affect the listener's attitude and in this way his behavior. Thus, Stevenson would doubtless consider the sentence "It's raining" as having purely descriptive meaning, to the extent that any expression can. But he would point out that while the most frequent use of the sentence "It's raining" is to record or communicate a belief, as in "It's raining" said in response to the question "What's the weather like there? " it could also be used dynamically, e.g. "It's raining" said in response to "Let's go for a walk." In the latter case "It's raining" is used primarily to change the first speaker's interest in going for a walk and, as such, has a primarily dynamic use. Likewise, Stevenson would not deny that expressions which have a primarily emotive meaning can be used descriptively. Thus, Stevenson would doubtless consider the sentence "It's good to be neat" as having primarily an emotive meaning. This on his view is especially appropriate for dynamic use, a use the sentence would have when, e.g., said in response to "Let's not bother to clean up the mess we've made." But it could be used descriptively, with the primary purpose of communicating information about the speaker's own attitudes, as might be the case when used to reply to the question "What are some of the things you think are good? " There is thus considerable flexibility in Stevenson's position. And by making these distinctions, it might be noted, he avoids an objection sometimes brought against the emotive theory of ethics, namely, that it confuses the meaning of an ethical judgment with the intended effect the speaker has in mind in making the judgment. Granted that the objector might say that the point of making an ethical judgment is often, perhaps typically, to alter the listener's feelings and attitudes, it does not follow that this is what the meaning of the ethical judgment consists in. Stevenson would agree that it does not strictly follow: he, too, wants to distinguish the intended effects of an utterance from its meaning. But he would still insist on holding that it is not purely accidental that ethical terms, having emotive meaning as they do on his theory, are typically used in a dynamic rather than a purely descriptive way. The fundamental fact, for Stevenson, is that ethical language is used dynamically rather than in a purely descriptive way, and for him it is primarily failure to recognize that fact which has led past thinkers to overlook the primarily emotive meaning of ethical terms and to treat them as if they were simply one special kind of descriptive expression.

In the preceding paragraphs I have tried to contrast Ayer's extremely simple version of the emotive theory with Stevenson's highly complex version. Although I do not wish to suggest that Stevenson in fact arrived at his position in this way, it can be understood as an attempt to present a plausible version of the emotive theory, one without the uninviting and paradoxical features of Ayer's version and, hence, one likely to attract a much wider philosophical following for the emotive theory than Ayer's statement of the theory seems likely to do. In the remaining paragraphs of this section I shall indicate some of the problems raised by Stevenson's statement of the theory in the 1937 article. My purpose here is not to show that the emotive thoery is untenable, even in Stevenson's sophisticated formulation of it, but only to suggest some of the difficulties which have to be dealt with to make it a fully tenable theory, difficulties which Stevenson himself has sought to deal with in his subsequent work.

(1) Stevenson, as stated above, does not deny that there is always a descriptive as well as an emotive element in ethical judgments, and it is at least natural to interpret this as meaning that ethical terms such as "good" and "right" have descriptive as well as emotive meaning for him. This makes Stevenson's position far more attractive to naturalists than Ayer's: it even seems to make it possible to regard his position as a kind of naturalistic theory. But what, a naturalist would be eager to know, *is* the descriptive meaning of, e.g., "good" according to Stevenson? Stevenson gives no very clear answer to this question, partly because he has little confidence that anyone can analyze an ethical term such as "good" with complete accuracy in the sense of providing some alternative expression which can be substituted for it in ordinary contexts without loss or change of meaning. But even such tentative analyses as Stevenson himself suggests are not very satisfactory. In the 1937 article he makes two tentative suggestions concerning the meaning of "good." The first is that "X is good" means something like "We like X" where "we" includes the hearer or hearers. This suggested analysis could be interpreted as meaning that "X is good" is an instance of an expression which has descriptive meaning ("We like X") used, however, not descriptively, not simply to record or report the fact that the speaker and hearers share a liking for X, but dynamically, to arouse or enhance an interest in X in the listeners. But on that interpretation, at least, of Stevenson's suggestion, "X is good" would, although not *used* descriptively but dynamically, have a purely descriptive *meaning*. Hence the analysis would go against Stevenson's central thesis that "good" and other ethical terms have a primarily emotive meaning. Stevenson himself points this out as a reason for

questioning "We like X" as an analysis of "X is good." "The word 'good' " he remarks, "has a laudatory emotive meaning that fits it for the dynamic use of suggesting favorable interest. But the sentence 'we like it' has no such emotive meaning. Hence my definition has neglected emotive meaning entirely." Stevenson's second suggestion is that "X is good" has roughly the meaning "I *do* like this: do so as well." (This suggestion is essentially repeated and discussed at length in *Ethics and Language* where, according to the "first pattern of analysis," "This is good" is synonymous with "I approve of this; do so as well." The difference is that in *Ethics and Language* Stevenson uses "approve" rather than "like.") Thus, in the 1937 article and in *Ethics and Language,* Stevenson was convinced that ethical terms such as "good" contain what can be called an autobiographical aspect, and that this aspect is part of the meaning of "good," not merely something that is suggested or implied in some loose sense by saying "X is good." Yet, Stevenson himself was not entirely sure that "I like X" or "I approve of X" fully or precisely states this autobiographical element. In a 1948 article, "Meaning, Descriptive and Emotive" (reprinted in *Facts and Values),* a clarification of his views on meaning in reply to some criticisms by Max Black, Stevenson, while again stressing the thesis that the autobiographical aspect is strictly part of the meaning of "good," also concedes again that the descriptive meaning of "good" is vague and that he could have mentioned other descriptive meanings in addition to "I approve of it," e.g. "I am inclined to have others share my approval." And, more important, in Essay 11 of *Facts and Values,* Stevenson takes the view that it would be a definite mistake to include any autobiographical element in the meaning of ethical judgments, on grounds that the reasons needed to support the ethical judgment do not include the reasons needed to support an autobiographical statement about the speaker's attitudes: when I say "Abortion is wrong" I do not and cannot support my ethical judgment by citing evidence to show that I do in fact disapprove of abortion and want others to share my disapproval. Hence the autobiographical aspect cannot by Stevenson's own later admission be the descriptive meaning of ethical terms such as "good"; what possibility remains? The 1937 article contains no further suggestion. But in *Ethics and Language* Stevenson discusses a "second pattern of analysis" whose general form is described as follows:

"This is good" has the meaning of "This has qualities or relations X, Y, Z. . . ," except that "good" has as well a laudatory
emotive meaning which permits it to express the speaker's approval, and tends to evoke the approval of the hearer. (*Ethics and
Language,* p. 207)

It might then seem that Stevenson would be prepared to accept some
naturalistic definition of "good," e.g. Spencer's definition of "good"
as "conducive to life in self or others" as a correct analysis, as long
as one is prepared to concede that "good" also has a laudatory emotive meaning. But anyone who has read Stevenson's ensuing discussion would recognize this as a radical misstatement of his position.
Stevenson's position is that all naturalistic definitions such as Spencer's are attempts to narrowly delimit the descriptive meaning of
"good" in order to gain approval for the specific qualities which the
definer himself approves of—in short, they are persuasive definitions
and as such are to be regarded as normative value judgments in
disguise rather than meta-ethical statements. Indeed, there is no such
thing on Stevenson's view as a "correct" second pattern definition of
"good" and other ethical terms. There are simply alternative definitions each of which expresses the definor's particular scheme of values. Stevenson does not and could not consistently (in his meta-ethical
work) himself give a second pattern analysis of "good" or any other
ethical term. And, hence, he could not himself specify the descriptive
meaning of ethical terms in this way either. At most, he could say that
the descriptive meaning of "good" is an indefinitely complex disjunction of this sort: "X is good" means (descriptively) "Either X has
qualities or relations X, Y, Z. . . . , or X has qualities or relations W,
X, Y. . . . , or X has qualities or relations V, W, X. . . , and so
on." But apart from the fact that Stevenson gives no hint as to how
one would decide what alternatives to include in the disjunction, Stevenson himself would doubtless regard it as giving a possible range of
descriptive meanings, rather than itself constituting an analysis of the
descriptive meaning. In sum, Stevenson's position is less attractive to
naturalists than it might at first sight appear to be, in the light of his
unwillingness or inability to specify what the descriptive meanings of
ethical terms are.

(2) Perhaps Stevenson's assertion, in the 1937 article, that ethical
judgments always have some descriptive element should be read as as-

serting that while in any particular occasion of their use an ethical term such as "good" always has a descriptive meaning, these descriptive meanings vary from occasion to occasion and from speaker to speaker. He is perhaps asserting, in short, that "good" always has *a* descriptive meaning but there is no such thing as *the* descriptive meaning of "good." There is little doubt that this would be Stevenson's explanation. But it raises the following difficulty. If the descriptive meaning of "good" and other ethical terms varies from occasion to occasion and speaker to speaker, then the meaning of "good" would change whenever the descriptive element changes. "Good" would then become a homonymous word, i.e. a word like "fast" (as in "fast dye" and "fast runner") or "bow" (in "bow of a ship" and "make a bow"), which has several different unrelated senses—is really several different words, one might say, which happen to be spelled and pronounced alike. True, "good" would not be completely homonymous: there would be a common emotive meaning. But insofar as the descriptive meaning is concerned, the word would be homonymous or at least radically ambiguous. One would have to say that if Mr. A. and Mr. B attach somewhat different descriptive meanings to "good" then when they both say "Mr. C is a good man" they are not, strictly speaking, saying the same thing. And when A and B disagree on whether to call C a good man, A saying "C is a good man" and B saying "C is not a good man," they would not, strictly speaking, be disagreeing since they are using "good" in somewhat different senses. Stevenson himself might accept these consequences. But problems of this kind have worried subsequent philosophers, notably R. M. Hare, who in his book, *The Language of Morals,* distinguishes the *meaning* of "good" and the *criteria* of goodness. Roughly (the notion of "criteria" is a highly difficult and problematic one) the criteria of goodness are the features of a thing by virtue of whose presence we call the thing good: to give the criteria is to give the test we employ in deciding whether to call the thing good or not. The point of the distinction is that it explains how "good" in "good strawberries," "good weather," "good sewage," "good man," etc. is not a mere homonym. More important, perhaps, it explains how it is possible to say that Mr. A and Mr. B in the above sort of example would be disagreeing when A says "C is a good man" and B says "C is not a good man." What Stevenson would call the descriptive meaning of "good" Hare would call the criteria, and would go on to say that while A and B are employing different criteria, they are in no way differing about the meaning of "good." There seems no reason why Stevenson could not accept this modification of his theory. But there are generally acknowledged difficulties in the notion of a criterion, and this modification would seem to move Stevenson's theory even further away from naturalism.

(3) As indicated above, Stevenson is able to avoid Ayer's conclusion that ethical terms are meaningless in a strict sense of "meaning" because of his notion of emotive meaning, a notion which is itself possible for Stevenson because of his pragmatic or psychological theory of meaning. But is this not a merely verbal advantage in Stevenson's version of the emotive theory? Could not Ayer reply that on Stevenson's view ethical terms (leaving aside the vexing question, discussed above, of their descriptive meaning) are entirely meaningless in the sense of "meaning" in which expressions such as "round" or "red" or "200° centigrade" are said to have a meaning? This sense, Ayer might say, involves the existence of empirical tests for the truth or falsity of statements ascribing to objects the properties designated by such expressions. And is it not Stevenson's view that (again leaving aside descriptive meaning) there are no empirical tests for the truth or falsity of sentences of the form "X is good" or "Y is right?" Is it not indeed Stevenson's view that such sentences are neither true nor false? As regards the last point Stevenson does, in Essay 11 of *Facts and Values,* make the point which it was suggested earlier that Ayer could have made, namely that saying " 'X is good' is true" is merely a way saying, with emphasis, "X is good": the fact that we can ascribe truth or falsity without linguistic impropriety to ethical judgments shows nothing, Stevenson argues, about their cognitive status. But the fact still seems to remain that, for Stevenson as for Ayer, ethical terms are meaningless as opposed to the sense of "meaningful" in which meaning is tied to empirical verifiability. Further, Ayer might argue, the price Stevenson pays for avoiding the conclusion that ethical terms are largely if not entirely meaningless is too great. Stevenson's general theory of meaning as stated in the 1937 article is that the meaning of an expression is its general and persistent tendency to express or evoke certain states of mind in the people who use the expression. But meaning in this sense is not exclusively a property of linguistic entities such

as words and sentences. Meaning in this sense could be a property of a wide variety of non-linguistic entities such as gestures, pictorial representations, conventional signs such as traffic signals, and so on: practically anything, in fact, could have a meaning in Stevenson's sense. Again, Stevenson's account of meaning as applied to strictly linguistic entities such as words and sentences has the consequence that a great many things we should not ordinarily consider part of an expression's meaning in any strict sense of "meaning" become so, e.g. one would have to say that since the word "Jesus" has a very general and widespread tendency to evoke the thought of a man dressed in white robes, that tendency is part of the meaning of the word "Jesus." In general, the price Stevenson has to pay for a conception of meaning according to which the emotive expressiveness and evocativeness of an expression is part of its meaning is that it becomes very difficult to distinguish in any precise and non-circular way between what a word means and what it merely suggests to most people in a given social or cultural group. Stevenson has sought to do this in chapter III of *Ethics and Language* and in "Meaning: Descriptive and Emotive." But it is not entirely clear he has succeeded.

(4) Stevenson, in the 1937 article and subsequently, appears to think of emotive meaning and descriptive meaning as simply two *kinds* of meaning, in the same way that, e.g., gas stoves and electric stoves are simply two kinds of stoves, rather than thinking of emotive meaning and descriptive meaning as involving two different *senses* of "meaning," as would be the case with, e.g., "stove" in "turning on the stove" and "stove in the side of the boat." Closely examined, however, Stevenson's account of emotive and descriptive meaning seems to involve two different senses of "meaning" rather than simply two different kinds of meanings. In the case of descriptive meaning, as Stevenson defines it in Chapter III of *Ethics and Language,* meanings are fixed by what he calls "linguistic rules." The descriptive meaning of a sign is said to be "its disposition to affect cognition, provided that the disposition is caused by an elaborate process of conditioning that has attended the sign's use in communication, and provided that the disposition is rendered fixed, at least to a considerable degree, by linguistic rules." In the case of emotive meaning, however, the meaning does not appear to be fixed in a similar way by any-

thing that could be called "linguistic rules." Indeed, in another footnote added to "The Emotive meaning of Ethical Terms" as reprinted
in the 1970 edition of *Readings in Ethical Theory,* Stevenson defines
emotive meaning without reference to linguistic rules at all: he there
defines emotive meaning as "a strong and persistent tendency, built up
in the course of linguistic history, to give direct expression (quasi-
interjectionally) to certain of the speaker's feelings or emotions or
attitudes; and . . . also a tendency to evoke (quasi-imperatively) corresponding feelings, emotions, or attitudes in those to whom the
speaker's remarks are addressed." In general, one would think that if
emotive meaning and descriptive meaning were simply two kinds of
meaning, then they would be distinguished in terms of the kind of
linguistic rule which fixes them. But Stevenson does not distinguish
them in this way: he distinguishes them in terms of the kinds of states
of mind expressed or aroused (affective or emotional states as against
cognitive states). Hence there is reason to think that emotive and
descriptive meanings are "meanings" in different senses, and are not
simply two kinds of meanings. But if they are not, then Stevenson has
again failed to show that ethical terms are meaningful in the sense in
which "round" or "red" or "200° centigrade" are meaningful.

(5) Stevenson's central thesis in the 1937 article is that ethical judgments of the form "X is good" and "Y is right" are used dynamically, with the purpose of influencing the listener's feelings and attitudes, and that this dynamic purpose is assisted by the emotive
meaning of ethical terms such as "good" and "right." But how central to ethical discourse is this dynamic use? And to what extent does
the notion of emotive meaning help explain how this dynamic purpose
is achieved? Both these questions have involved considerable controversy, and there is no general consensus that Stevenson's answers
are the right answers. As regards the first, there is little doubt that
ethical judgments are sometimes used dynamically in Stevenson's
sense. For example, they are used dynamically in cases where one person is seeking to persuade another to change his attitude or undertake
some course of action he is unwilling to undertake: e.g. "Eat some of
this asparagus: it's good!" or "We can't leave him lying there: it
wouldn't be right!" But even in such clear cases of dynamic use it
isn't obvious that the dynamic use is the only use. Stevenson himself
points out that a given utterance can be both dynamic and descriptive,

and it might be maintained that in cases such as the above there is both a descriptive and a dynamic use of "it's good" and "it wouldn't be right." And what about cases where the two persons are already agreed on their attitude, as in "She's an awfully good person, isn't she," or "I think we can trust Tom: he usually does the right thing." Some uses of "good" and "right," moreover, are not interpersonal at all, e.g. a person saying to himself privately "She's a good person but she talks too much." It would be implausible to hold that in saying "She's a good person" in such a case the speaker is seeking to influence his own attitudes. In general, Stevenson's thesis that ethical judgments are primarily dynamic, apart from a certain degree of vagueness (is it a matter simply of statistical frequency?), can be questioned. But granting this first thesis, what about the second thesis, that the dynamic use of ethical judgments can be accounted for in terms of their primarily emotive meaning? This too can be questioned. Words like "good" and "right" are not obviously emotive in the sense that words like "bastard" and "bitch" are. The emotive force of ethical terms seems not to reside so much in the terms themselves as in the tone of voice in which they are used, or the facial expression of the speaker, or his gestures, etc. The emotive meaning of ethical terms, granted it does exist in Stevenson's liberal sense of "meaning" is not obviously the major element in the meanings of such terms, a fact which has led such philosophers as Hare and Patrick Nowell-Smith, who fundamentally agree with Stevenson in holding that ethical language is not primarily descriptive, to abandon the notion of emotive meaning altogether. Probably that goes too far, but there are difficulties in the notion.

To summarize this section, there are highly important differences between Stevenson's version of the emotive theory of ethics as stated in "The Emotive Meaning of Ethical Terms" and Ayer's version. At the same time some of the differences may be more a matter of terminology than of fundamental doctrine. And in some basic respects Stevenson's position raises questions which have yet to be completely answered.

3 Stevenson's Theory of Ethical Disagreement

Stevenson's theory of ethical disagreement, as sketched in section V of "The Emotive Meaning of Ethical Terms" and presented in more detail in Chapter I of *Ethics and Language* and in his 1948 article "The Nature of Ethical Disagreement" (reprinted as Essay 1 of *Facts and Values*) can be summarized in the following way. Disagreements, Stevenson points out, can be of two quite different kinds (perhaps it would be better to speak of different senses of "disagreement"). One kind, which Stevenson calls "disagreement in belief," might be illustrated in its simplest form by, e.g., a disagreement over whether the capital of Massachusetts is Boston or Springfield, one person maintaining the former and the other the latter. In general, disagreement in belief exists when two persons hold beliefs which cannot both be true and when each person is not simply content to allow the other's belief to remain unchanged. The other kind, called by Stevenson "disagreement in interest" in the 1937 article and "disagreement in attitude" in *Ethics and Language* and in the 1948 article, exists when two or more persons have conflicting attitudes cooncerning something, one person favoring it and the other having a disfavorable or less favorable attitude toward it, and when neither is content to let the other's attitude remain unchanged.

Stevenson initially illustrates the second kind of disagreement by examples such as one person saying "Let's go to the movies tonight" and the other saying "No: let's go to the symphony concert"—examples of what could be called pure or nearly pure disagreement in attitude. But as his more complex example of the disagreement between representatives of management and labor over wage increases is intended to show, many disagreements involve both disagreement in attitude and in belief. Such a disagreement involves disagreement in attitude in that "the union is *for* higher wages; the company is *against* them, and neither is content to let the other's attitude remain unchanged." But there may also be disagreement in belief, e.g. about how much the cost of living has risen, or about the company's earnings. Stevenson's theory, in these terms, is that ethical disagreements are typically disagreements both in attitude and in belief, but that they are primarily disagreements in attitude in that (a) the parties to the disagreement only try to resolve those disagreements in belief whose resolution will help resolve the disagreement in attitude, and (b) argument ceases when disagreement in attitude ceases even though some disagreement in belief may presumably still remain:

Both disagreement in attitude and disagreement in belief are involved, but the former predominates in that (1) it determines what sort of disagreement in belief is relevantly disputed in a given ethical argument, and (2) it determines by its continued presence or its resolution whether or not the argument has been settled. (*Facts and Values*, p. 6)

As summarized thus far, a naturalist such as Dewey or Perry could accept Stevenson's theory of ethical disagreement as involving an important discovery about the nature of ethical disagreement which naturalists have overlooked, but which they need not deny—just as a naturalist could accept Stevenson's thesis that ethical terms have emotive meaning as long as this is not taken to deny that they also have descriptive meaning. The real issue between Stevenson and the naturalists concerning ethical disagreement concerns the extent to which ethical disagreement *can* be resolved by securing agreement in belief. The naturalist, as suggested at the end of the preceding chapter, holds in effect that ethical disagreement will cease when the parties to the disagreement have reached agreement will cease when the parties to the disagreement have reached agreement on all relevant matters of fact. Or at least some such assumption seems to lie at the basis of most if not all naturalistic ethical theories prior to Stevenson. Stevenson does not exactly reject this assumption. But he questions it. It is certainly logically possible, he argues, for two persons to agree on all the relevant facts concerning a certain thing or action and yet disagree concerning its value or rightness. And Stevenson himself is inclined to think this logical possibility may well be realized in practice, as the following passage suggests:

We usually *do not know,* at the beginning of any argument about values, whether an agreement in belief, scientifically established, will lead to an agreement in attitude or not. It is logically possible, at least, that two men should continue to disagree in attitude even though they had all their beliefs in common, and even though neither had made any logical or inductive error, or omitted any relevant evidence. Differences in temperament, or in early training, or in social status, might make the men retain different attitudes even though both were possessed of the complete scientific truth. Whether this logical possibility is an empirical likelihood I shall not presume to say; but it is unquestionably a possibility that must not be left out of account. (*Facts and Values*, p. 7)

Stevenson does not deny that all ethical disagreements can be *terminated* in some way or other; if not by rational methods, then by non-rational methods of persuasion, or by such methods as imprisoning or killing one's opponent. What he questions is whether all ethical disagreements can be *resolved*, understanding by the "resolution" of an ethical disagreement its rational termination by arguing deductively or inductively from mutually accepted factual premises. Naturalists, in effect, assuming that all disagreements in attitude are rooted in (to use Stevenson's expression) disagreement in belief, hold that in principle all ethical disagreements can be resolved. Stevenson's position is more pessimistic. Perhaps, he concedes, it may be discovered that all disagreement in attitude is rooted in disagreement in belief. But then again it may be discovered that they are not. In any event we are not now warranted in blindly assuming in ethical theory that the former is the case. Whether it is the case is something to be decided by discoveries in psychology and the social sciences, not by philosophical analysis. And if it turns out that to a significant extent conflicts in attitude are not rooted in disagreement in belief, we will have to conclude that many important ethical disagreements are not in principle resolvable.

The questions Stevenson raises in his account of ethical disagreement are clearly important, both for ethical theory itself and for their practical implications. The question concerning the extent to which ethical disagreement can be resolved, in particular, is a crucially important one both for theory and for practice. I shall try to deal with this question in the concluding section of this book. In the remaining paragraphs of the present section, I shall simply raise some critical questions concerning Stevenson's position, in hopes of somewhat clarifying the issue between Stevenson and the naturalist.

(1) The distinction between disagreement in belief and disagreement in attitude, while presented and illustrated by Stevenson with considerable lucidity, especially in "The Nature of Ethical Disagreement," is not without a certain degree of unclarity. Attitudes— that is, what we ordinarily call "attitudes," for Stevenson, as Urmson shows at some length, does not appear to mean by "attitude" quite what we ordinar-

ily mean—and beliefs are not, if ordinary language is any guide, necessarily two distinct things. Believing, or at least disbelieving, can themselves count as attitudes, as when we speak of a sceptical attitude or an attitude of disbelief. Insofar as this is so, there might be some justification for regarding disagreement in attitude as the more general phenomenon and disagreement in belief as one kind of disagreement in attitude, instead or regarding them as two separate species of disagreement as Stevenson does. Some of Stevenson's examples of disagreement in attitude, moreover, are not what we should ordinarily call instances of conflicting attitudes at all, at least not directly. If I want to go to the movies and my wife wants to go to the symphony concert, we have conflicting desires; but it would be somewhat odd to say we have conflicting attitudes (although perhaps our particular desires in some sense reflect or reveal our attitudes). Stevenson appears to count as attitudes mere particular likings or wantings, which is not how we commonly use the term "attitude."

(2) Perhaps the last point made above is merely terminological, and Stevenson's terms "attitude" and "belief" should be taken as technical or quasi-technical expressions. But in that case one would expect Stevenson to be somewhat more worried than he appears to be at his admitted inability to give a very clear and precise explication of what he means by "attitudes." In *Ethics and Language* he gives the following (admittedly rough) characterization of an attitude: "It [an attitude] is, in fact, itself a complicated conjunction of dispositional properties . . . marked by stimuli and responses which relate to hindering or assisting whatever it is that is called the 'object' of the attitude." This suggests that by "attitude" Stevenson primarily has in mind being "for" or "against" something. But this is too narrow a conception of what we ordinarily mean by attitudes. Thus, we speak of a cheerful or hopeful attitude concerning something, and these do not obviously involve a disposition either to hinder or to assist something. And clearly neither are involved in an attitude of indifference. The truth seems to be that Stevenson is heavily influenced in his conception of an attitude by Perry's conception of an "interest" (as was mentioned above, Stevenson's original expression in the 1937 article was "disagreement in interest" rather than "disagreement in attitude"). What Perry meant by an interest is, or could be, a particular kind of attitude, namely an

attitude of favor or disfavor concerning something; something involving a "tendency to create or conserve, or an opposite tendency to
prevent or destroy." Perry never suggested, however, that "interest"
and "attitude" are even roughly synonymous, and it is clear that in ordinary usage "attitude" is by far the broader term. Stevenson's terminology is possibly somewhat misleading then: it might have been less
so had he preserved the term "interest" used in the 1937 article.

(3) If it is roughly correct, as suggested above, to say that in using the
term "attitude" Stevenson intends to mean what Perry meant by "interest," then the thesis that ethical disagreements are primarily disagreements in attitude becomes a highly arguable one. For, offhand at
least, there seems a radical difference between judging something
good or bad on the one hand, and on the other hand liking it or dislik-
ing it, having feelings of desire or aversion toward it, or having a tendency to assist or hinder it. There is doubtless an important connection
between these two kinds of things: it is no doubt the case that a person
who judged something ethically or morally good but had no liking for
it, no desire for it, and no tendency to seek it and to create and conserve it, would as a general rule be considered insincere in his judgment. Yet the connection is not quite an entailment, even. Certainly I
may sincerely say that so and so is a good person without particularly
liking him, wishing to seek his company, wanting to assist him, etc. It
seems a commonplace of the moral life, indeed, that one's likes and
dislikes, desires and aversions, etc. are frequently in conflict with
one's judgments as to what is good and bad or right and wrong. It may
well be, to use Stevenson's example, that the representatives of management do not deny that the workers have a morally defensible claim
to receive higher wages. Yet they may well dislike this, work against
it, and generally display a negative attitude toward it. Stevenson's account would have to be that there is something at least insincere or
deceptive in the conduct of the representatives of management in such
a case. But while that could in some instance be the case, it need not
be: the representatives of management could quite frankly admit that
they were subordinating considerations of justice and morality to considerations of self interest. This would doubtless reflect on their moral
worth as persons, but it would not necessarily be the deception or in-
sincerity it would have to be on Stevenson's theory. Or, to make the

same point in a somewhat different way, there is a great difference between thinking I have a moral claim to something, and simply favoring it as something which I like or desire or tend to want to assist. In the first case one is morally indignant if one is prevented from having the thing, in a way that one would not be if it were merely a case of having one's interest opposed or hindered. Stevenson's analysis of ethical disagreement seems in fact to miss the very thing that is central in such disagreement and distinguishes it from a mere conflict of interest, namely, that the parties to the disagreement think, mistakenly or not, that their desires have a kind of moral backing or justification which does not itself simply reduce to the fact that they strongly want their desires or interests satisfied.

(4) If Stevenson's analysis of ethical disagreement as primarily a disagreement in attitude (in Stevenson's sense of "attitude") were correct, then it can hardly be doubted that arrival at agreement in belief is often not sufficient to end the disagreement, and that, therefore, the ethical disagreement can often not be resolved. For a disagreement in attitude in Stevenson's sense is characterized by a conflict of interest where neither side is content to let the other side's interest be satisfied at what he considers his own expense. It is quite clear that such conflicts of interest are often not rooted in disagreement in belief, if by "rooted in" one means "caused by." It is obvious that what causes such conflicts is very often factors such as those Stevenson mentions, e.g. differences in temperament, or in early training, or in social status. And, it likewise appears obvious, it is frequently the case in such conflicts that no amount of agreement in belief is sufficient to resolve the conflict in the sense of changing the feelings or desires of one or both parties to the dispute. Thus, in a simple case of disagreement in attitude such as the disagreement between my wife and I about whether to go to the movies or to the concert, it could be and often is quite obvious that the disagreement is not caused by any disagreement in belief (at least barring unconscious beliefs) but by the mere fact that we want different things which, in the circumstances, we cannot both have. Stevenson raises the question whether, in general, reaching agreement in belief is sufficient to bring about agreement in attitude. The answer is obviously no: the only puzzling thing is why Stevenson thinks this is even an open question for whose answer we have to wait

on the future findings of psychology and the social sciences. But the conclusion, that disagreements in attitude can very often not be resolved, is not as threatening as many of Stevenson's readers seem to have supposed. There are methods of conflict resolution which do not presuppose an agreement in attitude, and it may prove possible to use some of these methods in ethical disagreements. Thus, to take a hypothetical simple case, A may think it would be wrong to do X, and B may think it would be wrong not to do X, A having a strongly disfavorable attitude toward X and B having a strongly disfavorable attitude toward non-X. The conflict could be resolved without any change in attitude if we could point out that there is an alternative to X, namely Y, which both favor and, further, which is such that B's favorable attitude toward Y outweighs his unfavorable attitude toward non-X. In such a case they could agree that it would be right to do Y instead of X, even though the original incompatible attitudes in a sense remain the same. (As an actual attempt to compromise in this way, one might mention the recently proposed educational voucher system. Some strongly oppose aid to private religious schools in the form of tax credits, others think it wrong not to provide such aid. The suggested compromise is to provide aid on an equal basis to all schools, in hopes that while those who in principle oppose aid to religious schools will not like the voucher system in its aspect of aiding religious schools, they will prefer it to no aid at all.) Even, therefore, if one were to grant that Stevenson's analysis of the nature of ethical disagreement as primarily disagreement in attitude is correct, the frequent impossibility of resolving the disagreement through reaching agreement in belief, while almost certainly a consequence, need not necessarily be seen as threatening. In any event, to the extent that Stevenson's analysis of the nature of ethical disagreement is still in doubt, it is still an open question as to whether all ethical disagreements are in principle resolvable. The naturalist, as indicated at the end of the preceeding chapter, thinks that in the case of all ethical disagreements, there is some set of non-ethical facts such that all persons who agree on these facts will share the same ethical judgments. Or *would* share the same ethical conclusions to the extent that they are rational. What the naturalist thinks is that to the extent that men and women are able and willing to draw all and only logically warranted conclusions from factual premises, to that extent they will agree in their ethical conclusions. Whether men and women actually are rational in that sense is not a matter a naturalist need commit himself on. Probably no naturalist has ever thought that people are completely rational, and in any case it is certain that a faith in human rationality is no part of naturalism as a meta-ethical theory. Thomas Hobbes was, or can with plausibility be read as, a naturalist, but few philosophers have had less faith in human rationality than Hobbes.

To summarize, I have tried to suggest that while Stevenson has raised a question of fundamental importance, both theoretical and practical, concerning the resolvability of ethical disagreement, his own analysis of ethical disagreement as primarily disagreement in attitude leaves several questions unanswered. The principle question, I should say, is this: granting Stevenson is right in maintaining that ethical disagreement typically involves non-cognitive conflicts of attitudes, and that failure to see this was a serious oversight in previous ethical theories, cannot a naturalist accommodate Stevenson's discovery and still maintain his own thesis that in all cases of ethical disagreement there is available, or could become available through sufficient further empirical inquiry, a set of non-ethical facts such that all who accept these facts would, if they were rational, come to the same ethical conclusions? It is not clear to me that Stevenson's account of ethical disagreement shows conclusively that this thesis must be given up. And in section 4 of the Conclusion I shall argue that even if what Stevenson mentions as a possibility is a frequent actuality, namely that ethical disagreements are rooted in disagreements in attitudes rather than disagreements in beliefs, it may still be possible to resolve these disagreements in a rational way, by ordinary inductive and deductive reasoning from factual premises.

V

NON-COGNITIVISM: HARE

IN THE COURSE OF the preceding chapters I have already mentioned some of Hare's views, notably in the first section of Chapter III where I discussed Hare's characterization of naturalism in his 1963 book, *Freedom and Reason.* In the present chapter I want to discuss certain aspects of Hare's ethical theory in a more systematic and critical way. In the first section I shall discuss Hare's attempt, in his 1952 book, *The Language of Morals,* to restate Moore's refutation of naturalism in a way designed to free the anti-naturalist argument from the criticisms that have been made of Moore's statement of the argument. In the second section I shall discuss what I take to be the main or at least one of the main positive lines of argument in *The Language of Morals,* namely, that since the function of moral judgments is to guide choices, they cannot be merely statements of fact but must contain an irreducibly prescriptive (as opposed to descriptive) element. And in the third section I shall discuss what I take to be the main positive thesis advanced in *Freedom and Reason,* which is, that while moral judgments are subject to a certain formal requirement, namely that they must be universalizable, the principle of universalizability is only a logical principle, true of moral judgments because they have descriptive as well as prescriptive meaning, and that nothing of moral substance can be derived from the principle.

1   Hare's Refutation of Naturalism

Hare has expressed the view that although Moore's refutation of naturalism was badly stated and has been widely criticized, it nevertheless rests on secure foundations: "there is indeed," Hare asserts, "something about the way in which, and the purposes for which, we use the word 'good' which makes it impossible to hold the sort of position which Moore was attacking, although Moore did not see clearly what this something was." Moore's argument, as I tried to show in Chapter 1, is (or can be understood as) an argument of this general form: naturalism, if true, implies that certain ethical sentences are analytic; but ethical sentences are never analytic; hence naturalism is false. Hare himself sometimes argues as if it were evident, and needed no further argument, that ethical sentences are not analytic. Thus, he asserts:

> Suppose that someone were to maintain that "It is not right to do A" is entailed by "A has been forbidden by the ruler of our State," we should only need to point out that in that case "It is not right to do what has been forbidden by the ruler of our State" would be entailed by the analytic sentence "What has been forbidden by the ruler of our State has been forbidden by the ruler of our State," and would therefore be itself analytic, which in ordinary usage it is not. (*The Language of Morals,* p. 155)

Generally, Hare's argument in this passage is that no ethical sentence, in ordinary usage, is analytic. But if this were Hare's argument, his refutation of naturalism would not be a substantial improvement over Moore: Moore, too, without using the term "analytic", in effect based his argument on the principle that ethical sentences are never analytic. Further, as I have suggested in discussing Moore's argument, it is not altogether clear what sort of evidence would go to show that in ordinary usage ethical sentences are never analytic. It is certainly true that naturalists have used sentences such as "Whatever is pleasant is good" in order to make analytic sentences, and while such usage may not be part of what is presently considered ordinary usage, there seems no very good reason for thinking that it could not at some future time become so.

The clearest statement of Hare's refutation of naturalism is contained in the following passage:

> Now our attack upon naturalistic definitions of "good" was based on the fact that if it were true that "a good A" meant the same as "an A which is C," then it would be impossible to use the sentence "An A which is C is good" in order to commend A's which are C; for this sentence would be analytic and equivalent to "An A which is C is C." (*The Language of Morals*, pp. 90–91)

By saying that we use sentences of the form "An A which is C is good" to commend A's which are C, Hare presumably means more than saying that we apply an ethical word to A's which are C. If this were all that commending means, it would be trivially true that by commending A's that are C's we are not saying that A's that are C are C (when C is replaceable by a non-ethical expression). In order to understand and evaluate Hare's argument we have to know what Hare means by commending.

Hare describes commending as follows: "When we commend or condemn anything, it is always in order, at least indirectly, to guide choices, our own or other people's, now or in the future." Hare's refutation of naturalism might, then, be restated as follows:

1. If naturalism is true, then some ethical sentences of the form "Whatever is F is good" are equivalent to "Whatever is F is F."
2. Sentences of the form "Whatever is F is F" are never used to guide choices.
3. But ethical sentences of the form "Whatever is F is good" are used to guide choices.
4. Hence sentences of the form "Whatever is F is good" are never equivalent to "Whatever is F is F" and, hence, naturalism is false.

Formally the argument is valid. But what evidence does Hare have for saying that sentences of the form "Whatever is F is good" are always used to guide choices? A naturalist could say (for some non-ethical expression F) such sentences are analytic, and hence do not guide choices. In reply to this, Hare might simply argue that in fact such sentences do guide choices. How is such a dispute to be settled; how is one to go about deciding whether a given sentence does or does not guide choices? Hare gives no way of deciding such a question.

A further question can be raised concerning Hare's argument. Hare holds that sentences of the form "Whatever is F is F" cannot be used to guide choices, whereas sentences of the form "Whatever is F is good" are used to guide choices. But is it impossible for a sentence of the form "Whatever is F is F" to be used in order to commend F's? It would probably be granted by anyone, naturalist or intuitionist, that such sentences are not used in order to guide choices. But it is not so clear that sentences of the form "All F's are good" are never used to guide choices when "F" and "good" are synonymous. A hedonist, for example, might want to say that since "pleasant" and "good" are synonymous, the sentence "All and only pleasures are good" is equivalent to "All and only pleasures are pleasant." But he might also want to say that while the latter sentence does nothing to guide choices, the former sentence does guide choices, because the word "good" guides choices in a way in which no synonym of "good" does or can do. In general, a naturalist might argue, two expressions can be synonymous even if sentences containing one expression are not equivalent to sentences containing the other expression. For example, it might be argued that the sentence "She is an elderly unmarried woman," and the sentence "She is a spinster" are not equivalent, in the sense that the latter conveys overtones and suggestions, and hence guides choices, in a way in which the former sentence does not. Yet, "elderly unmarried woman" and "spinster" can be counted as synonyms. Similarly, the naturalist could argue that the expressions "pleasant" and "good" can well be synonymous, even though replacement of "pleasant" by "good" might result in a sentence which guides choices in a way in which the former sentence does not.

In reply to the question just raised, Hare might of course reply that if one sentence, S_1, guides choices, while another, S_2, does not guide choices, and the two sentences only differ because S_1 contains an expression E which does not occur in S_2, then the expression E cannot be synonymous with the expression E_1 which replaces E in S_2. In other words, Hare might want to make the choice-guiding usage or function of expressions a criterion of synonymity, so that it can never be the case that one of a pair of synonyms guides choices while the other does not. This criterion, plus the empirical fact (if it is a fact) that ethical words such as "good" or "right" guide choices whereas non-ethical expressions such as "pleasant" do not, would be sufficient to refute naturalism.

In reply to Hare's argument as sketched above, a naturalist could however reply (1) that he does not accept choice-guidance as a criterion of synonymity, and (2) that it is not in fact true that ethical words guide choices whereas non-ethical expressions never do. As regards (1), there does seem to be some reason for rejecting choice-guidance as a criterion of synonymity. Consider, for instance, the expressions "X told a lie" and "X knowingly uttered a falsehood"; dictionaries tell us these are interchangeable and synonymous, but it is at least plausible to hold that the first has an effect on choices which the second does not have. In general, there are many expressions which are interchangeable without change of truth-value, and in that sense synonymous, which affect listeners in different ways and guide their choices in different ways: one might say that advertising is made possible by this fact. Of course Hare can still contend that interchangeability without changing truth-value is not a sufficient criterion of synonymity. But Hare's argument would then rest on an unusual and arbitrary proposal about synonymity. As regards (2), a naturalist might well argue that non-ethical expressions do in fact guide choices (One assumes that guiding choices is not a criterion of being an ethical word; if it were, then it would of course be trivially true that no non-ethical expressions guide choices). When someone says, for example, "There is a law against X," he usually intends to, and often does, guide our decision to do or not to do X. Hare might reply that this is so only because we understand the speaker to have implied an additional premise to the effect that whatever is illegal is wrong, the inference then being that X is wrong. But what reason is there to suppose that such an inference takes place in all cases? The assertion that it must take place seems to amount to nothing more than saying, in a complicated and misleading way, that the sentence "There is a law against X" does in fact guide choices. I conclude that the naturalist would have some reason for rejecting Hare's argument; it does not seem to be generally true that, since ethical words guide choices and non-ethical expressions never do, the two sorts of expressions are never synonymous. Hence, I conclude, Hare has not been entirely successful in showing that sentences of the form "Whatever is F is good" can never be analytic—suggestive as his argument undoubtedly is—and hence he has not succeeded in giving a final refutation of naturalism.

Can there be a final refutation of naturalism? I should say that in any case naturalism cannot be refuted by any direct appeal to matters of fact. Underlying every naturalistic theory is an assertion that an ethical expression is synonymous with a non-ethical expression. In general, an assertion that expressions are synonymous can be understood as an empirical assertion about ordinary language, or as a proposal which is one of the rules of an artificial language. In neither case, however, is the truth of naturalism a simple empirical question. The assertion that, e.g. "good" and "pleasant" are synonymous in ordinary language cannot be decided without deciding on a criterion of synonymity, and in the previous discussion I have tried to show that disputes about synonymity may be an important part of disputes about naturalistic definitions of ethical terms. If, on the other hand, naturalism is viewed as based on a rule in an artificial language, acceptance of naturalism depends on adopting that artificial language. In neither case is the acceptance or rejection of naturalism a straightforward empirical issue; the refutation of naturalism, then, cannot be an argument that naturalistic theories are contradicted by the facts.

2 Prescriptivism

In the *Language of Morals* Hare argues that since the function of moral judgments is to guide choices they cannot be merely statements of fact but must contain an irreducibly prescriptive element:

> Moral philosophers cannot have it both ways; either they must recognize the irreducibly prescriptive element in moral judgments, or else they must allow that moral judgments, as interpreted by them, do not guide actions in the way that, as ordinarily understood, they obviously do. (*The Language of Morals*, p. 195)

Granting that moral judgments do in some sense guide choices and actions, why must they therefore contain a "prescriptive element"?

(Stevenson, it may be recalled from the preceding chapter, seemed prepared in his 1937 article to grant that a statement could have a dynamic use, and in that sense presumably guide choices, and still have a purely descriptive meaning.) Hare's answer to this question is as follows:

> To guide choices or actions, a moral judgment has to be such that if a person assents to it, he must assent to some imperative sentence derivable from it; in other words, if a person does not assent to some such imperative sentence, that is knock-down evidence that he does not assent to the moral judgment in an evaluative sense—though of course he may assent to it in some other sense. . . . This is true by my definition of the word evaluative. . . . We are therefore clearly entitled to say that the moral judgment entails the imperative; for to say that one judgment entails another is simply to say that you cannot assent to the first and dissent from the second unless you have misunderstood one or the other; and this "cannot" is a logical "cannot"—if someone assents to the first and not to the second, this is in itself a sufficient criterion for saying that he has misunderstood the meaning of one or the other. (*The Language of Morals*, pp. 171–72)

If moral judgments are to guide choices, then, they must entail imperatives. And according to Hare no merely factual statement can entail an imperative; if a judgment entails an imperative the imperative must already be contained in the judgment itself:

> Nothing can appear in the conclusion of a valid deductive inference which is not, from their very meaning, implicit in the conjunction of the premises. If follows that, if there is an imperative in the conclusion, not only must *some* imperative appear in the premises, but that very imperative must be itself implicit in them. (*The Language of Morals*, p. 32)

At the risk of considerable oversimplification and distortion (in the Introduction to *Freedom and Reason* Hare remarks that he was not using the term "imperative" in quite the narrow sense ascribed to him by some of his critics) these passages can be pieced together to obtain the following line of argument: (1) the function of moral judgments when used evaluatively is to guide choices, (2) when judgments guide choices they entail imperatives, (3) judgments which entail imperatives must contain imperatives as part of their very meaning, and therefore (4) when *moral* judgments are used evaluatively they must contain imperatives as part of their meaning. And (5) since moral judgments (used evaluatively) do have an imperative element in their meaning, they cannot be merely statements of fact. A bit more formally, the argument might be outlined as follows:

1. To say that a judgment is used evaluatively is to say that it is used to guide choices.
2. If a judgment guides choices, it must entail an imperative.
3. If a judgment entails an imperative, then it must itself contain an imperative.
4. Therefore, when moral judgments are used evaluatively, they must contain an imperative (i.e. a prescriptive) element, and cannot be merely statements of fact.

In the following discussion I will use this argument as a kind of model, without claiming it is necessarily a true-to-life representation of Hare's position. But in criticizing the argument I hope to bring out more clearly some possible difficulties in Hare's position. I will discuss these three questions: (1) Is it true that to say a judgment is used evaluatively is to say that it is used to guide choices? (2) Is it true that if a judgment guides action or choices it must entail an imperative? (3) Is it true that if a judgment entails an imperative, it must itself contain an imperative as part of its meaning? In the case of (1) I will argue that there are a number of uses of moral judgments which are not in any obvious way choice-guiding, even indirectly, but which are usually called evaluative: further, there is no clear way of showing these uses are logically dependent on the choice-guiding use. In the case of (2) I will argue that judgments need not entail imperatives in order to guide choices, and in one sense of "guiding choices" cannot entail an imperative—at least as imperatives are commonly understood. In the case of (3) I will argue that on Hare's criterion of entailment it is not true that if a judgment entails an imperative it must contain an imperative as part of its meaning. For judgments do sometimes have a purely descriptive meaning but also entail an imperative in this sense: if someone assents to the judgment but dissents from some imperative which is not stated but is, as we say, "implied," then in Hare's words "this is in itself a sufficient criterion for saying that he has misunderstood the meaning of one or the other.'' The purpose of this criticism is not to argue that moral judgments *never* have an irreducibly prescriptive element. Nor is it to argue that moral judgments *are* always, or even sometimes, merely statements of fact. I do not wish to challenge what I take to be the widely held view among contemporary philosophers that Hare is right in stressing the typically prescriptive use of moral judgments, although I should be prepared to argue that this is a point a naturalist need not deny. The purpose of the following discussion is, rather, to suggest that the logical characteristics of moral judgments are more complex than Hare's argument might lead one to think, There are other uses of moral judgments besides the choice-guiding use, and there is no reason to think there is a clear order of logical priority among these uses: the choice-guiding role of moral judgments is not explained by saying that they entail imperatives, and in any event entailing imperatives is not peculiar to any kind of language use except, tautologically, prescribing or commending uses.

1. In a passage quoted above Hare makes it ''true by my definition of the word evaluative'' that when a moral judgment is used evaluatively, it entails an imperative. But this cannot be an arbitrary definition, introduced without regard to any previous meanings of ''evaluative.'' If that were so Hare could have no objection to the naturalist, who makes it true by *his* definition of the word ''evaluative'' that a moral judgment is used evaluatively only if it is used to describe a certain kind of fact. Further, Hare believes that this definition will prove illuminating. Behind the proposed definition, according to Hare, there are important facts, namely these: there is a class of sentences containing value words, some of these sentences entail imperatives, and it is this subclass which is ''of primary interest to the logician who studies moral language.'' But to say this is to assume that we can already pick out sentences containing value-words, and that what is to count as a value-word is already to some degree fixed. And this is to assume that some meaning has been given to the expression ''value-word''; that there is some standard by which to include or exclude an expression from the list of value-words. What is this standard? Hare has, I think, already at least suggested an answer. And the answer is this: value-words are expressions used in order to ''guide choices, our own or other peo-

ple's, now or in the future.'' In general, according to this reading of Hare, to say of an expression that it is a value-expression is to say that it is used to guide choices. In particular, to say that a moral judgment is a value-judgment is to say that it is used in order to guide choices. This is the thesis I want to question.

If a moral judgment is used in order to guide choices, then it must be directly or indirectly aimed at some agent—the speaker himself, or someone else, or some group of agents. And the person making the judgment must at least believe the following things to be true: the agent is in a position to hear and understand the judgment, and is capable of making choices. If a moral judgment is *not* addressed to some agent, or the person making the judgment does *not* believe that the agent is in a position to hear and understand it, or that he is in a position to make a choice, then we can be certain that the judgment is not being used to guide choices. But moral judgments are used (1) to appraise actions and choices, without being addressed to the agent, and (2) when the agent is not in a position to make a choice. And there seems nothing unnatural in calling these uses evaluative. Thus, (1) moral judgments are used to appraise actions of people who are complete strangers and where we have no intention of guiding the agent's action (''He oughtn't to smoke in that railway compartment''), and also to appraise actions by people no longer living (''Jones ought to have included his first wife in his will''). Further, moral judgments are used in the context of hypothetical or counterfactual judgments, to appraise actions of an unknown or non-existent agent (''Whoever is looking after those children shouldn't let them play in the street like that''; ''If someone *had* been looking after those children, then *he* ought to have kept them from playing in the street''). And moral judgments are also used to appraise actions and choices in works of fiction. In these uses we make judgments *about* actions, but the judgments are not addressed to the agent, and are not intended to guide an agent's choices: one cannot be said to guide the choices of an agent who is no longer living, or not known to exist, or known not to exist, or known to exist only in a work of fiction. Yet, it is natural to call these judgments value-judgments. (2) Moral judgments are used to appraise actions or choices where the agent addressed (ourselves or other people) is not in a position to make a choice: because the situation referred to in the judgment no longer exists (''I ought to have kept the children from playing in the street'') or because circumstances make it impossible to act otherwise (''I ought to be paying him more, but can't afford to''). The point of such uses cannot be to guide choices: one cannot guide someone's past actions, or guide someone's actions in a situation where circumstances prevent him from acting differently. In sum, there are many uses of moral judgments other than that of guiding choices. It cannot therefore be true that to say a moral judgment is used as a value-judgment is to say that it is used in order to guide choices.

In reply to this objection, Hare might argue as follows: although moral judgments do have uses besides guiding choices, these uses are all logically dependent on the choice-guiding use, in the sense that if we did not first understand the choice-guiding use, we could not understand the other uses. Therefore (so the argument might run) these other uses are all secondary, derivative. And to identify the evaluative use of moral judgments with their choice-guiding use is simply a way of stressing this fact—the fact that the choice-guiding use is basic, and all the others are logically dependent on it. But *are* all the uses that are not choice-guiding uses logically dependent? Is it true, for example, that one could not understand the use of ''ought'' in judgments such as ''He ought not to have smoked there'' unless one first understood the use of ''ought'' in such judgments as ''You ought not to be smoking in here''? The truth of this claim is not obvious, nor is it very clear how one would go about establishing it. It *is* plausible to say that in order to understand what a moral judgment is, one must understand the choice-guiding use of moral judgments. But it is equally plausible to say that it is necessary to understand the uses that are not choice-guiding. It is equally plausible to say, for exmple, that in order to understand what a moral judgment is, one must understand the uses of moral judgments to appraise the actions and choices of persons no longer living, or of remote strangers, or of merely hypothetical persons. But there is no obvious sense in which all the other uses are logically dependent on the choice-guiding use. Hare does point out certain ''inverted comma'' uses of moral judgments that are logically dependent on some other use: e.g., ''I ought to do X'' used to mean roughly ''Most people would say 'X is what ought to be done' '' or ''The people I respect would say 'X is what ought to be done.' '' But he does not argue that whenever a moral judgment is used for some purpose other than guiding choices, it is used in one of these logically dependent *senses*. Nor would such an argument be convincing: it is not convincing to say, for example, that whenever we make a judgment about the actions of someone no longer living, we are merely acknowledging what most people would say, or saying something "just because everyone else does," or using moral language in an ironic sense or in some other logically secondary sense. The choice-guiding use, then, has not been shown to be logically prior to all the other uses: therefore, there seems to be no good reason for holding that moral judgments are used evaluatively only when they are used to guide choices.

2. In the preceding part of this section I have tried to show that there are many uses of moral judgments besides guiding choices, and that these uses have not been shown to be logically dependent on the choice-guiding use. In the present part, I want to question briefly the second step in Hare's argument as I have outlined it: the assertion that if a judgment guides actions or choices, it must entail an imperative. In questioning this assertion I hope to forestall an objection to what I have said above. I have assumed (so the objection runs) that when we use moral judgments simply to *appraise* actions and choices, without attempting to *guide* someone's actions or choices, we still use words such as "ought," "oughtn't," "good," etc. with the same meanings they have when used to guide choices. But the meanings cannot be the same, and the evidence is this: when these words are used in order to guide choices ("You oughtn't to be smoking in here") the judgments in which they occur have a special logical characteristic, namely entailing imperatives ("Don't smoke in here"). But when these words are not used to guide choices, this logical characteristic is absent. Hence (the objection concludes) moral words used for purposes other than guiding choices *cannot* have the sense they have when used to guide choices: therefore it is at least misleading to say that moral judgments have many uses besides guiding choices, since in these other uses moral words have different meanings. This objection depends on the assertion that when moral judgments are used to guide choices, they are marked off by a special logical characteristic—entailing imperatives. And this is the assertion I want to question.

To guide someone's choices is not necessarily to point to a particular course of action and say, or imply, "Do this." We can guide someone's choices by telling him what the alternatives are and what their consequences are likely to be, without telling him what choice to make. Or, we can give reasons for making one choice rather than another, again without telling the agent what choice to make. Further, there is a variety of forms of speech used in guiding choices which are much weaker than an imperative, and do not in any obvious way entail an imperative: e.g. "I advise you to do X" or "I would do X if I were you." Formulae of this sort are deliberately used in order to avoid the imperative "Do X." In general, then, a judgment need not entail an imperative (in the ordinary sense of "imperative") in order to guide choices. There is even a sense in which to guide someone's choices is to refrain from saying or implying "Do X." To guide someone's choices is to give him some kind of support in making his own choices, while to tell someone what choice to make is, in effect, making the choice for him. Tautologically, if a judgment is used to guide choices in the sense of telling someone what choice to make, then it must assert or imply "Do X." But that is not the only, or even the most familiar sense of the expression "guiding choices."

Hare does have an apparently convincing argument for the claim that moral judgments addressed to persons faced with making a choice *do* entail imperatives. The argument, quoted previously, is this:

> If he professes to assent to the moral judgment, but does not assent to the imperative, he must have misunderstood the moral judgment (by taking it to be non-evaluative, though the speaker intended it to be evaluative). We are therefore clearly entitled to say that the moral judgment entails the imperative; for to say that one judgment entails another is simply to say that you cannot assent to the first and dissent from the second unless you have misunderstood one or the other. . . . (*The Language of Morals,* p. 172)

The argument might be outlined as follows:

1. To say that one judgment entails a second is to say that if both are understood, one cannot (logically) assent to the first and dissent from the second.
2. If moral judgments of the form "I (you, we) ought to do X" are understood as value-judgments, one cannot (logically) assent to them and not assent to the imperative "Do X."

3. Therefore if moral judgments of the form "I (you, we) ought to do X" are understood as value-judgments, they entail the imperative "Do X."

If this argument were conclusive, Hare's point would be established. One would have to agree that although the fact that a judgment is used to guide choices does not prove that it entails an imperative, moral judgments (used evaluatively) *do* entail imperatives, when addressed to agents faced with making choices. But the argument is not, I think, conclusive. It is not immediately obvious that when we assent to judgments such as "I (you, we) oughtn't to be smoking in this compartment," understanding them as value-judgments, we must assent to the imperative "Don't smoke in this compartment." It is not obvious that someone who says "I know I oughtn't to smoke in the compartment but I'm going to have a cigarette" *cannot* be using the expression "I oughtn't to smoke" in an evaluative sense, but only in some descriptive sense such as "The railway forbids smoking" or "Most people would disapprove of my smoking." Further, there is no way to test this claim. In order to test it, we would need some independent way of knowing whether the person who says "I know I oughtn't to smoke in this compartment" *has* understood "I oughtn't to smoke" in an evaluative sense. Hare provides no such independent way of knowing this. And if one were to say that "understanding a judgment in an evaluative sense" here simply *means* "understanding a judgment in such a way that one cannot assent to it and not assent to the imperative," then the argument becomes question-begging.

Hare does suggest a way of telling whether someone has assented to a moral judgment in an evaluative sense, namely, by studying what he *does*. But Hare himself points out that this test cannot be conclusive: it would only be conclusive if it were "analytic to say that everyone always does what he thinks he ought to (in the evaluative sense)" which is "not how we use the word 'think.' " Using "assent" in the ordinary way, then, we cannot tell whether someone has assented to a moral judgment in an evaluative sense by studying his actions, although this may help us decide whether he has. But in the absence of any conclusive independent test of assenting to a moral judgment in an evaluative sense, we have no assurance that it is ever impossible to assent to a moral judgment in an evaluative sense but not assent to the imperative. Consequently, Hare has not established the claim that moral judgments ever entail imperatives. There may *be* imperative-entailing uses, but it is not clear what they are.

3. In the preceding part of this section I have argued that when moral judgments are used to guide choices they need not entail imperatives. Further, I have argued that there is no way to prove that moral judgments ever do entail imperatives when used evaluatively. In this way I have tried to meet the objection raised earlier: the objection that since moral judgments used to guide choices have a logical characteristic (entailing imperatives) absent in other uses, the value-words in these other uses cannot have the same meanings they have in guiding choices. Since it is not clear that moral judgments used to guide choices do entail imperatives, we are not entitled to say that there must be a difference in meaning. We are not entitled to say, for example, that "ought" in "Someone ought to have kept the children from playing in the street" must have a different meaning than in "You ought to keep your children from playing in the street."

But even if moral judgments do sometimes entail imperatives, according to Hare's criterion of entailment, it still does not follow that they cannot be merely statements of fact but must contain an irreducibly prescriptive element. For according to Hare's criterion of entailment, it is not in general true that if a judgment entails an imperative, it must itself contain an imperative. Suppose A (a conductor) tells B (a passenger) "You oughtn't to be smoking in this compartment." It is at least plausible to say that on Hare's criterion A's judgment entails the imperative "Stop smoking": if B understands how A is using the judgment "You oughtn't to be smoking in this compartment" he could hardly be said to assent to it without assenting to the imperative. But it does not follow that A's judgment contains an imperative. The judgment itself might be correctly rephrased as a statement of fact, e.g. as "There is a railway rule against smoking in this compartment." And B might correctly understand A's judgment in this sense. In general it is not true that when a judgment is used in a way that entitles us to infer an imperative from it, the judgment itself must contain an imperative and cannot be a mere statement of fact. What entitles us to infer the imperative may be the circumstances in which the judgment is made, rather than an imperative element implicit in the judgment itself. It might be argued that whenever a judgment is used in circumstances which entitle us to infer an imperative, it is *used as* as imperative and not as a mere statement of fact. Further (the argument might run), to say that a judgment contains an imperative is simply to say that it is used as an imperative. So it is true that whenever a judgment entails an imperative, it must contain an imperative. But how can we know that a judgment *is* used as an imperative except by knowing that it entails an imperative? And we may not be able to know this from the meaning of the judgment itself: we may have to consider the circumstances. Even granting that moral judgments do entail imperatives, then, I do not think it has been shown that when they do so they must contain a prescriptive element as part of their very meaning and so cannot be merely statements of fact.

To summarize this section, I have tried to show, first, that moral judgments have other uses besides guiding choices and that these other uses are not in any clear way logically secondary; second, that in order to guide choices a judgment need not entail an imperative, and third, that even if there are uses of moral judgments in which they entail imperatives they need not therefore contain an imperative. There may well be some sense in which the primary use of moral judgments is to guide choices. And there may be some sense in which judgments cannot guide choices unless they are irreducibly prescriptive. But I do not think Hare is entirely successful in making these senses clear. As a result, it has not yet been proved that since moral judgments guide choices they must have logical characteristics similar to those of imperative sentences.

3   The Universalizability Principle

My purpose in the two preceding sections of this chapter has been to raise the question whether, first, Hare's refutation of naturalism in the *The Language of Morals* is altogether conclusive, and, second, whether the line of argument by which Hare reaches the conclusion that moral judgments cannot be merely one kind of factual statement but are rather essentially prescriptive really does establish that conclusion with complete certainty. In the present section I want to discuss certain questions concerning Hare's treatment of what he terms the universalizability of moral judgments in *Freedom and Reason*. In particular, I want to discuss the question whether the principle that moral judgments must be universalizable is, as some of Hare's critics have maintained, an empty and trivial one, and, second, whether Hare is right in explaining the universalizability principle in the way he does, namely, as a logical consequence of the fact that moral judgments have descriptive as well as prescriptive meaning. In regard to the first question I shall argue that the universalizability principle as applied to moral judgments is not trivial—understanding the principle as Hare apparently wants it understood, or at least as it could be understood. But in regard to the second question I shall question whether Hare's explanation of the truth of the universalizability principle is correct. I want to suggest that the principle is true by virtue of the meaning of the term "moral": the principle that moral judgments are universalizable is explicative of the concept of a moral judgment as contrasted with a non-moral statement of fact.

In approaching the questions about the universalizability principle I want to discuss, it may be well to ask, first, what the principle as applied to moral judgments asserts, as Hare understands the principle. What, in short, is the universalizability principle? Hare's answer is given in a general way in the following passage:

> Let us merely observe that in an apparently trivial, but at any rate unobjectionable sense, any singular descriptive judgment is universalizable: viz. in the sense that it commits the speaker to the further proposition that anything exactly like the subject of the first judgment, or like it in the relevant respects, possesses the property attributed to it in the first judgment. (*Freedom and Reason,* p. 12)

In general, Hare means by "universalizability" that feature of a singular statement of the form "a is an F" according to which if a is an F, then anything exactly like a, or like a in the relevant respects, is also an F. Thus, to say "John is tall" is universalizable is to say that anyone exactly like John, or like John in the relevant respects (i.e. in respect to height), is also tall. As applied to moral judgments, then, to say that singular or particular moral judgments of the form "X is good" or "Y is right" are universalizable is to say that anything exactly like X, or Y, or like X or Y in the relevant respects, is also good or right. To say "It was good of John to spend so much time with his younger brother" is universalizable is to say that it would be good for anyone exactly like John, or like John in the relevant respects, to do so; to say "In telling the truth, John did the right thing" is universalizable is to say that it would be right for anyone exactly like John, or like John in the relevant respects, to tell the truth. The principle of universalizability, then, is that all moral judgments are in the above sense universalizable; it could be stated as follows:

(1) Whenever a moral or ethical predicate such as "good" or "right" is ascribed to a particular subject A, the same predicate must be ascribable to anything exactly like A, or like A in the relevant respects.

Stated simply in this way, however, the principle could be interpreted (or misinterpreted) in such a way as to make it trivial or, even, actually false. Thus, as stated above, the principle seems to say that if it is right for a particular person A to do an action X, then it must likewise be right for any person exactly like A to do X. But the expression "exactly like A" could, aside from the fact that it is unnecessary (if it is right for anyone relevantly similar to A to do X, it will necessarily be right for anyone similar to A in *all* respects and, in that sense, exactly like A) be taken in such a way as to make the principle false. Taking the expression "exactly like A" in one common meaning, one would have to say that if, e.g., it is right for A to have sexual relations with his wife, it must likewise be right for anyone exactly like A, say A's twin brother, to do so (I owe the example to Marcus G. Singer). It might, therefore, be better to drop the expression "exactly like A" and state the principle as follows:

(2) Whenever a moral predicate such as "good" or "right" is ascribed to a particular subject A, it must likewise be ascribable to anything like A in the relevant respects.

But still another misinterpretation is possible, one according to which the principle would be, while true, utterly trivial. If by "like A in the relevant respects" one had in mind being like A in being good or right, then the principle would become a mere tautology. The principle would then merely say that if a particular thing A is good, or right, then any other thing which is also good, or right, is necessarily good or right—undeniably true but trivially so in that a tautology is entailed by any statement whatever. Hare himself does seem to suggest that universalizability as applied to some non-moral descriptive statement amounts to a triviality of this sort: he seems to suggest that what it means to say that, e.g., "A is red" is universalizable is merely that anything which is like A in respect to color is likewise red—i.e., that whatever is red is red. But as applied to moral judgments the principle is not meant to be trivial in this way. What the principle asserts as applied to moral judgments is that in the case of any particular thing A which is right or good there is some set of features X, by virtue of which A is right or good—a set of features logically distinct from A's goodness or rightness—and, further, that anything else which has that same set of features is likewise good or right. Thus, if it was good of John to spend so much time with his younger brother, it was good of him to do so because of some set of features or characteristics of his doing so: the universalizability principle asserts (1) that there is such a set of features and (2) that anything which has this same set of features will likewise be good. The principle, then, might be restated as follows to bring out the fact that it really has two parts in its application to moral judgments:

(3) Whenever the predicate "good," "right," etc. is ascribed to a particular subject A, then (1) it is so ascribed because A has some set of features or characteristics X which is the reason why "good," "right," etc. is ascribed to A, and which is not merely the feature of being good or right, and (2) anything which is similar to A in having the set of features or characteristics X is likewise good, right, etc.

The point of the first part of the principle is that when ethical or moral predicates such as "good," "right," etc. are ascribed to a particular subject, they are always so ascribed because of some feature or set of features (not the feature of being good or right: Hare's view is that, strictly speaking, there is no such feature) which could be called the basis of ascription. Or, to use somewhat different language, the principle asserts in its first part that a particular thing or action is good or right because it has what Ross called a "good-making" or "right-making" characteristic. The point of the second part of the principle is simply that everything which has the same good-making or right-making feature is likewise good or right. Thus, if I say that in telling the truth John acted rightly I must (if the universalizability principle is true) be prepared to say that John acted rightly because of some feature of the action logically independent of his acting rightly—which in this case might be simply the fact that in acting as he did he was telling the truth—and that anyone acting as John did in this situation would be acting rightly.

In order to forestall still another possible misinterpretation of the universalizability principle which might seem to make the principle false, it may be well to restate it in still another way. To see this possible misinterpretation, consider the following case. Suppose I say that John acted rightly in doing what he did, and give as my reason the fact that in doing what he did, he was telling the truth. It would seem to follow that if my judgment is universalizable, I must be committed to saying that anyone who tells the truth is acting rightly—in other words that "tell the truth" is a moral principle which applies to everyone alike and which has no exceptions. But few would want to say that the moral rule "tell the truth" has the status of a moral principle in that sense: few would want to say that there are absolutely no exceptions to the rule "tell the truth." How then is the universalizability of the judgment that in telling the truth John acted rightly to be understood? The answer is that the principle is to be understood in such a way that the good- or right-making features or characteristics of the thing or action to which goodness or rightness is ascribed include not simply what we should commonly think of and mention when asked "Why do you say that is good?" or "Why do you say that is right?" but *all* the features or characteristics involved in making the thing or action good or right. The point is like a point sometimes made in connection with the notion of the "cause" of an event, namely, that the cause of an event, strictly speaking, should be understood to include all the antecedent conditions which, taken together, are sufficient to produce the effect, not simply those antecedents which we might commonly think of when asked what the cause is. Similarly, the good- or right-making features of a thing or action should be understood to include all the features, including features of the situation in which the thing or action occurred, which taken together are the basis for ascribing goodness or rightness to the thing or action in question. Thus, in the above sort of case, most of us would probably want to say that what makes John's action right is not simply that in acting as he did he was telling the truth, but also that the situation or circumstances had certain features, understanding by "features" the absence of certain features—just as "the cause" of an event may be said to include the absence of certain antecedent factors, as when we say that the cause of death was lack of oxygen. To make this point explicit, the universalizability principle might be restated again as follows:

> (4) Whenever the predicate "good," "right," etc. is ascribed to a particular subject A, then (1) it is so ascribed because A has some set of features or characteristics X, or there is some set of features or characteristics, positive or negative, in the situation or circumstances in which A occurred, which is the reason why "good," "right," etc. is ascribed to A, and which is not merely the feature of being good or right, and (2) anything similar to A in having the features or characteristics X, or in being in a situation in which X is present, must likewise be good, right, obligatory, etc.

One final point may be worth making before turning to the question of the principle's alleged triviality. In my discussion of Prichard in Chapter II, I said that according to Prichard there is no ulterior reason, in the case of actions such as telling the truth, or paying one's debts, or showing gratitude, why the action is right: that there is no answer to the question, e.g. "Why is it right, or obligatory, for me to tell the truth in this case?" beyond, tautologically, that doing so is right or obligatory. But to the extent that Prichard's view is plausible, it might seem to cast doubt on the truth of the first part of the universalizability principle as I have restated it. For the first part of the principle appears to say that there always is some ulterior reason why an action is right or obligatory. One might of course simply say that Prichard was mistaken, and that there always is some ulterior reason: e.g. that when we say that in telling the truth John was acting rightly, there is some ulterior reason why we ascribe rightness to his act of telling the truth. But that kind of answer to the intuitionist would be unsatisfactory. It would leave the universalizability principle a matter of philosophical controversy as to its truth. That would, to be sure, suggest the principle is not trivial: we do not argue over trivialities. But it would leave the principle as something whose truth is not likely to be readily acknowledged by everyone who understands it, which is the status Hare (and I) want to claim for the principle.

A better answer to the difficulty seems to me to be the following. As I have stated it, the principle assumes that the particular thing A to which "good," "right," or "obligatory" is ascribed has not been so fully described as to make all the good- or right-making features of A themselves a part of the description of A. Thus, if I said that John's telling the truth in circumstances C was right, and fully specified the circumstances, it is undoubtedly true, as Prichard would want to say, that there is no *further* feature on the basis of which "good" or "right" is ascribed to John's action. But if, on the other hand, John's action is simply described as that of telling the truth, or, more clearly, if it is simply described as that of uttering the sentence S, then it could hardly be denied that there is some ulterior right-making feature. In general, the point to be made here is that when we say of some thing or action that it is good or right, we generally describe the thing or action in such a way that the question why the thing or action is good or right is a morally significant question. Otherwise there would be little point in taking the trouble to say that the thing or action is good or right. But we could, as indicated above, give what may be called a morally complete description of the thing or action, that is, a description which includes all the good-making or right-making features of the thing or action, including the features of the agent and of the circumstances, which, taken together, constitute the basis of an ascription of goodness or rightness. In that case there would be no further feature or characteristic of A which makes it good or right, and hence part (1) of the principle as stated above would in a sense not apply. But that is not because the principle as stated is false, but because the principle as stated envisages a case in which a morally complete description of A has not been given. To meet that case, still another restatement of the principle might be worth making. Let us call all the features of the particular situation—which, taken together, are the basis for ascribing "good" or "right" to a thing or action—the morally essential features of the situation: this could include features, positive or negative, of the agent, of his action, and of the accompanying circumstances. The principle could then be stated in this way:

(5) Whenever the predicate "good," "right," etc. is ascribed in a particular situation S, then (1) there is some feature or set of features of S which is morally essential in that it is what

makes us ascribe "good," "right," etc. in S and (2) "good," "right" must likewise be ascribable in any other situation S_1 in which the same feature or set of features is present.

Thus, in the case of an ascription of rightness to John's telling the truth, at least part of the morally essential features of the situation would be that in saying what he did, John was telling the truth: this would probably be what we would commonly think of as *the* morally essential feature. To that extent Prichard would be right. But as suggested above and in the discussion of intuitionism, it may well not be the only morally essential feature. I should say it would not be: features of the accompaniments and consequences would also be, strictly speaking, morally essential. Indeed, the point of the universalizability principle is in part to show that what we often take as the morally complete description of the action is not really complete. If we took such features as the fact that the action was an act of telling the truth, or paying one's debts, for example, as *the* morally essential feature in a strict sense, then, by the universalizability principle we should have to say that all acts of telling the truth or repaying one's debts were right—which by no means everyone would accept.

In the foregoing discussion I have tried to clarify somewhat the universalizability principle as a basis for considering the two questions I said I wanted to deal with in particular, namely, whether the principle is trivial as applied to moral judgments, and whether Hare is right in explaining the principle as a result of the fact that moral judgments have descriptive as well as prescriptive meaning. What, first, should be said concerning the triviality question? Basically the principle has been alleged to be trivial on grounds that the principle itself does not in any way indicate, or provide a way of telling, what the morally essential features of the situation are by which the predicates "good" or "right" are ascribed—and that therefore one could always take as morally essential some feature which is in fact unique to the particular situation in question. The result would then be, it is alleged, that the particular ascription of goodness or rightness would be universalizable in only a trivial and empty sense. Thus, suppose that in the above mentioned case of John's telling the truth, one took as the morally essential feature of the situation some feature of the situation that in fact applied only in that situation: e.g. the fact that John was the student seated fourth from the left in the front row in Philosophy 104 on Monday, April 23, 1973. One could, as far as anything actually in the principle as I have stated it is concerned (it might be alleged), take this or any other unique feature as the morally essential feature. But the judgment that "right" applies in the situation would only be universalizable in a completely formal and empty sense. In saying "John acted rightly" one would be committed to "Any student seated fourth from the left, etc. who tells the truth is acting rightly"—but this is a "universal" principle which in fact applies to only one case.

There is a certain sense, I should say, in which the charge of triviality as just sketched cannot be answered. For it is indeed true that the principle does not itself indicate how one is to pick out the morally essential feature of a situation. But it hardly follows that we can pick out arbitrarily any feature of the situation we want to and call it "morally essential." If that were possible, it is hard to see what the expression "morally essential" would mean. What the triviality objection shows, I should say, is that to use the principle in the way it is intended to be used, one needs some *criterion* for what is to count as morally essential in given situations. The principle in fact presupposes there are such criteria. And while in the absence of such criteria the principle would indeed be trivial, or rather, I should say, meaningless as I have stated it in form (5), it does not follow that in the presence of such criteria the principle is trivial. But are there any such criteria, it may be asked? The answer to that question, it seems to me, should be that we do have criteria to the extent that everyone would agree that certain features are *not* a part of the morally essential features in a situation in which "good" or "right" is ascribed, but that we do not have a fully complete set of criteria either, to the extent that there is considerable disagreement about what, positively, should be included in the morally essential features. Thus, no one would seriously argue that, e.g. the exact height of a person is morally essential in a situation where rightness is ascribed to his act of telling the truth. But, on the other hand, there may well be serious disagreement over the extent to which the consequences, for example, of his telling the truth are morally essential. In general, then (I should maintain), while the triviality objection makes a point about the principle that is true and important— namely that in the absence of criteria of relevance, or, as I have stated the principle, of moral essentiality—the principle has not really been shown to be trivial, at least not by the kind of argument sketched above. And I know of no other better way of trying to show the triviality of the principle. I conclude, then, that Hare is quite right in taking the universalizability principle to be both true and morally significant.

Where I wish to take issue with Hare is, as indicated at the beginning of this section, in his account of the basis of the universalizability principle. The question, basically, is this: granted the principle is true, why is it true? What makes it true? Hare's answer, in brief, is that what makes the universalizability principle as applied to moral judgments true is (1) that all statements of the form "a is an F," or at least all such statements which are descriptive, are universalizable in the sense indicated in my first statement of the principle, and (2) that since statements of the form "X is good" or "Y is right" are (partly) descriptive, they too are universalizable. I do not wish to question Hare's view that the universalizability principle in some general sense applies to all descriptive statements, and I certainly do not wish to question his view (in *Freedom and Reason*) that moral judgments have descriptive meaning. But it does not seem to me that these two facts taken together really explain why the universalizability principle as applied to moral judgments is true, at least as I have stated the principle in forms (3), (4), and (5). Hare himself recognizes that there is an important difference between the universalizability principle as applied to what we might call purely descriptive statements, e.g. "Snow is white," and to moral judgments. Consider the case of "Snow is white": what does it mean to say this sentence is universalizable? All it seems to mean, on Hare's account, which I am not denying as an account of the universalizability of non-moral descriptive statements, is that anything which is similar to snow in respect to color is likewise white. But this seems only to be a way of saying that whatever is white is white, an obvious tautology. Yet, it is clear that Hare is right in not regarding the principle as applied to moral judgments as tautological. How, then, can the fact that moral judgments are (in part) descriptive explain the truth of the universalizability principle as applied to moral judgments? It could only explain its truth if it were taken in a trivial sense, not in an interesting sense. But what needs explanation is the sense in which the principle is both true and interesting. In the trivial sense, what the principle would say is something like this: if A is right, then anything similar to A in being right (or in respect to its moral rightness) would likewise be right—i.e., a principle whose truth needs no explanation at all. It is not, then, the fact that in the case of an ascription of moral predicates to things or actions these predicates have descriptive meaning which makes the universalizability principle true, at least not in the sense in which the principle is both true and important.

What, then, is the explanation of the principle if not the fact that ethical predicates such as "good" and "right" have descriptive meaning? The answer I want to suggest, without arguing for it at any length here, is that the principle is true by virtue of the meaning of the term "moral." It is part of the meaning of "moral" (I should maintain) that moral judgments are always rational in the sense that particular moral judgments are always instances of some general rule which is to be taken as impartially applicable in all relevantly similar cases. Hence, it is a part of the concept of a moral judgment that we are or should always be prepared to back up our particular moral judgments with reasons which have a general, or at least potentially general, application. This, I should say, is part of the meaning of "moral judgment" in a way that is not obviously the case with all non-moral statements of fact. Thus, if I say "My foot hurts," there seems to me no interesting sense in which my statement is universalizable: I do not make the statement on the basis of any *reasons* at all. I could say, to be sure, that it would be true of anyone who feels the same sensation in his foot that I do, that his foot hurts. But "the same sensation" can only be described as the sensation of hurting, so that my universal statement really only says that if anyone's foot hurts, then his foot hurts—undeniably true, but a mere tautology. There could perhaps be a conception of morality—that is, a concept similar in a number of interesting ways to our concept of morality—in which "moral" judgments are not in the above sense universalizable. And we certainly could extend our concept of a morality to include these. But this would be to change our concept of a morality, not to falsify the principle. The principle itself cannot be falsified, for to state it is to state what we mean, in part, when we speak of morality.

VI

THE GOOD REASONS APPROACH

IN THE PRESENT CHAPTER my aim is to examine critically the position in recent ethical theory which, for the sake of convenience, I shall call the good reasons approach. According to this position, as I would characterize it, normative ethical judgments, while never equivalent in meaning to any set of non-ethical statements of fact, can be and quite commonly are supported or established—proved, one might say, except that "proved" might suggest they are conclusively established by deductive reasoning, which the good reasons approach denies—by non-ethical statements of fact, those non-ethical statements of fact constituting good and in many ordinary cases entirely adequate *reasons* for accepting the normative ethical conclusion. But further, according to this position, the kind of reasoning by which we go from non-ethical factual premises to normative ethical conclusion is neither deductive nor inductive, as logicians commonly understand deduction and induction, but is rather a special kind of reasoning peculiar to ethics or at least to reasoning concerning values—evaluative reasoning, it might be called. In the first section I shall discuss this point of view as stated in Stuart Hampshire's important article "Fallacies in Moral Philosophy" (*Mind*, 1949), as developed in Stephen Toulmin's 1950 book *An Examination of the Place of Reason in Ethics*, and as recently stated and defended by Carl Wellman in his 1971 book *Challenge and Response: Justification in Ethics*. The general conclusion about this theory I shall arrive at in this section is that while the good reasons approach is highly plausible, more so I should say than intuitionism and the emotive theory, it has not been shown with complete success that ethical reasoning cannot in some cases be ordinary deductive or inductive reasoning, especially inductive reasoning.

In the second section of the chapter I shall discuss the question, naturally raised by the good reasons approach, as to what exactly constitutes a good reason in ethics, and the further question of whether the acceptance of a non-ethical statement of fact as, by itself, a good reason for a normative ethical conclusion is itself in some important sense a matter of moral decision, as Hare has maintained, or whether the notion of a moral or ethical reason is, to some important extent at least, determined by the notion of morality itself, as Toulmin has maintained. I shall argue that ultimately there is no clear way to decide this last question, since it appears to depend on how narrow or wide a concept of morality one has, and there seems no good reason to think that everyone's concept of morality is the same in this respect. But I am inclined to think that if the question is about the most frequently encountered concept of morality, then Toulmin is right: that the acceptance of a factual statement as a good reason (or its rejection as not a good reason) for a normative ethical conclusion is not in general best viewed simply as a matter of moral decision, on which moral agents may disagree, but that the concept of morality itself determines to an important degree what can constitute a morally good reason, or what cannot constitute a morally good reason, for a normative ethical conclusion.

1   Ethical Reasoning as *Sui Generis*

In his article "Fallacies in Moral Philosophy" Hampshire maintains that the following four mistakes underlie the typical post-Kantian approach to moral philosophy: (a) "the assimilation of moral or practical judgments to descriptive statements" which is associated with "con-

centration on the use of moral terms in sentences expressing a spectator's praise or blame," (b) "the inference, from the fact that moral or
practical judgments cannot be logically derived from statements of
fact, that they cannot be based on, or established exclusively by reference to, beliefs about matters of fact," with a resulting view of ethics
as non-rational or emotive, (c) "the assumption that all literally significant sentences must correspond to or describe something" and (d)
"the confusion between clarifying the use of ethical terms with dis-
covering definitions of, or verbal equivalencies between, these
terms." Like Stevenson, then (and, as I have argued, like Dewey),
Hampshire rejects the view that moral judgments are merely equivalent in meaning to some non-ethical statement of scientific or empirical
fact, on grounds that moral judgments are prescriptive. As Hampshire
himself expresses this, "it is the distinguishing characteristic of practical judgments that they have a prescriptive or quasi-imperative force
as part of their meaning." It is important to recognize here that when
Hampshire speaks of moral judgments as "practical judgments" he is
apparently thinking of what he calls a "pure primary moral judgment"—a judgment of the form "X is the best thing to do in the circumstances" or "Y is the right thing to do in the circumstances"
which represents the solution of a practical problem, in that it represents an agent's own conclusion as to what it would be best or right
for him to do in a situation actually facing him, the conclusion being
reached after a process of genuine, serious, moral or ethical deliberation on the part of the agent himself.

I have argued in the previous chapter that Hare does not conclusively show that moral judgments necessarily contain as a part of their
meaning an imperative element. But while Hampshire in the 1949 article presents no argument for that thesis, as Hare does in *The Language of Morals,* it does seem reasonable to hold that in the kind of
situation Hampshire envisages as a case of making a "pure primary
moral judgment" there is at least a quasi-imperative element (a
slightly more cautious statement of the thesis than Hare's possibly
misleading statement that moral judgments actually contain an imperative element) in moral judgments. It does seem plausible to hold that
when an agent says to himself, after some deliberation, "I ought not
to smoke in this compartment" he is in some sense telling himself not
to smoke in this compartment. His judgment does seem clearly to have

a prescriptive force which would be overlooked in an analysis which treated the statement as simply one special kind of descriptive statement. To that extent, I should say, prescriptivism (to use Hare's term) hardly seems open to serious argument, although I should maintain that (1) prescriptivism is held by some philosophers such as Dewey who have still wished to regard themselves as naturalists and (2) there is also the appraisal use of moral judgments as in some of the examples suggested in the preceding discussion of Hare, e.g. judgments about the actions of a purely hypothetical agent, which also need to be considered in a fully comprehensive theory of the meaning of moral judgments. Indeed, prescriptivism as Hampshire presents it is, I should say, almost analytic. We should hardly say that the conclusion "X would be the best thing to do in these circumstances" represents the agent's own *conclusion* if he is not in some sense prepared to assert to himself "Do X," understanding the situation as one in which the agent is in point of fact trying to make up his mind what to do. And to the extent that precriptivism is analytic it cannot of course be denied.

Apart from prescriptivism, the central thesis that Hampshire presents in the 1949 article is that the kind of reasoning by which moral judgments, at least pure primary moral judgments, are derived from non-ethical statements of fact is neither deduction nor induction, but a kind of reasoning which is special to ethics. Or, if that is not what Hampshire actually says, it is a possible reading of the position he intends to suggest. What he actually says is that there is a wider sense of the expression "rational argument" than the sense in which logicians commonly understand it: "Arguments," he asserts," may be, in the ordinary and wider sense, rational, without being included among the types of arguments which are ordinarily studied by logicians, since logicians are generally concerned exclusively with the types of argument which are characteristic of the a priori and empirical sciences." And, Hampshire goes on to say, these arguments, of which ethical argumentation is one kind, are rational in the same general sense as deductive and inductive arguments are rational—namely, in being governed by what might be called rules or standards of argumentation: "they are more or less strictly governed by recognized (though not necessarily formulated) rules of relevance."

Several questions can be raised concerning Hampshire's position as sketched above. (1) What reason does Hampshire have for holding that inductive and deductive argumentation cannot establish moral or ethical conclusions? That is, why can we not argue from non-ethical scientific or factual premises to normative ethical conclusions by ordinary inductive or deductive procedures? And (2) what exactly does Hampshire have in mind by "rules of relevance" which are said to govern moral reasoning? Hamphire gives no suggestion which would serve to answer the second question (the article is apparently somewhat programmatic, leaving it open to others to work out the details). There is, however, in the article a suggested answer to the first question. The line of reply, in brief, would be that moral judgments cannot be arrived at by inductive or deductive reasoning from non-moral factual premises just *because* moral judgments are prescriptive and therefore neither true nor false. The underlying argument, apparently, is this. If an argument is inductive or deductive, the conclusion must have a truth value. For what it means to say that an argument is deductively valid is that the truth of the premises entails the truth of the conclusion (or, that in any argument of that form, if the premises are true then the conclusion is always true); what it means to say that an argument is inductively valid is that the truth of the premises increases the probability of the conclusion's being true. Hence if moral judgments are neither true nor false—and Hampshire in the article does suggest they are not properly so called—it would follow that moral reasoning cannot be either inductive or deductive, as induction and deduction are commonly understood by logicians.

How sound would this argument be? It is not easy to say. In discussing Ayer's version of the emotive theory of ethics I have argued that it is highly implausible to say that moral judgments are neither true nor false. If my argument has any force, Hampshire is simply mistaken in holding that the expressions "it is true that" and "it is false that" never in ordinary language precede an ethical sentence. To be sure, it might be said that "true" and "false" as applied to moral judgments do not mean what they mean when applied to non-moral statements of fact. It might be held that in the case of non-moral statements of fact, what it means to say that a statement is true is that it corresponds with some independent objective fact or state of affairs, whereas in the case of moral judgments there simply are no objective states of affairs or moral facts to be corresponded to. Very possibly Hampshire has something like this in mind: in (c) above he is apparently denying that moral judgments "correspond to or describe something." But if this is the argument, one might reply that while moral facts or states of affairs may seem like queer entities, facts or states of affairs generally— as opposed to things and properties—seem somewhat queer entities. Further, this line of argument would seem to show that logical relations, i.e. what logicians commonly take to be logical relations, can only hold among statements which are true or false in the correspondence sense of "true" and "false," which would be to tie logic to a particular theory of truth in a way it is not commonly thought to be tied. And, perhaps another way of making the same point, no one seems to have any objection to the common assumption that logical relations hold between moral judgments: e.g. no would object to saying that the inference from "X is the best thing to do in the circumstances" and "If X is the best thing to do in the circumstances, then I should first do Y" to "I should first do Y" is deductively valid. Yet, the conclusion is certainly prescriptive if any moral judgment is. Finally, Hampshire himself appears not to deny that moral judgments are *partly* descriptive: at least he does not show why that could not be the case. And if they are partly descriptive, it might be held that they do in part correspond to something and hence can be true or false in the correspondence sense of "true" and "false." In sum, then, the arguments Hampshire suggests for the thesis that the logic of moral reasoning cannot be deductive or inductive do not really succeed in establishing that thesis, and it is not clear what general argument would establish it.

One of the questions asked above was what exactly does Hampshire have in mind by "rules of relevance" and what *are* the rules of relevance governing ethical reasoning? Hampshire suggests no general answer to this question: indeed, his discussion of the capital punishment example suggests he may be inclined to think that on each particular moral question we can recognize what constitutes good and bad moral reasoning without being able to say in general what makes a non-ethical statement of fact a good or bad reason for a normative ethical conclusion. A general answer to this question is, however, provided in Stephen Toulmin's book *An Examination of the Place of Reason in Ethics*. Toulmin's position is highly involved and complex, and I shall in no sense try to summarize it. But he does give an answer to the above question which can be stated quite simply and briefly. In the case of particular actions, the fact that the action is in accordance with the existing moral code is, generally speaking, a good reason for judging it to be right:

> On most occasions it is a good reason for choosing or approving of an action that it is in accordance with an established maxim of conduct, for the existing moral code, and the current institutions and laws, provide the most reliable guide as to which decisions will be happy—in the same kind of way as codes of standard practice in engineering. (*The Place of Reason in Ethics,* p. 223)

In the case of moral codes, institutions, and laws themselves, a good reason for judging them good or right is the fact that their adoption will reduce conflict of interests and will be conducive to the ideal of a harmonious and fulfilling satisfaction of interests: "If the adoption of the practice would genuinely reduce conflicts of interest, it is a practice *worthy of adoption,* and if the way of life would genuinely lead to deeper and more consistent happiness, it is one *worthy of pursuit"* (*The Place of Reason in Ethics,* p. 224). The "rules of relevance" Toulmin proposes are, then, (1) in the case of particular actions one may, generally speaking, infer that an action is right from the fact that it is in accordance with an established moral code and (2) one may infer that a moral code or practice is right from the fact that it reduces conflict of interests.

Toulmin's answer (viewing it as an answer) to the question I raised concerning "rules of relevance" is a plausible one—and, I think, one that would be highly attractive to at least some naturalists: his emphasis on reduction of conflicts of interest and harmonious satisfaction recalls Perry's conception of a morally right act as an action such that no other act would produce more harmonious satisfaction of the interests of the persons whose interests are affected by the action, the main difference being that Perry is answering the question of what it means to say of a particular action that it is morally right, whereas Toulmin is answering the question of what counts as a reason for the moral rightness of a moral code or practice. Yet, attractive as Toulmin's answer may be to some naturalists, it does raise certain questions. (1) Why not say that the logical relation between "X is in accordance with an established maxim of conduct" and "X is right," or between

"Y reduces conflicts of interest" and "Y is right" is an ordinary inductive one? (In a moment I shall consider Carl Wellman's reply to this question.) (2) Is not the account of moral reasoning which Toulmin gives really an assertion of a particular normative ethical theory, a theory which has come recently to be called "rule utilitarianism," rather than a logical or meta-ethical theory? Are not Toulmin's "rules of relevance" really normative ethical principles, with which one could conceivably disagree on moral or ethical grounds? I shall try to deal with this question in the next section, in connection with a discussion of Hare's criticisms in his review of *The Place of Reason in Ethics*. (3) Is not Toulmin's account of what constitutes good reasons in ethics, whether it be meta-ethical, or normative, or possibly both (at the outset of this work I suggested that possibly the categories "metaethical" and "normative" should not be taken as necessarily exclusive: some assertions may be both at the same time) at any rate unacceptable on normative ethical grounds?

In regard to the last mentioned question, I think there is room for doubt as to whether Toulmin is right in incorporating, as it were, rule utilitarianism in the form he does in his account of moral reasoning. It would certainly be a mistake, as Richard Brandt has argued in his article "Some Merits of One Form of Rule Utilitarianism," to hold that accordance with an *existing* moral rule or code is, in general, either sufficient or necessary to establish the moral rightness of a particular action. That view, which Brandt calls "actual rule utilitarianism," is indefensible: the defensible form of rule utilitarianism is what Brandt calls "ideal rule utilitarianism," according to which an action is morally right if it is in accordance with a moral code which is ideal for the society to which the agent belongs, i.e. is such that its general adoption in that society would have the maximum utility. (There are problems, even, with ideal rule utilitarianism: e.g. what unit, as it were, constitutes "the society" to which the agent belongs? His country? His social class? Or what? Also, many of us are inclined to think that in some important matters such as choice of marriage partner or family size moral legislation is undesirable, even though an ideal moral code—if that just means a code which would maximize utility if generally adopted and acted on—would perhaps contain strict rules concerning such matters.)

Toulmin, to be sure, does not say that it is always or even ever a *sufficient* reason for saying that a particular action is right that it is in accordance with an established moral rule. He only says, cautiously, that it is generally *a* good reason. Similarly, he only says that the fact that a code or practice reduces conflicts of interest is *a* good reason for judging it morally right, not that this is the only good reason. Hence he might reject the suggestion that he incorporates some form of rule utilitarianism in his account of moral reasoning. But then, one wonders, what are the other reasons which count as evidence for the moral rightness of actions and practices? And assuming there may be cases where there is a conflict between utilitarian considerations and some other kind of consideration, what more ultimate rule can we appeal to in order to resolve the conflict? Toulmin's account, one might say, is involved in something of a dilemma. Either his account of moral reasoning does in effect incorporate what Brandt calls actual rule utilitarianism, in which case it is open to unanswerable objections at the level of normative ethics, or it does not, in which case it is open to the charge of being seriously incomplete and, possibly, incompletable.

Leaving aside the question of the defensibility of some form of rule utilitarianism, what reasons are there for holding that accordance with an existing (or ideal) moral code, or conduciveness to the ideal of mutual harmonious satisfaction of interests, cannot support in an ordinary deductive or inductive way the judgment that an action or practice is right? Why, in general, cannot moral reasoning be deductive or inductive? A recent careful examination of this question is contained in Chapter 1 of Carl Wellman's book *Challenge and Response: Justification in Ethics,* in which Wellman argues both against what he calls "deductivism," the view as he states it that *all* ethical reasoning is deductive, and "inductivism," the view that ethical reasoning is inductive (Wellman does not seem to make it entirely clear whether inductivism is the thesis that all ethical reasoning is inductive, or only that some important instances or types of ethical reasoning are inductive). His main argument against deductivism is that moral reasoning is typically not conclusive in the way that a deductive argument always has to be. There are, as Wellman points out, typically several sides to be taken in a serious moral issue, with something to be said on both sides—otherwise, one might say, it would not be a serious moral issue. Thus, I might argue as follows: "You ought to tell him the truth: he wants to know." This seems like a valid argument morally speaking, and the premise, let us assume, is true: he does want to know. But one might counter with "You ought not to tell him the truth: it may cause a severe depression." This too could be a valid moral argument with true premises. But both arguments cannot be deductively valid: if one were, the conclusion of the other could not be true and hence—since a deductively valid argument is one in which the truth of the premises guarantees with certainty the truth of the conclusion—the other one could not be deductively valid. Insofar as this is Wellman's point, it seems sound enough. But it hardly need worry a naturalist or even a moderate deductivist: he could simply concede that while not all and even perhaps not the most typical and important kinds of moral reasoning are deductive, some are.

Wellman does not deny that some cases of ethical reasoning are deductive. But the ones he allows are relatively non-controversial, such as the derivation of a less general ethical conclusion from a more general ethical premise—as in "You ought to tell him the truth because a friend always ought to tell the truth and you are his friend." This is non-controversial because one of the premises is itself an ethical judgment. What is controversial is whether an ethical conclusion can ever be derived solely from non-ethical statements of fact. My own view is that it has not been shown that it cannot be, and an instance of such a derivation is given by John Searle in his article "How to Derive 'Ought' From 'Is' " in which the conclusion that Jones ought to pay Smith five dollars is derived by a series of deductive steps from the initial premise that Jones uttered the words "I hereby promise to pay you, Smith, five dollars." Searle's derivation has been a subject of considerable recent controversy, and in section 3 of the Conclusion I shall try to show that the objections raised to it are not conclusive. But even if it were shown that Searle has failed to derive deductively an "ought" from an "is", it is not clear to me what general argument there is that shows this to be in principle impossible. And even if that were shown, it is not clear what general argument there is that shows that ethical reasoning is not inductive—all that a naturalist need hold in the somewhat wide sense of "naturalism" suggested earlier in this work. Wellman's main argument against inductivism is that what he terms "thought experiments" in ethics, in which one imagines a situation and then makes a moral judgment based in some sense on one's experience of the imaginary situation, are not really like scientific experiments at all in that one does not simply wait and see, as it were, what the outcome of the experiment is, as in scientific experiments, but rather infers the outcome by a process of moral reasoning which Wellman later calls "conduction" as opposed to either deduction or induction.

Wellman's point here is convincing as far as it goes, but it does not seem to show that there are not other kinds of cases of moral reasoning which are inductive in an ordinary sense. It may be said that inductive arguments give a certain degree of probability to their conclusions, and that we do not speak of moral judgments as more or less probable. But we can and do speak of moral judgments as probable in some cases, as in e.g. "You told him you would be in your office this afternoon, so you probably should be there." A non-inductivist might reply that this is not really an inductive argument but a deductive argument with one of the premises unstated, the unstated premise being that if you tell someone you are going to do a certain thing, you should probably do it (barring a particular reason not to do it). But to make that reply is to make the mistake that Wellman points out the deductivist makes, namely, the mistake of assuming that all valid arguments are deductive. Unless one takes this extreme deductivist line, there seems to me no reason to deny that there may be valid inductive moral arguments just as most logicians would probably agree that there are valid inductive arguments (as opposed to deductive arguments with unstated premises).

It is sometimes said against the suggestion that some moral arguments are inductive that in the case of genuine inductive inferences, there is some way to test the conclusion independently of the evidence used to arrive at it in that particular argument. But why could we not arrive at the same moral conclusion by several independent routes? Indeed, Wellman gives this fact of converging moral arguments as an objection to deductivism. It is not clear, moreover, that a fact or set of facts cannot be considered as inductive evidence for a particular conclusion unless there is some independent way of establishing the truth of that conclusion. To suppose there must be is, in effect, to take a side in a number of important philosophical controversies quite unrelated to the question of whether moral reasoning can be inductive. Thus, the supposition that there must be independent evidence for the conclusion would cast doubt on the view that our knowledge of what other people are thinking or feeling is arrived at inductively from observation of their behavior—on grounds that there is not any way other than behavior to know about these thoughts and feelings. Or, it would cast doubt on arguments for the existence of God which purport to argue inductively from the observed order in nature. I am not arguing that the supposition is false, only that it involves general and controversial philosophical issues which go far beyond ethical theory. Insofar as these general issues are unresolved, I should say, one cannot dismiss as obviously mistaken the view that some ethical reasoning is inductive in a quite ordinary sense. I am not suggesting that all ethical reasoning is inductive: I should maintain that in many cases of ethical reasoning, perhaps the most important and typical, there is some logical connection between the facts stated in the premises and the conclusion, whereas in ordinary inductive reasoning the relation is purely contingent. But I see no reason to reject the possibility that some ethical reasoning, of the sort illustrated above, may well be inductive.

To summarize this section, I have argued that while the good reasons approach has considerable inherent plausibility, the negative aspect of this approach, its denial that ethical reasoning from nonmoral factual premises to normative ethical conclusions can be deductive or inductive as logicians ordinarily conceive deduction and induction, has not been established in anything like a conclusive way. There may well be a special kind of reasoning peculiar to ethics—what Wellman calls "conduction." But that would not by itself go to show that there are not also very many cases of moral reasoning from non-ethical premises to normative ethical conclusions which are quite ordinary cases of inductive or deductive reasoning. (I would be prepared to argue, for example, that an inference from "This action is in accordance with an established moral maxim" to "This action is probably right" is an inductive inference: the connection between the fact stated in the premise and the conclusion seems to me a contingent one.) The whole issue, to be sure, is a highly controversial one, and in the conclusion I shall try to give a fuller account of my reasons for holding there may be such cases. But in any event I think it has yet to be conclusively shown that deductive or inductive ethical reasoning in an interesting sense is in principle impossible.

2   Could a Moral Principle be Anything

In the preceding section I have tried to sketch the main ideas involved in the good reasons approach and to raise certain questions about them, in particular about the idea that ethical reasoning is *sui generis*. In the present section I shall deal with the question about Toulmin which I said I would consider here, namely, whether Toulmin's "rules of relevance" (to use Hampshire's expression) are not really normative ethical principles rather than logical or meta-ethical rules or principles—the status which Toulmin apparently means to ascribe to them. I shall begin by considering some remarks made by Hare in his review of *The Place of Reason in Ethics* (the review appears in *The Philosophical Quarterly,* July, 1951), and then discuss the general question whether Hare is right in suggesting that the claim that a set of non-ethical facts F is a good reason for accepting a normative ethical conclusion E should itself be regarded as a normative ethical assertion and, moreover, as one of the premises which entitles us to infer E from F.

Hare, in his review of Toulmin's book, raises essentially the question just mentioned, namely, whether what Toulmin apparently regards as a meta-ethical assertion about what constitute good reasons in ethics is not really a normative ethical assertion. What Toulmin has actually done, according to Hare, is to transform the normative ethical principle that if the adoption of a practice would genuinely reduce conflicts of interest, then it is a practice worthy of adoption, into a "rule of inference," the rule as Hare states it being that "This practice would involve the least conflict of interests attainable under the circumstances" is a good reason for "This would be the right practice." The assertion just mentioned—" 'This practice would involve the least conflict of interests attainable under the circumstances' is a good reason for 'This would be the right practice' "—looks like a meta-ethical statement: it is a statement *about* ethical statements. But as I indicated at the very beginning of this study it is not sufficient that a statement be about normative ethical statements. If it is to be meta-ethical, it must itself not be a normative statement. Hare's claim is that the above statement is in point of fact really itself normative, as is indicated by the fact that it is equivalent to the clearly normative assertion that if the adoption of a practice would genuinely reduce conflicts of interest, then it is a practice worthy of adoption. Further, Hare argues, this statement is not a "rule of inference" as Toulmin regards it, asserting that one may validly infer that a practice is right from the fact that it reduces conflicts of interests. It is rather, according to Hare, one of the premises needed to infer that a practice is right from the fact that it reduces conflicts of interest. And given this as an additional premise the inference in question turns out to be a quite ordinary kind of deductive argument. The inference, in brief, is that (1) if a practice reduces conflicts of interest, then it is right, (2) this practice reduces conflicts of interests, therefore (3) this practice is right. But this is merely an instance of the deductive argument form:

$$\text{If } p \text{ then } q$$
$$p$$
$$\overline{}$$
$$q$$

Toulmin's account is thus mistaken on two counts, according to Hare. First, he takes as logical or meta-ethical a statement which is really normative. And second, he regards this statement as a rule of inference rather than as one of the premises needed to validate the inference.

In regard to Hare's first point, it is, I think, correct to say that what Toulmin has done is to translate, as it were, what was traditionally conceived as a normative ethical principle—that rules and practices are right insofar as their adoption reduces conflicts of interest—into a meta-ethical statement about ethical reasoning. But it is not altogether clear that this is wrong or even necessarily misleading. Indeed, I have suggested that Hare himself does something like this in connection with the universalizability principle, which was traditionally conceived (by Sidgwick for example) as a high-level normative principle or "axiom." Hare seems to suggest that the principle in some sense remains normative even as restated by Toulmin as a statement about good reasons. But Toulmin could, I think, claim that as he restates it, the principle is no longer normative but logical. It does, to be sure, contain the word "good." But "good" as used in the principle does not mean "morally good." It means something like "valid" or "logically adequate." Nor is Hare's main argument for regarding the principle as normative entirely conclusive. Hare's main argument is that one can imagine a man who, holding that struggle and conflict are morally good things, says that the fact that a practice reduces conflicts of interest is *not* a good reason for judging the practice to be right. Such a man would, if anything, regard this fact as a good reason for judging the practice to be wrong. Hence, Hare holds, what one takes as a good reason depends on, or perhaps one should say is constituted by, one's normative ethical principles. This argument certainly has some weight, but it is not conclusive either. One could reply that a man who denies the principle (or rule) in question simply shows he has failed to understand what a good reason in ethics is—that he lacks our concept of ethical reasoning. To that extent, one might say, he has failed to grasp our concept of morality, in somewhat the same way in which we might say that a man who fails to universalize his ''moral'' judgments shows thereby that he does not have our concept of morality, although he might have a concept interestingly similar in a number of respects to our concept of morality.

It may be said that to take this line of reply is to adopt a narrow-minded and provincial concept of what a morality is. But while that might in a sense be true, Toulmin might reply that he is not saying what our concept of a morality ought to be, but what it in fact is. In general, then, I see no way to resolve the disagreement between Toulmin and Hare on this issue. Nor am I clear about what hangs on deciding it one way or the other. Perhaps the conclusion to be drawn is that a statement can be interpreted with equal justification as normative and as meta-ethical: that the distinction does not, as it were, pick out one group of statements from another, but picks out a way of regarding given statements. If one thinks that philosophical ethics should restrict itself entirely to conceptual analysis, and still wants to arrive at ethically significant conclusions, there may be some motive for holding with Toulmin that the acceptance of the principle or rule in question necessarily follows from analysis of our concept of a good reason in ethics, rather than representing a particular ethical commitment as Hare would hold. But if one is quite prepared to accept normative ethics as a legitimate part of philosophical ethics as is done by Brandt and many other contemporary philosophers, no such motive would be present. One could simply go ahead and argue for the acceptance of some form of rule utilitarianism as a normative ethical theory as Brandt has done in his above mentioned article, ''Some Merits of One

Form of Rule Utilitarianism.'' That leaves one without any particular motive for resolving the disagreement in one way rather than another, and perhaps there is no need to do so as a general matter. One could simply say that some people have a concept of ethical reasoning such that a man could not logically deny that the fact that a practice reduces conflicts of interest is a good reason for judging it right, whereas others have a somewhat broader concept according to which this could be denied. There seems no reason why there could not in this way be narrower and wider concepts of morality, and if there are, it is simply impossible to decide the question at issue. The principle could be either normative or meta-ethical depending on whose concept of morality you happen to pick out for analysis.

In regard to Hare's argument that the principle in question—that the fact that a practice reduces conflicts of interest is a good reason for judging it morally right—should be regarded as one of the premises from which we infer that practices are morally right rather than as a rule of inference, I should say that while Hare's position does sound plausible, it should be regarded with some suspicion. If Hare were right, one would have a quick and easy a priori way of proving that it is never possible to derive an ethical conclusion from non-ethical factual premises. The argument would run somewhat as follows. Let F be the non-ethical factual premises and E be the normative ethical conclusion. The argument would be that E cannot be derived from E alone: to validate the argument, one needs the further premise ''If F then E.'' But such an argument, I should say, is question begging. For one thing it appears to involve the deductivist assumption that all valid arguments are deductive. But also, the alleged necessary premise ''If F then E'' is completely unnecessary and redundant if the inference from F to E is in fact valid—which is the question to be decided. To argue in this way would, in fact, be to commit the fallacy involved in the so-called ''paradox of inference,'' according to which an argument is not valid unless one includes as a premise the further premise that the original premises entail the conclusion. The fact is, however, that one does not need this further premise—if one did, there would be an infinite regress. Similarly, the point in saying that E can be derived solely from F is that one needs no further premise: to assume one needs in addition the premise ''If F then E'' is to assume it cannot be so derived. Perhaps it cannot be, but to assume it cannot without argu-

ment is to beg the question. Hare may be right in holding that the principle in question should be regarded as a further premise, but I can see
no way to show that it must be so regarded. Here again, I should say,
it is not clear how to decide the issue between Toulmin and Hare (or
more generally, between those who hold that normative ethical conclusions can be derived logically from purely non-ethical factual premises, and those who deny it). The most one can do is to show the in-
conclusiveness of arguments purporting to prove that normative
conclusions cannot be derived from purely factual premises, and invite
the non-derivablist (as he may be called) to consider plausible cases of
such derivations—as Searle does in "How to Derive 'Ought' from
'Is.' "

In the preceding part of this section I have considered the issue between Toulmin and Hare as to whether the statement "If a practice
reduces conflicts of interest, there is good reason for judging it morally
right" is in some sense analytic (and true by virtue of the meaning of
"good reason"), or a synthetic normative moral principle as Hare
would hold. In the remainder of this chapter I will discuss briefly the
more general question as to whether there are *any* material restrictions,
as it were, involved in our concept of ethical reasoning: whether, that
is, what is to count as a good reason or not a good reason in ethics is
to any extent determined by our concept of ethical reasoning. This, in
effect, is one of the issues raised by Philippa Foot in her essay "Moral
Beliefs" (published in *Proceedings of the Aristotelian Society*, Vol.
59, 1958–59, and reprinted in her 1967 book, *Theories of Ethics*). As
Philippa Foot formulates the question, it is the question whether the
meaning of "good" connects goodness with any particular evidence,
as the naturalist holds, or whether, as an extreme anti-naturalist might
hold, the meaning of "good" does not connect goodness with any particular evidence whatever, so that anything imaginable could be given
as evidence of something's goodness, and whatever is offered as evidence for something's goodness could be rejected as no evidence
without thereby in any way revealing a failure to grasp the concept of
goodness. The extreme anti-naturalist (my term, not hers) holds the
following, as Philippa Foot characterizes him: "one man may say that
a thing is good because of some fact about it, and another may refuse
to take that fact as any evidence at all, for nothing is laid down in the
meaning of 'good' which connects it with one piece of 'evidence'

rather than another." On this view, as she goes on to point out, there would be nothing *logically* or conceptually odd in claiming the most seemingly irrelevant fact as evidence that something is good: "It follows that a moral eccentric could argue to moral conclusions from quite idiosyncratic premises; he could say, for instance, that a man was a good man because he clasped and unclasped his hands, and never turned N.N.E. after turning S.S.W. He could also reject someone else's evaluation simply by denying that his evidence was evidence at all."

The issue here is in essence the same as that considered in the preceding chapter in connection with the principle of universalizability: there, the issue was stated as the issue whether there are any criteria by which to pick out the morally essential from the morally inessential or irrelevant features of situations. What Philippa Foot clearly intends to suggest by her example is that we do have such criteria, to the extent at least that we can quite unhesitatingly rule out certain features as morally irrelevant, and that these criteria are in some sense involved in understanding what the word "good" means. I should say this is clearly right: we do have criteria, although it is perhaps equally clear that we do not have a fully complete set of criteria. And to the extent that knowing the meaning of a word or expression is or involves having the ability to apply it or withhold it in given situations, I should say that these criteria constitute part of the meaning of ethical words such as "good." To that extent—and I take this to be Philippa Foot's suggestion—the naturalist appears to be making a basically sound point. At the same time it must, I think, be conceded that one can always say, heroically, that any fact is equally good evidence for an evaluative conclusion—or as the view should perhaps be stated, that there is no meaning in talking of factual evidence for a normative ethical judgment—and that it is always logically possible to deny that any suggested evidence that something is good or right is really evidence at all. And it is not clear how one would go about refuting one who did take that extreme anti-naturalist position. For the anti-naturalist does not deny that we do regard certain facts as good and even as conclusive evidence for a thing's goodness or rightness, and other facts as no evidence at all. But he simply considers this to be our particular normative ethical commitment which could theoretically be rejected without changing the concept of morality itself. Here, I should say what I said in the case of the issue between Toulmin and Hare over the status of Toulmin's "rules of relevance," namely that it may depend on what a particular person's concept of morality happens to be. I am inclined to say that a person who regarded the facts of a man's clasping and unclasping his hands as, without any further background, evidence of his moral goodness does not share my concept of moral goodness—that our disagreement is conceptual, not moral. But one could have a much wider concept of morality in which the view that such facts count as evidence of moral goodness is a genuine although presumably mistaken moral judgment.

Whether it is equally plausible to say that certain facts are positive evidence of goodness or rightness (as opposed to saying that certain facts are *not* evidence and cannot be evidence by themselves given our concept of goodness) by virtue of our concept of goodness or rightness is not so easy to say. Offhand it does seem plausible to hold that if a person maintains that the fact that a man is generous, kind, sympathetic, etc. is no evidence at all that he is a good man, then he has failed to understand the concept we have of moral goodness. But there is always the Nietzschean who would say these qualities are evidence of moral badness rather than moral goodness. Should we say that we and the Nietzschean have two different *concepts* of moral goodness? Or simply that there are two different moralities? Once again it is not clear how to go about deciding the question, nor is it clear what hangs on deciding it one way rather than another. I myself am inclined to say we have to deal here with two different concepts of morality, but I should also emphasize the fact that there is no way to refute the antinaturalist who, employing a broad concept of morality, speaks of us and the Nietzschean as having two different moralities.

To summarize this chapter very briefly, I have argued that while the good reasons approach rightly emphasizes the existence of logical relations between non-ethical statements of fact and normative ethical conclusions, the negative part of the position, that this relation cannot be an ordinary deductive or inductive one, is not obviously true and has not been conclusively proved. Perhaps ethical reasoning is a third kind of inference, peculiar to ethics or, more generally, to evaluative arguments. Certainly nothing I have said goes to show that it is not the case. But it would seem that, in the interests of simplicity if nothing else, it would be preferable to take the position that there is nothing peculiar to ethical reasoning which distinguishes it from the kinds of reasoning commonly recognized by logicians. And in the following and concluding chapters I shall try to give some reasons for thinking that ethical reasoning can be viewed as in at least some cases not different in kind from the reasoning we employ in everyday (non-ethical) life and in the sciences.

VII

THE RETURN TO NORMATIVE ETHICS: SINGER AND RAWLS

THE ISSUES between Hare and Toulmin discussed in the preceding chapter could be regarded as expressions of a different answer to the question of how far to go in making traditional ethical principles (a) normative ethical principles which express basic evaluative decisions (Hare's view) or (b) in some important sense meta-ethical and ingredient in the concept of morality itself or of moral reasoning (Toulmin's view). To a certain extent Toulmin's attempt to view fundamental ethical principles as rules of moral reasoning—the rules of inference of ethical argumentation, as it were—represents the ultimate logical outcome of relocating the questions of ethical theory from the normative level to the meta-ethical level. The ultimate outcome of the shift from normative ethics to meta-ethics described in the foregoing chapters of this work would be to regard all fundamental moral rules and principles, such as "It is wrong to tell a lie" or "No one should cause another person unnecessary suffering" or "Do unto others as you would have them do unto you," as analytic statements known to be true by virtue of a conceptual analysis of moral concepts such as "wrong," rather than as statements of basic normative commitments. This line of thought would make normative ethics itself a mere part, although very likely the most important part, of meta-ethics. There is, however, an opposite line of thought, which is to give up altogether the notion that philosophers should restrict themselves to meta-ethics, and deal with normative ethics in a traditional philosophic way with the new factor of a recognition of the existence of meta-ethical questions as to a degree separable or at least distinguishable from the normative questions. In the present chapter I shall deal quite briefly with two recent examples of the return to normative ethical theory in this sense: Marcus G. Singer's ethical theory as set forth in his 1961 book, *Generalization in Ethics,* particularly Chapter 4, "The Generalization Argument," and John Rawls's 1971 book, *A Theory of Justice,* particularly Chapter 7, "Goodness as Rationality." My aim in discussing these two recent and primarily normative ethical theories is to show how it has now become possible to develop and set forth normative ethical theories which at the same time recognize the line of development in meta-ethics discussed earlier in this book.

1   The Generalization Argument

The subtitle of Singer's book, *Generalization in Ethics: An Essay in the Logic of Ethics,* suggests that Singer is intending to deal with questions generally considered to be meta-ethical rather than normative in the period of ethical theory we have already discussed. In one sense that is certainly the case. One of Singer's main aims, certainly, is to demonstrate the validity, in a straightforward sense of "validity," of what he terms the "Generalization Argument," the argument that since the results of everyone's doing a certain action are undesirable, therefore no one ought to do that action. Briefly, Singer's defense of the validity of this kind of argument is that the argument becomes valid when understood as involving two unstated premises, both of which Singer would regard as essentially normative basic ethical principles: (1) the Principle of Consequences, which states that if X's doing A has undesirable results, then X ought not to do A, and (2) the Generalization Principle, which states that if some persons ought not to do Z, then no person who is in a similar case in regard to his characteristics and the characteristics of the situation he is in, ought to do A. The first principle, the Principle of Consequences, cannot as just stated serve as a premise in the generalization argument. But the Principle of Consequences can, Singer suggests, be itself expanded and generalized so as to yield the following principle, the Generalized Principle of Consequences: if the consequences of everyone's doing A are undesirable, then not everyone ought to do A, i.e. some persons ought not to do A. The second part of the principle, that not everyone ought to do A, taken together with the Generalization Principle, which states that if not everyone ought to do A, then no one ought to do A, yields the conclusion that no one ought to do A, i.e. that anyone would be acting wrongly in doing A. In other words, the statement that not everyone ought to do A, taken in conjunction with the principle that what anyone has a right to do, everyone has a right to do—or, the principle that what someone has no right to do, no one has a right to do—entails the conclusion that no one ought to do A. For if there are some persons who ought not to do A, and if from the Generalization Principle one can infer that what is true morally of any given individual is true morally of all similarly constituted and similarly situated individuals, then one can infer that no individual ought to do A, and hence you, the person to whom the argument is addressed in its actual use, ought not to do A. The line of argument contained in the Generalization Argument—the "what if everyone did it?" argument—is thus summarized by Singer himself as follows:

> It may be useful to display in one place . . . this deduction of the generalization argument from the generalization principle and the principle of consequences. The principle of consequences (C) states that: If the consequences of A's doing x would be undesirable, then A does not have the right to do x. The following principle (GC) is what I have called a generalization from C: If the consequences of everyone's doing x would be undesirable, then not everyone has a right to do x. Now the generalization principle (GP) may be stated as follows: If not everyone has the right to do x, then not anyone (no one) has the right to do x. The generalization argument (if the consequences of everyone's doing x would be undesirable, then no one has the right to do x) clearly follows from GP and GC. (*Generalization in Ethics,* p. 66)

Broadly speaking, two sorts of questions can be asked about Singer's analysis and defense of the "What if everyone did it?" argument. First, there is the question of the logical validity of the argument as he reconstructs it. And, second, there is the question of the truth or adequacy of the principles used as premises in the argument: in particular, a question concerning the truth and adequacy of the Generalization Principle. In the following paragraphs that remain in this and the following section, I shall discuss each of these questions in turn.

The sort of argument which Singer tries to reconstruct and explain as the Generalization Argument could be illustrated by the following exchange:

A. Why should I vote: it's a considerable inconvenience to me, and my vote won't make any difference to the outcome of the election.

B. If everyone argued as you do, no one would vote and our political system would collapse: therefore you ought to vote.

Singer's point, as far as the validity of B's argument is concerned, seems to be the following. The inference from "If everyone failed to vote, then our political system would collapse" to "You ought to vote" requires the additional unstated premises that (1) it would be wrong or in some sense undesirable for everyone to fail to vote, since this general failure would result in the collapse of our political system, which presumably no one, including A, really wants, and (2) it would be wrong for A to claim to have a right (not to vote) which he is unwilling to grant to everyone else in similar circumstances. The first unstated premise is, roughly speaking, an instance of the Generalized Principle of Consequences: it has the form of an assertion that if the results of everyone doing a certain action are clearly undesirable, then it is not the case that everyone should (or has a right to) do that action. The second unstated premise is simply the Generalization Principle itself: it asserts that a given individual cannot arbitrarily treat himself as an exception, as it were. He cannot claim a right to do something which he is unwilling to grant a right to do to all similar persons in similar circumstances. Adding these premises and trying to formulate B's argument in a slightly more rigorous way, the logic of B's argument, on Singer's account, appears to be something like this:

1. The results of no one's voting would be undesirable (this is an evaluative statement, but one concerning which practically everyone would agree there can be strong factual empirical support).
2. If the results of no one's doing x would be undesirable, then not everyone should fail to do x (Generalized Principle of Consequences).
3. Not everyone should fail to vote: i.e., some persons should vote (from 1 and 2 by the principle that p, and if p then q, entail q).
4. If some persons should do an action, then all similar persons in similar circumstances should also do the action (Generalization Principle).
5. All those who are similar persons in similar circumstances (to those who should vote) should likewise vote (from 3 and 4 by the principle that p, and if p then q, entail q).
6. A, in particular, is similar to those who should vote (this is presumably an empirically verifiable statement of fact).
7. A, in particular, should vote (from 5 and 6 by the principle that p, and if p then q, entail q).

The argument stated in this way is strictly speaking valid. But it does raise a serious question of interpretation. Steps 3 and 4 together establish that there is a class of persons who should vote, a class presumably picked out by the possession of certain features such that having those features is a sufficient condition for having an obligation to vote. This class is presumably what is referred to in step 5 as "All those who are similar persons in similar circumstances." Yet, the argument itself does nothing to even suggest what defines or characterizes this class. All we know, as far as the argument is concerned, is that there is such a class. Hence, it would seem impossible to actually establish the conclusion of the argument sketched above without some independent knowledge of the class characteristics of those who should vote: only when this has been antecedently decided, can one proceed to speak of a given individual person A being in a similar case, morally speaking, to the other members of this class. Clearly, the class has to be defined in the right way: e.g. one would not want to make the class of those who ought to vote equivalent to the class of those who are over 45, or of those who voted in the last election, or of those persons who earn more than $15,000 a year. But as far as the argument itself is concerned, these would all be possible ways of picking out the class referred to in step 3 as those "persons who should vote." And if this were done, then one could of course easily argue that a particular person A is not similar to those who should vote and hence is under no moral obligation to do so. The problem is reminiscent of the problem raised earlier concerning Hare's universalizability principle: the principle seems empty until we know what count as the morally essential features of a given situation. Similarly, Philippa Foot's view that only certain empirical features can count as evidence of moral goodness assumes we can distinguish the morally relevant from the morally irrelevant features of the case. So in the case of Singer's generalization argument: it assumes that we know the basis, so to speak, for the construction of the class of those having a certain obligation, so that we can say of a given individual that, having the morally required features, he too has the moral obligation that is in question.

Perhaps the above difficulty might be removed by restating step 3 in the argument sketched above in the following way:

3' Some, or at least one, should vote.

and then rephrasing the remaining steps in the following way:

4' If at least one should vote, A either ought to be the one to vote, or else ought to be able to give a reason why he is not the one to vote, or among the class of those who should vote.
5' A cannot give a reason why he should not vote.
6' A ought to vote.

An argument of this sort could then be repeated, using the Generalization Principle as expressed in step 7 below, as an argument designed to show that any given individual B, C, D, etc. ought to vote if he is relevantly similar to A. This argument would take the following form:

6' A ought to vote.
7. For any individual B, C, D, etc., if it is the case that A ought to vote, and if B, C, D, etc. are in a morally similar case to A, then B, C, D, etc. ought likewise to vote.
8. B, C, D, etc. ought to vote.

The problem with the argument as reconstructed in this way is that no reason is given, as far as the argument itself is concerned, for singling out A in step 4' as the one who ought to vote, unless there is some extenuating circumstance, overriding obligation, etc. which takes away the burden of proof laid on A to vote. Why, without any antecedent justification, is it assumed that A ought to be the person, or the member of the class of persons, who ought to vote unless one can show some good reason to the contrary? It certainly seems not to be the case that in general, given that some one ought to do an action X, one can arbitrarily pick any given individual and say that he ought to do X unless he can give some good reason to the contrary, thus placing the burden of proof morally speaking on that particular individual. Thus, it would be unfair in a situation where there is some unpleasant task which someone in a group must do—acting as secretary for the meeting, say—to argue that since someone must perform the onerous unpaid task of secretary, therefore A should do so unless he or she can give a reason why not. Justice seems to require the burden be distributed or assigned in a fair way among those qualified for the task, rather than simply placing the burden on some particular arbitrarily selected member. As sketched above, the argument seems in step 4' to depend on a principle that amounts to the direct opposite of the Generalization Principle, namely, a principle which could be termed the "Singularization Principle" according to which one can say of any given individual A arbitrarily picked out from the entire class of individuals who are in some sense qualified or possible recipients of a benefit or burden that this individual A ought to receive the benefit or burden unless some good reason to the contrary can be given. But this principle, when openly stated, seems grossly unfair. Why should any particular individual at all be arbitrarily selected as the one who bears the burden of proof?

Still another suggestion might be that the argument could be rephrased in the following way:

4' ' If some should vote, all should vote (Generalization Principle).

5' ' All should vote (from 3 and 4' ' by the principle that p, and if p then q, entail q).

6' ' A should vote (from 5' ' and the principle of instantiation).

But surely the Generalization Principle is not so strong as to imply that in general, if a certain group of individuals have some obligation, therefore everyone, or even everyone remotely similar, has that obligation, even as a prima facie obligation. Thus, one could not argue that because some of A's friends and acquaintances should visit A when he is in the hospital, all of A's acquaintances should do so: it is sufficient if a certain relatively small group of them visit him. Or, one cannot argue that because some married couples ought to have children, all married couples have even a prima facie obligation to have children. In general, there seem to be at least three distinct kinds of obligations. (1) Some obligations are restricted to a certain limited class of persons picked out by common possession of some feature, where not even a prima facie obligation holds for those that are not members of the class in question: e.g. parents have certain obligations to their own children which no other persons have. The Smiths have a special obligation of providing care and affection for their own children, and no similar obligation for anyone else's children; whereas the Joneses have no similar obligation to the Smiths' children, and no comparable obligation at all in the case that they have no children. (2) In the case of some obligations we say generally that "someone" ought to do so and so without being able to pick out the individual persons who have the obligation. Thus, we say that someone ought to serve as secretary to the club, or someone ought to look out for the children playing in the street, but we cannot say of anyone in particular that he has the obligation. (3) There are, thirdly, certain general obligations which we are generally thinking of when we refer to a person's moral obligations; these would include such things as the obligation to tell the truth, to keep a promise, to refrain from injuring another person or to commit any act of violence against others, and so on. In the example in question, voting, the obligation presumably belongs to the first class. But if it does, then to put A into the class of voters already seems to presuppose that he has at least a prima facie obligation to vote. But the latter is what the argument is supposed to establish: an apparent circle is involved here.

The problem raised above in understanding Singer's explanation of the generalization argument could conceivably be a difficulty resulting from a peculiarity of the example chosen, namely voting. It is a question whether the obligation to vote is a moral obligation at all, and if it is, it clearly belongs to the first class of obligations restricted to a definite limited class and is not a general or unrestricted obligation such as veracity or sexual integrity or promise-keeping are generally assumed to be. But while this point may in itself be a good one, it does not seem to meet the difficulty encountered above in Singer's argument. A similar difficulty can be raised with an unrestricted obligation of the third kind, veracity for example. Thus, consider the following exchange:

A. Why should I tell the truth: a lie will get me out of trouble and no one will be injured by my telling a lie.

B. If everyone lied just to get themselves out of some trouble, the results would be undesirable: no one would trust another's statements. Therefore you ought to tell the truth.

This exchange, while not exactly as natural sounding as the voting example was, still seems a conceivable example of the actual use of the Generalization Argument. But to what extent does Singer's analysis of the Generalization Argument explain the force of B's answer to A? Singer's analysis of B's reply to A would appear to be roughly the following:

1. The results of everyone lying just to avoid trouble and inconvenience for themselves are undesirable.

2. If the results of everyone doing X are undesirable, then not everyone should do X (Generalized Principle of Consequences).

3. Not everyone should lie to avoid trouble and inconvenience for themselves—i.e. some should be truthful even when it involves trouble and inconvenience (from 1 and 2 and the principle that p, and if p then q, entail q).

4. If some should be truthful, all should be (Generalization Principle).

5. All should be truthful (from 3 and 4 by the principle that p, and if p then q, entail q).

6. A should be (or at least has a prima facie obligation to be) truthful (from 5 and the principle of instantiation).

In this case the force of the argument may be more apparent, even, than the argument in the voting example. The natural rejoinder in the argument just sketched concerning lying would be to question the step from 3 to 5 by way of 4. One might well want to say that while some and perhaps even everyone has an obligation not to lie, the reason is not that general or universal lying has undesirable consequences. Some should not lie, the objection might run, but surely all persons need not be always truthful to avoid these undesirable consequences. The reply Singer would presumably make to this rejoinder is that it would be in an important sense unfair to avoid the undesirable consequences by imposing, as it were, the burden of truthfulness on some and not equally on others. If some are to be truthful, fairness requires that all be truthful unless they can show some difference in their case which removes from them the general obligation. In this instance, then, and generally, the Generalization Argument appeals to a sense of fairness: it is wrong in the sense of unfair to claim an exeption for oneself from some general moral obligation, without granting to everyone else the same right to make an exception in his or her favor also. This is what Singer presumably has in mind when he calls the Generalization Principle a principle of justice or equity. But while it certainly is unfair to claim an advantage for oneself that one is not prepared to grant to others—and being unfair is certainly morally wrong in at least a prima facie sense of "morally wrong"—it is not, on the other hand, obvious that this is *the* reason, in the sense of the *only* reason or even the *main* reason, why a particular individual ought not to lie. It can easily be argued that the moral objection to lying is simply that the consequences of everyone lying to avoid a difficulty would be undesirable and hence—assuming a Utilitarian principle that one ought not to do an action, or has at least a prima facie reason against doing an action, which has a tendency to produce undesirable results—morally wrong. In that case the argument would not need to make use of the Generalization Principle at all: its structure would be roughly as follows:

1. The results of everyone lying to suit their convenience would be undesirable.
2. If the results of everyone doing an action X would be undesirable, then no one should do action X (The rule-utilitarian principle according to which actions that tend to have undesirable results ought not to be done).

    3. No one should lie (from 1 and 2 by the principle that p, and if
p then q, entail q).

An argument of this general sort would seem a much simpler and more
direct reply to A in the exchange outlined above; much simpler and
more direct, that is, than the argument suggested by Singer which
employs the Generalized Principle of Consequences and the Generalization Principle. (The Rule-Utilitarian principle allows one to infer directly that an action is wrong, and hence that everyone has a prima
facie obligation not to do it, from the fact that if everyone, or a significant number of persons, do the action, the results are undesirable. The
Generalized Principle of Consequences would only allow one to infer
from this fact that it is not the case that everyone, or a certain significant number of persons, should do the action). Further, it seems to
correspond more closely to Singer's own view as to what constitutes
the wrongness in lying. Singer argues in connection with lying that the
real objection is the Utilitarian consideration that general lying would
have highly undesirable consequences and that hence, as a direct consequence, no one should lie—as if it were not the Generalization Principle which is needed to demonstrate the wrongness of lying, but a
Rule Utilitarian Principle according to which actions are to be judged
right or wrong depending on the consequences of that kind of action's
being generally done. Thus, when he addresses himself specifically to
the question of lying, Singer speaks very much as a Rule Utilitarian:

> Lying is wrong because of what would happen if everyone lied. It
> would be nothing short of disastrous if everyone were to lie
> whenever he wished to, if lying became the rule and truth-telling
> the exception, which is, however it may seem, actually not the
> prevailing practice. It follows that lying is generally wrong, or
> that no one has the right to lie without a reason, and that the mere
> wish or desire to lie is never a sufficient justification. (*General-
> ization in Ethics,* p. 121).

No mention is made here of the Generalization Principle as such, nor
does that principle seem to be necessarily involved.

    It is true that the Generalization Principle might in certain circum-
stances become involved in an argument concerning the right to lie. A
might agree with B that people should in general be truthful, but that
in his particular case and in any other particular case relevantly similar

to his, no harm is done by lying but, rather, a good is achieved. A, in other words, might claim a special exemption for himself, and were he to do so, a "What if everyone did it?" argument would have to include a reference to the principle that what is right for one is also right for all—that is, a reference to something like the Generalization Principle. It could also be the case that the particular obligation in question *is* the obligation to be fair, and in such an instance, the Generalization Principle might be essentially involved. The difficulty here, however, is that if it is the obligation to be fair which is in question, it is not likely to be effective to use a principle of justice or fairness (as the Generalization Principle is, on Singer's view) to convince a person that he has a moral obligation to be fair. Thus, imagine the following exchange:

A: I don't see why I shouldn't cheat on my income tax return: no one will know and I need the money more than the government.

B: But what if everyone did the same: our system of voluntary tax collection would be impossible, which is undesirable to all; therefore you ought to make an honest tax return.

Here it would probably do little good to explain the force of B's argument as an appeal to the Generalization Principle. If that were done, B's argument would have something like the following form:

1. If all took unfair advantage of our voluntary system of tax collection, the result would be undesirable.
2. Not all should take unfair advantage of our tax system.
3. No one should take unfair advantage of our tax system.
4. A, in particular, should not take unfair advantage of our tax system.

This argument, which depends on the Generalization Principle to derive 3 from 2, is odd in that it is an argument appealing basically to A's sense of fairness, when A himself only argues as he does because of his very lack of a sense of fairness. B's argument is valid enough, but is would seem to lack any moral or perhaps, better expressed, any rhetorical force against A in the situation imagined. One can't very well seek to use an argument based on the principle of fairness against one who, judged by his remarks which inspire the argument, lacks any real sense of fairness to begin with. Hence the very kind of argument which essentially uses the Generalization Principle seems ineffective, whereas an effective use of the argument seems to be a utilitarian kind of argument that does not explicitly rely on the Generalization Principle at all.

To summarize, insofar as the Generalization Argument seems a natural kind of argument to use, as it does in the voting example indicated above, it leaves open the crucial question of whether the individual in question does or does not fall within the class of those who are morally similar as far as the obligation, e.g. to vote, is concerned. On the other hand, in cases where this problem does not arise because the obligation is a general or unrestricted one, as in the case of veracity and honesty, the use of the Generalization Principle seems to be to an important degree pointless and redundant. Further, insofar as the Generalization Argument as Singer analyzes it appeals more or less openly to a sense of justice or fairness, it would not be the kind of argument most naturally used against one who deliberately and consciously proposes an action in itself unfair or otherwise in itself immoral. This is not to say that the Generalization Argument as Singer analyzes it is entirely without point or relevance. Singer seems clearly right in holding, (1) we very often do in fact use a line of argument that is well represented by Singer's Generalization Argument, (2) this argument does in some sense depend for its validity on acceptance of something like Singer's Generalization Principle and Generalized Consequences Principle, and (3) the latter two principles are clearly normative in the sense that they are in some instances logically necessary premises in arguments establishing substantive normative ethical conclusions. But what exactly is the status of these principles themselves: how could they be supported or in some sense vindicated if one wanted to challenge them? In the following section I shall discuss briefly this important question, hoping to show that in spite of many problems attending his view, Singer is essentially right in wanting to regard these principles as normative ethical principles with substantive ethical content, and at the same time as necessary truths known to be true by an essentially meta-ethical analysis of the meaning of ethical discourse.

2   Singer on the Status of Moral Principles

Singer's analysis of the "What if everyone did it?" argument does not in itself commit him to any particular analysis of the status of moral principles, in particular the Generalized Principle of Consequences or the Generalization Principle. It does, however, commit him to the view that these principles are logically necessary to reach certain particular normative ethical conclusions which could not be reached without them. And his considered view is that these principles should be viewed as both substantive moral principles with normative force, and also as necessary truths deriving their force from the very meaning of ethical expressions such as "right" and "obligatory." Thus, Singer summarizes his view on this subject as follows:

> I conclude from this that the generalization principle, and the associated generality of moral judgments, does have moral consequences. Moral judgments can be based on this characteristic of moral judgments. To claim that this is to confuse logical considerations with ethical ones (or language with morals) is to invoke a dogma, and one that has not been shown to have any relevant application in the present context. This illustrates something, I think, concerning the nature of facts about "moral language," and about the possibility of a "morally neutral" ethics. (*Generalization in Ethics,* p. 50)

Singer is certainly running counter to a widespread feeling that general principles such as the Generalization Principle or the Principle of Consequences must be either normative ethical judgments or analytic statements owing their truth entirely to the meanings of ethical words, and not both. But his view that they can be both is neither very obviously impossible in itself nor without precedent in other philosophic areas: such basic philosophical principles as the law of excluded middle or Leibniz's law of the identity of indiscernibles, too, could be and have been viewed both as purely formal and linguistic in some sense, and also as substantive metaphysical principles. More exactly, perhaps, it is not obviously impossible to hold that basic moral principles can legitimately be regarded as either linguistic, or analytic, and at the same time normative. There is, of course, no difficulty in a statement being linguistic in the sense of being about language, and at the same time being normative, as in e.g., "You ought not to have used the word 'Polack' in his presence." But what many would find difficult is the view that a statement can be classified as being true by virtue of linguistic conventions, and hence necessary, and also true by virtue of some extra-linguistic fact or state of affairs. Singer's view might be expressed, however, as the view that while basic moral principles cannot at the same time and in the same respect be viewed as both linguistic and normative, they can equally well be so viewed at different times and in different contexts: in short, that they are sometimes best viewed in one way, and sometimes best viewed in the other way.

What is open to serious question in Singer's account of the status of moral principles is whether the Principle of Consequences, which he regards as essential for the validity of the Generalization Argument, really can claim to be a necessary truth as Singer maintains. Singer's view on this subject is given in the following passage:

> The principle of consequences is a necessary ethical or moral principle. It is necessary not only in the sense that its denial involves self-contradiction. It is necessary also in the sense that like the generalization principle, it is a necessary presupposition or precondition of moral reasoning. There can be sensible and fruitful disagreement about matters within the field delimited by it, but there can be no sensible or fruitful disagreement about the principle itself. We might say that, like the generalization principle, it is both necessary and fundamental. (*Generalization in Ethics,* p. 64)

The main difficulty here as far as the Principle of Consequences is concerned is that it simply is not obviously the case that a person who denies it has contradicted himself. In what sense has a person contradicted himself when he says "I grant that the consequences of A's doing X would be undesirable, but nonetheless A ought to do X"? We certainly seem able to imagine circumstances in which such a statement might be made, and even carry with it a degree of moral plausibility: e.g. as said by a person who concedes that the result of telling a person truthfully that he has an incurable illness will be undesirable, and yet maintains that if he is asked, he ought to tell the truth. It would seem indeed to be the position of the intuitionists such as Ross and Prichard that it is often the case that actions have undesirable consequences, all things considered, and yet still ought to be done. One hesitates to say that such philosophers have been misled by their theories into making a self-contradictory assertion. And ordinary persons too seem to agree that having undesirable consequences is not a sufficient condition for making an action wrong. One could, to be sure, always save the principle by holding that the committing of an immoral act is itself one of the undesirable consequences, or that refraining from committing an immoral act is to be counted among the desirable consequences. But in that case it becomes apparent that the Principle of Consequences is a mere tautology, saying nothing but that if an act ought or ought not to be done, then it ought or ought not to be done—certainly a statement whose denial is self-contradictory, but not one which can count as a substantive moral principle. In general, then, there is in the case of the Principle of Consequences a special problem, not simply the general problem of understanding how a statement can be one which owes its truth to linguistic conventions and also owes its truth to some extra-linguistic reality. The special problem is that of understanding how the Principle of Consequences (the same problem exists for the Generalized Principle of Consequences) can be understood as a necessary truth (assuming that "necessary truth" means roughly "analytic" or "true by virtue of linguistic conventions") when it seems quite possible to make up a story, so to speak, in which the principle is intelligibly denied. It would seem that if a statement is true by virtue of linguistic conventions, then we could not make up any coherent story in which it would be false: we could not imagine what it would be like for it to be false, to use still another criterion of necessity. But insofar as the Principle of Consequences is a substantive moral principle, it would seem that we *can* make up such a coherent story, thus throwing doubt on the claim that the Principle is necessary in the sense that its denial involves a self-contradiction.

It may be noted that there is a further problem with the Principle of Consequences in addition to the problem outlined above. This is the connection between the Principle of Consequences (PC) and the Generalized Principle of Consequences (GC). As Singer's critics have been quick to point out, GC (which says that if the results of everyone doing an action is undesirable, then not everyone ought to do the action) does not obviously follow from PC (which says that if the results of A's doing an action are undesirable, then A ought not do the action). There appear to be cases where one individual person ought not to do an action because of its undesirable consequences when done by a single person, but where there would be desirable results if large numbers of persons were to do the action. Thus, if I as an individual break some immoral law such as a segregation law, the results will be probably undesirable, whereas if everyone disobeys it, the results will be desirable in that the law becomes unenforceable and will probably be repealed. And, to take the reverse case, there are instances where good results, or no particular bad results, follow from a single individual's doing an action, but where bad results ensue if everyone does the action, e.g. talking for half an hour at a time on the telephone. One cannot, therefore, necessarily argue that because if one or a few doing an action has bad results, therefore bad results follow from everyone doing it, or vice versa: it is therefore hard to see how there can be any strict entailment between the Principle of Consequences and the Generalized Principle of Consequences. The truth seems to be that these are independent principles, both of which are, if Singer is right about their status (and I am not denying he is right), to be taken as ultimate necessary ethical truths, neither having nor needing any further support by some more basic process of ethical reasoning.

The problem raised above with PC and GC was that it is not easy to see how they are necessary truths in the sense that their denial involves a self-contradiction. Further, neither seems to entail the other. The problem with the Generalization Principle (GP) itself is that while it very well can be understood as a necessary truth, it seems to be such only by emptying it of all moral content, so to speak, and making it trivially true. GP says that if it is right or obligatory for one individual A to do X, it is also right or obligatory for any other individual B, C, D, etc. who is similar to A. The problem is that while the principle so stated is irrefutable, it would seem, just because no counter-instance can be imagined, to lack moral content. Faced with an apparent discrepancy, where it is right for A to do X, and not right for B, who is similar, to do X, one can always find some difference which can then be used to suggest that A and B are not really similar cases and hence need not have the same rights and obligations. Thus, a racist can argue that there are racial differences which make it right for members of one race to vote in a certain election and not right for otherwise similar members of a different race: we may dispute his theory of racial differences, but we cannot say he has violated the principle of treating similar cases similarly (another way of stating the Generalization Principle). My own view on this matter is that the difficulty just pointed out does not empty GP of *all* substantive moral content. For the principle still requires one to make out a case that in seemingly similar cases there is some relevant difference—and not just some arbitrary selected difference—to explain the differential treatment morally speaking. But it must I think be conceded that in view of the difficulty or, one might say, impossibility of producing a counter-instance to the principle, it is more like an analytic statement, true by virtue of linguistic convention, than it is like a substantive moral truth.

To summarize, there seems no conclusive general reason why, as Singer suggests, basic moral principles such as PC, GC, and GP cannot be viewed as substantive moral principles and also count as linguistic or conceptual truths—in the sense that if one were to deny them as moral principles, one could fall back on their status as necessary truths which cannot coherently be denied. At the same time these particular principles do present difficulties in their interpretation: PC and GC are difficult to regard as necessary truths, and GP is easy to regard as morally vacuous. But without denying these problems, Singer is, I should say, importantly right in challenging what seems to be a prevailing meta-ethical dogma which regards the distinction between truths based on a conceptual analysis of moral language and moral truths possessing positive normative force as an absolutely rigid and exclusive distinction in kind.

3 Rawls: Goodness as Rationality

In the two preceding sections I have discussed Singer's attempt to regard basic moral principles of the right and the obligatory as both in some sense meta-ethical truths and also fundamental normative ethical principles, an attempt which is significant as indicating a move from meta-ethics back to normative ethics. In this remaining section of this chapter I shall deal briefly with John Rawls's definitions of 'good' in Chapter 7 of his book *A Theory of Justice,* viewing Rawls as giving naturalistic definitions of "good" in several senses including the specifically moral or ethical sense of "good." To the extent that Rawls's definitions of "good" are acceptable, they represent not only a return to normative ethics, in so far as naturalistic definitions can be viewed

as a kind of value-judgment as suggested in the beginning of this work
in connection with Stevenson's concept of a persuasive definition.
They also represent a frankly naturalistic approach to the problem of
the meanings of basic normative ethical concepts and, as such, provide
support for the basic positive argument in this work, which may be
summarized as the argument that in many respects naturalism is the
most plausible meta-ethical position in ethical theory and at the very
least still remains a viable alternative in ethical theory which has yet to
be decisively refuted. Accordingly, I shall in no sense seek to criticize
Rawls's definitions of "good." Rather, I shall simply present the definitions in a way close to the way Rawls himself presents them, attempt
some explanation and clarification, and try to meet some of the more
obvious and likely objections that could be raised. My overall aim, as
suggested above, is to make use of Rawls's theory of the good as a
support for the naturalistic position I am trying to advance in this
work: in the Conclusion I shall attempt a more direct defense of naturalism or, at least, of certain theses in ethical theory generally identified with ethical naturalism.

In section 61 of Chapter 7 of *A Theory of Justice,* Rawls presents
three definitions of "good," none of which is likely to arouse great
controversy in that "good" in these senses is not necessarily being
used, nor does Rawls claim it is being used, in a specifically moral or
ethical sense. These are: (1) A is a good X if and only if A has the
properties (to a higher degree than the average or standard X) which it
is rational to want in an X, given what X's are used for, or expected to
do, and the like, (2) A is a good X for K (where K is some person) if
and only if A has the properties which it is rational for K to want in an
X, given K's circumstances, abilities, and plan of life, and (3) A is a
good X for K if and only if A has the properties which it is rational for
K, given his plan of life, to want in an X and, further, K's plan of life
or the relevant part of it is itself rational. Definition (3) raises the question of the meaning of a "rational plan of life," a question Rawls answers as follows in section 63: A person's plan of life is rational if and
only if (a) it is "one of the plans that is consistent with the principles
of rational choice when these are applied to all the relevant features of
his situation" and (b) "it is that plan among those meeting this condition which would be chosen by him with full deliberative rationality,
that is, with full awareness of the relevant facts and after a careful
consideration of the consequences." Finally, in section 66 ("Good

applied to persons'') Rawls defines good in the sense in which goodness is ascribed only to persons: ''A good person, then, or a person of moral worth, is someone who has to a higher degree than the average the broadly based features of moral character that it is rational for the persons in the original position to want in one another,'' or, alternatively, ''a good person has the features of moral character that it is rational for members of a well-ordered society to want in their associates'' (p. 437).

We sometimes speak (a) of things as ''good of their kind'' where we are thinking primarily of tangible possessions such as cars, books, etc., sometimes (b) of activities and pursuits such as getting regular exercise or marrying and having children as good, and sometimes (c) of persons as a whole as good when we describe a person as ''a good person'' or ''not a good person.'' Rawls's definitions of ''good'' could be used to define ''good'' in each of these three ways, without, I think, departing too far from what his definitions intend to imply:

1. A thing (e.g. a book, a car) is good of its kind if its qualities are such as to make it rational to choose that thing from among the other available things of that kind.
2. An activity or pursuit (e.g. marrying) is a good thing to do or have if it is rational for a person to do or have that thing in the light of his life's activities or pursuits as a whole.
3. A person is a morally or ethically good person if rational people would regard that person as someone to be chosen as an associate if they were free to choose the people they are to associate with in daily life.

I am not at all claiming to literally follow Rawls here in these three definitions of ''good.'' But something like these three definitions is at least suggested by Rawls's remarks, and they have the advantage of relating Rawls's definitions to the three classic kinds or senses of ''good'': ''good'' as applied to things, or ''good of its kind,'' ''good'' as applied to actions, and ''good'' as applied to persons. In the remaining paragraphs of this section I will discuss each of these three characterizations of ''good,'' hoping to show that at least some of the more obvious objections can be dealt with in fairly direct fashion.

(1) Clearly, the first sense of ''good'' is not specifically a moral or ethical sense: one can imagine a potential murderer hefting a gun or

some other lethal weapon and saying "This is a good one," which it well might be in the first sense. The point holds equally well when "good" in this first sense does apply to persons, as when someone, a burglar say, is described as "a good man for the job." But this is no objection to the thesis that "good" sometimes has this meaning, and that Rawls's analysis of it as an object of rational choice correctly captures what is intended by "good" in this usage. It might perhaps be suggested that if one had a wildly irrational desire to drink a glass of mud, say, a certain glass of mud might be good in this sense although we should hesitate to say that it would be rational to choose this glass of mud as darker and more evil smelling, say, over other substances. But that objection only shows that rationality here is to be understood as relating to the means used to satisfy some desire, regardless of the rationality or irrationality of the desire or urge itself. If I am a confirmed cigarette smoker, it may be rational to choose a cigarette with more nicotine and tar as providing more smoking satisfaction, even though the desire to smoke itself can, on the basis of the second sense of "good," be condemned as bad.

(2) Sense (2) of "good" defines an activity or pursuit as good insofar as it is a coherent part of a rational plan of life, and this definition raises immediately the question of the value of rationality. Why, an objector might say, should value be placed on a rational life in this way, as if rationality itself were an unquestioned good. Perhaps the best activities—a passionate love affair, for example, that is clearly destined to lead to mutual misery—are not parts of rational life plans, while other activities that are highly important to a rational life, such as having a socially useful job or not speaking habitually so as to antagonize others, are without any real value whatever as far as ethical or moral value is concerned. Some thinkers, indeed, seem to condemn rationality on moral or quasi-moral grounds, as inimical to individuality and freedom: how, then, can one assume that the goodness of an activity is measured by or even correlates in any clear way with the coherence of that activity with a rational plan of life? This sort of objection is a very natural one to raise. But its apparent force rests, I should say, on an unduly narrow conception of "rationality." Rationality often carries with it the connotation of living by a limited set of rules which are rigidly adhered to regardless of particular circum-

stances and impulses: a fixed, inflexible kind of life that allows little or no real spontaneity. But while "rationality" certainly does have that connotation on occasion, nothing in definition (2) requires "rational" to be understood in that sense. If a person's plan of life is such as to give high priority to, say, passionate love affairs, even when they are the causes of misery, it would be rational and hence good for such a person to engage in such affairs, although it might be objected to as irrational in the light of the prevailing conception of a rational plan of life. All (2) really says is that activities are good insofar as they form a rational, coherent part of a general plan of life: nothing is stipulated as to what that rational plan of life is like in the sense of what priorities it assigns to different kinds of experiences (Rawls himself would of course maintain here that, rationally speaking, high priorities should be given to certain goods in all plans of life, e.g. liberty of thought and action, on grounds that these are necessary conditions of forming and following any plan no matter how "irrational" it might conventionally be judged to be).

A possibly more serious objection to definition (2) is that it relativizes "good" to individual life plans: an activity might be good when done by A, as fitting in in a rational way with his plan of life, but might be bad as done by B, as conflicting with his plan of life. (This objection is in a sense the opposite of the one considered above: that objection was that the definition of "good" as applied to activities is too rigid in equating goodness with rationality, while the present objection is that the definition is too loose and tolerant, making the goodness of an activity a function of a particular individual's goals and plans). The obvious reply to this objection, it seems to me, is that the relativity of the goodness of an activity to an individual's goals, desires, aspirations, etc. is so fundamental and important a part of the notion of "good" that any account of "good" that denies it must be radically unacceptable. Surely we want to say that it is impossible to judge, say, marrying, or having children, or pursuing a certain career, etc. as being in general good or bad: it all depends on the individual and the life plan being discussed at the time. This is not to relativize goodness in any objectionable way, but simply to recognize the fact that persons and their circumstances differ very widely, so that what is rational activity for one is by no means necessarily rational activity for someone else—just as what is the right amount of exercise, or the proper medical prescription for one is not necessarily the same for someone else. It is a strong point in definition (2) that goodness in this sense is made relational, not an objection.

(3) Few would probably deny that a person judged to have a good moral character is in fact a person it is desirable to associate with, if one had one's pick of associates: whether this can be interpreted as a definition of a "morally good person" is another matter. An objector might attempt an open question argument here. He might argue that the question "Is that morally good person one whom a rational person would want to associate with?" is a significant question, which it would not be on definition (3) in the sense that its answer would be an obviously analytic truth. In reply to that line of objection, I should simply say that it is not clear that the statement "A morally good person is one whom it is rational to want to associate with" is not analytic, and I see no clear way to demonstrate that it is not analytic. Further, it does seem clear that when the association in question involves a common sharing of burdens, and moral goodness is taken as meaning in large part the quality of fairness, it becomes plainly obvious and indeed self-evident that, other things being equal, a morally good associate is a more rational choice of an associate than a morally bad associate, no matter what other desirable qualities from some non-moral point of view (having a good sense of humor, for example) the person to be associated with may have. In general, it seems highly plausible to say that we want our associates to have as many good qualities as possible, some of them moral, such as fairness and veracity, and others non-moral, such as an attractive and cheerful personality. But in the case of the moral qualities, we insist on our associates having these qualities, and feel we have a right to complain and even reject them if they fail; whereas in the case of the other non-moral qualities, we tend to think of them as a bonus whose deficiency or absence we have no right to complain about. Hence, it does not seem at all implausible to take qualities that are rational to choose in an associate as a defining feature of morally good qualities, and if that is so, a strong prima facie case can be made for the acceptability of definition (3).

To summarize, there are reasons for thinking Rawls has suggested a possible set of naturalistic definitions of "good" both in the moral and in the non-moral sense of "good." Doubtless other objections will be raised. But the attempt is sufficiently plausible to add something to an argument supporting the naturalistic definability of basic ethical words and expressions.

CONCLUSION

1 Normative Ethics and Meta-Ethics Again

THE PERIOD IN ETHICAL THEORY I have discussed in the preceding chapters, roughly the period from 1900 to 1970, exhibits an increasingly single-minded concentration on meta-ethical questions and issues: it might be called the era of meta-ethics or, perhaps more descriptively, the era of analysis in ethics. Yet, if there is any weight to the conclusions reached in the preceding chapters, in particular in the chapter on the emotive theory, the philosophical grounds for the shift to meta-ethics are very shaky indeed. Insofar as there is now a move back to normative ethics, this book has been a defense of it. I suggested in the introduction that Ayer's paradoxical remark that "a strictly philosophical treatise on ethics should make no ethical pronouncements" was largely inspired by the view that since philosophy is a cognitive activity, a search for truths, and since on Ayer's view ethical judgments are neither true nor false, therefore philosophers as such should not make ethical judgments. The argument is valid enough, but the premise that ethical judgments are neither true nor false is at least doubtful and, if I am right, simply false. (I shall resume the argument on this point in the next section, in which I shall argue that the distinction between factual and evaluative statements is untenable when taken, as I think it still generally is, as an instance of what Carl Hempel has called "classificatory types" as contrasted with "extreme types.")

There may, however, have been a more widely held view during the period I have discussed which, while not necessarily agreeing with Ayer and the non-cognitivists in holding that ethical judgments lack truth values, does support a similar conclusion about the desirability of concentrating on meta-ethics at the expense of normative ethics. This view could be expressed as follows. Whether or not ethical judgments are cognitive claims which have truth-values—this itself is a meta-ethical question whose answer involves considerable thought and discussion—there is, at any rate, reason to think that philosophers would do well to avoid controversial normative ethical questions (they would hardly be interesting if they were not controversial) and concentrate on meta-ethical questions. For (the view might be expressed) the normative questions are ones which have long been discussed without any successful resolution, in the sense that no generally acceptable solution has been or seems likely to be reached. Nor do the new philosophical methods and techniques developed in the course of twentieth century British and American philosophy seem likely to help very much in arriving at such generally acceptable solutions. Meta-ethical questions, on the other hand, do not have the same history of unsuccessful discussion. And (the view holds) it is reasonable to think that by careful use of the new methods and techniques, generally acceptable solutions *can* be found. If something like this is the more widely held reason for the shift to meta-ethics, the hope on which it is based has not been entirely fulfilled. Moore, the first to make the shift in question, regarded what we should call his meta-ethical theories as the most certain and secure part of his contribution to ethics. But it seems safe to say that very few philosophers indeed would now consider Moore's meta-ethical theories to be acceptable or even plausible. And one could say the same thing about intuitionism, the emotive theory, and many other meta-ethical theories developed since Moore. It appears we are as far from consensus on basic meta-ethical questions as we were when the development started.

I do not wish to suggest that no progress has been made. If nothing else, a number of issues have been formulated with some clarity which cannot now be ignored by any serious ethical theory, e.g. concerning the meaning and force of ethical terms, the cognitive status of ethical judgments, the possibility of deriving ethical conclusions from nonethical factual premises, and the nature and possible resolution of ethical disagreement. Further, it is possible that the actual amount of disagreement existing among those who hold different meta-ethical theories may have been exaggerated for polemical purposes or for purposes of emphasizing differences which would otherwise be unnoticed—as for example the differences between Dewey, Stevenson, and Hare. An impartial spectator might well hold that the agreements are more important than the disagreements. Thus, it seems widely accepted that Moore showed something by his open question argument (however much disagreement there might be concerning what exactly he did show), or that ethical disagreement is not usually *simply* a matter of cognitive differences, or that the notion of prescriptive meaning or force, however difficult to characterize in any precise way, is somehow important in the analysis of ethical judgments. And so on. These could be counted as discoveries which all must now reckon with in setting forth a meta-ethical theory that hopes to gain any kind of general hearing. All the same, it still remains true that serious disagreements divide contemporary meta-ethical theorists, disagreements which appear not to be easily resolvable by means of current philosophical methods. And one might therefore wonder whether the situation in meta-ethics is really all that different from the situation in normative ethics. Perhaps there are some important general points of agreement in normative ethics too: if there are, the conclusion to be drawn may be, not that we should be as sceptical of meta-ethics as some philosophers have been of normative ethics, but that just as the presence of unresolved and possibly unresolvable disagreements is not a good reason for giving up meta-ethics as a philosophical investigation, so we need not fear getting involved in normative ethics just because there are normative questions that appear unresolved and possibly unresolvable by rational argument and discussion.

Apart from the question about the extent to which the development of ethical theory since Moore has borne out the hope that meta-ethics will prove productive of positive results to a much greater degree than normative ethics has been able to do, there is likewise the question, raised earlier, whether it is strictly possible to confine oneself to meta-ethics. The question I began by asking, whether philosophers should confine themselves to meta-ethics, assumes there is no serious problem about making the distinction between doing meta-ethics and doing normative ethics. But one of the conclusions that could be drawn from a survey of the history of recent ethical theory such as I have attempted in the foregoing chapters is that it is not all that easy to make the distinction. Consider for example the question raised by Moore as to whether "good" can be defined empirically. Is this a purely meta-ethical question? In some sense it certainly seems so. Yet, if by a meta-ethical question one means a question whose answer has no implications whatever for normative ethics, it is not clear that this question can be regarded as purely meta-ethical, or indeed that there are any purely meta-ethical questions. For suppose I say that "good" *can* be defined empirically: it would follow that normative ethical judgments can be obtained from a definition plus some set of empirical facts. Suppose for example I say "good" means "productive of pleasure": this definition plus the fact, say, that books are productive of pleasure entails that books are good—clearly normative. Or, more simply, since the meta-ethical statement " 'Good' means 'productive of pleasure' " entails "Things that are productive of pleasure are good," and since the latter is normative, a meta-ethical statement about the word "good" can directly entail a normative judgment that is not about the word "good" at all but about things that are good— just as the assertion that the word "vixen" means "female fox," (an assertion that is in a sense not about foxes at all but about words) allows one to assert that vixens are foxes (apparently, at least, a statement about foxes). Of course if Moore was right, then no such definition of "good" can be given. But if the question at issue is whether meta-ethical statements can have normative implications, it would be question-begging to reject an empirical definition of "good" such as the above *on the grounds that* a non-evaluative statement about words would then entail an evaluative statement about values.

It may be true that if one is entitled to assume initially that no ethical terms such as "good" can be defined empirically, then one can hold that meta-ethical assertions have no normative implications. But then one would only hold the separability of meta-ethics from normative ethics by holding a particular meta-ethical theory.

It is, moreover, possible to hold that in a very general sense of "normative," the meta-ethical assertion that "good" does *not* mean "productive of pleasure" could be taken as entailing a normative statement. For the assertion " 'Good' does not mean 'productive of pleasure' " entails "It is possible for a thing to be productive of pleasure and not good," and it is not altogether clear why the latter statement could not be considered normative. Certainly "There are things that are productive of pleasure that are not good" is normative, and "It is possible that there are things that are productive of pleasure that are not good" differs from the clearly normative statement only in its modality. But why should a difference in modality of a statement change it from a normative to a non-normative statement? Why should the assertion of p as a contingent truth be normative whereas its assertion as a possible truth not be? Again, if "It is true that whatever produces pleasure is good" is normative, as it surely seems to be, why shouldn't its denial—"It is not true that it is true that whatever produces pleasure is good"—likewise count as normative, on grounds that if a statement is normative, its negation should likewise be normative. Yet, the non-cognitivist's assertion that ethical judgments lack truth values is commonly considered purely meta-ethical, not normative. One wonders, then, whether a double standard may not be operating in regard to whether meta-ethical assertions can have normative implications, or perhaps in regard to what is considered to be a "normative implication": it is assumed that meta-ethical assertions cannot have normative implications, and then in some cases not being equivalent to or entailed by a meta-ethical assertion is made a criterion of being normative; whereas in other cases, such as the assertion that "good" means "productive of pleasure," it is argued that since this meta-ethical assertion would, if true, have a normative implication, it must not be true. Fairness would seem to require either drawing a similar conclusion that the apparently normative conclusion is not really normative, or, better I should say, abandoning the initial assumption that a meta-ethical assertion cannot have normative implications.

The above discussion raises a question central in deciding the relation of meta-ethics to normative ethics, namely, what *is* a normative ethical judgment? More exactly, is there any way of answering the question "What is a normative ethical judgment?" that does not already commit one to a particular analysis of normative judgments, that is, to a particular meta-ethical theory? This question is not easy to answer. Offhand one might say that any sentence actually ascribing an ethical predicate such as "good" or "right" or "obligatory" to some subject counts as ethical or at least as evaluative, and hence as normative. But then what about the use of ethical sentences in the context of hypothetical statements, such as "If Smith is giving the party, it will be a good one," or in counterfactuals such as "If Smith had given the party, it would have been a good one." Such statements do not actually ascribe goodness to anything, yet they would certainly be counted as normative.

Perhaps the above account of normative judgments might be revised as follows: a normative judgment is one that ascribes goodness, etc. to some subject *or* implies such an ascription. Then it could be said that the above statements, while not actually ascribing goodness to anything, do imply such an ascription—that parties given by Smith are or tend to be good. But this account of normative ethical judgments immediately raises a meta-ethical question. On some meta-ethical theories, non-normative statements of fact can imply normative ethical judgments: if one said that every judgment entailing a normative ethical judgment is itself normative, one would be ruling out such theories at the outset by virtue of the definition of "normative judgment." That is too quick and easy a way of refuting naturalism, and in any case one ought, it would seem, to be able to define "normative judgment" without committing oneself on one of the major issues of meta-ethics.

Perhaps, as a third suggestion, it might be said that a normative ethical judgment can be defined simply as the categorical *or* hypothetical ascription of goodness, etc. to a subject. But if hypothetical ascriptions of goodness count as normative judgments, it can easily be shown that non-normative factual statements can entail normative judgments. Let "If Smith has good taste in music, then he enjoys Mozart" be the hypothetical normative statement. This statement is entailed by "Smith enjoys Mozart," as an instance of the logical principle that q entails that if p then q. (Similarly, since it is also a logical principle that not p entails if p then q, one could derive the hypothetical normative statement "If Smith likes opera, then he ought to visit

Europe" from "Smith does not like opera.") If hypothetical ascriptions of goodness, etc. count as normative, one would thus have to say that naturalism is true, not, I should say, in itself an undesirable consequence, but undesirable insofar as the truth of naturalism would immediately follow from one's definition of "normative judgment"—too easy and quick a way of proving naturalism, I should say. One could in desperation simply define a normative ethical statement as an ascription of goodness, etc. which does not follow logically from any set of purely factual non-ethical statements. But this would so obviously beg an outstanding meta-ethical issue that few would be willing to go so far. Few would want to say that it is the very meaning of an "ought" statement that it cannot be derived from an "is" statement. In sum, it is not at all easy to define "normative judgment" without, in doing so, deciding by definition some crucial meta-ethical question.

In the preceding paragraphs I have argued that because of the difficulty in characterizing what is meant by "normative judgment" without committing oneself to a particular meta-ethical theory, it is hard to decide whether and to what extent meta-ethics and normative ethics are independent of one another. The difficulty of characterizing what is meant by "normative judgment" may be worth stressing further, in a way that suggests that the meta-ethics/normative ethics distinction, important as I think it is, is also to a considerable degree an artificial one. Thus, consider the suggestion that the distinction between a normative ethical judgment and a meta-ethical judgment is that whereas the former is *about* such things as actions, persons, motives, intentions, etc., the latter is about statements about such things. There are questions to be raised about this way of making the distinction, quite apart from the problem mentioned in the Introduction, namely, that while all meta-ethical statements are statements about normative ethical statements, the converse is not true: some statements about normative ethical statements are themselves normative rather than meta-ethical. Suppose, for example, one says that the only things that can be intrinsically good or bad are a person's intentions—a rough paraphrase of Kant's remark that the only thing in the world or even out of it that is good without qualification is a good will. It is at least highly plausible to take this remark as a normative ethical judgment, although certainly a highly general one. But the remark in question could easily be restated as an apparently meta-ethical remark to the effect that statements ascribing "good" and "bad" in the sense of "intrinsically good" and "intrinsically bad" are always statements about a person's intentions. On the definition in question, at least, this last statement is certainly meta-ethical.

Confronted with this problem, one might say that Kant's remark about a good will, despite appearances, is really meta-ethical: what it really says is that there is a peculiarly ethical sense of "good" in which "good" only applies to an agent's intentions as opposed to his outward actions. But if Kant's remark can be understood in this way as meta-ethical, why cannot one equally well understand as meta-ethical the hedonist's claim that all and only pleasurable experiences are good, by understanding it as the claim that there is a peculiarly ethical sense of "good" in which it applies only to pleasurable experiences. But hedonism would then become a meta-ethical theory on the notion of meta-ethics in question: it would be the assertion that statements ascribing "good" in its ethical sense are always statements about pleasurable experiences. We certainly do commonly understand the hedonist's position as normative, and rightly so I should say. But if one had some reason for doing so, one could state it in the formal mode, as it were, rather than in the material mode, as a statement about ethical statements, in which case it would not be normative at all but meta-ethical according to the criterion in question.

Considerations like those indicated above, suggesting that the meta-ethical/normative ethical distinction is to a degree an artificial one, may also result from reflecting on other possible ways of characterizing a normative judgment, e.g. as one *using* as contrasted with *mentioning* an ethical word, or as one in which an ethical word or sentence occurs essentially, as opposed to judgments in which ethical words or sentences occur vacuously. Thus, "John was a bad king" is certainly normative, and uses "bad" in an ethical sense: but if one had any reason for doing so, the statement could be rephrased as "The term 'bad' applies to King John" in which case the statement would mention the word "bad" rather than using it and, hence, would count as meta-ethical rather than normative on the test in question. Or, to take an example where there might be some real question as to whether a statement is normative or meta-ethical, consider the principle that (as it might be stated) "ought" implies "can." As I have just stated the principle it would mention the words "ought" and "can" and hence counts as meta-ethical rather than normative. But a real doubt could exist here: the statement '' 'Ought' implies 'can' '' entails such statements as "If Smith can't keep his promise, then it is not the case that he ought to," and the latter is normative, at least in the sense that it uses rather than mentions ethical words. I would not myself hesitate to see this as a case where a meta-ethical statement entails a normative judgment, but if one is committed to the view that no such entailments exist, one would have to give up the use–mention distinction as a way of drawing the line between meta-ethical and normative statements. Similarly, the suggestion that normative statements use ethical words and sentences essentially as opposed to using them vacuously, i.e. such that substituting other words or sentences in their place does not affect the truth value of the statement in which they occur, does not altogether succeed in helping one draw an absolutely sharp line between meta-ethics and normative ethics either. There is, for one thing, the kind of difficulty mentioned earlier concerning hypothetical and disjunctive statements in which ethical words and statements occur essentially, and hence would be normative on the proposed test, and yet which by ordinary logic are entailed by one of their parts which is non-normative. Thus, "Either Smith is a no-good liar or there are no tigers in Africa" would be normative insofar as "no-good liar" is a normative expression, but as Arthur Prior pointed out in an article entitled "The Autonomy of Ethics" (*Australasian Journal of Philosophy,* 1960) that statement is entailed by "There are no tigers in Africa" on the general principle that p entails either p or q. Again I should not myself regard this consequence, that a normative ethical judgment can be logically entailed by a non-normative statement of fact, as in itself undesirable. But if one does not accept it, there is a difficulty with the proposed test of "normative judgment" which allows that consequence. It is true that in this case and perhaps generally, one could point out that the entire statement "If there are no tigers in Africa, then either Smith is a no-good liar or there are no tigers in Africa" does not contain an essential occurrence of any ethical word or sentence. One could substitute any other sentence for "Smith is a no good liar" and the statement as a whole would still be true. But that does not, I think, affect the point at issue, which is that a statement which to all appearances is normative on the proposed test would be entailed by a non-normative statement of fact.

To conclude, it is very hard indeed to maintain the thesis that meta-ethics has no normative ethical implications. To a large extent one's position depends on what one takes to be a normative ethical judgment, and I have tried to show that on the most obvious ways of characterizing a normative judgment it is simply not the case that normative statements and meta-ethical statements are logically independent. At the same time I do not want to suggest that the distinction between meta-ethics and normative ethics should be altogether rejected. The problem at the present time may in fact be to maintain the distinction in view of the current renewed interest in normative ethics. To a very large degree, I should say, meta-ethics can, if one wants, be pursued as an autonomous (i.e. normative free) philosophical inquiry: insofar as the development from Moore to the present discussed in this book shows that meta-ethics so pursued can have substantial positive results, this book itself constitutes a defense of the autonomy of meta-ethics.

2   Fact and Value: An Untenable Dualism?

In Chapter 3 I said that insofar as this book attempts to defend a particular meta-ethical theory, it is intended as a defense of naturalism. And while my main aim throughout the preceding chapters has not been to present such a defense, I have made some attempt at suggesting it to the extent at least of arguing that the main existing refutations of naturalism are inconclusive. In this and the two following sections I shall try to give a somewhat more positive defense of certain theses at least closely associated with theories commonly called "naturalistic." In this section I shall argue in support of the view that "factual" and "evaluative" are not exclusive terms, in that an evaluative statement can be to a degree factual and a factual statement to a degree evaluative: the distinction is one of degree rather than a distinction in kind. In the following section I shall argue that even if one were to assume that the predicates "factual" and "evaluative" are exclusive, or rather to leave it an open question whether they are, it is still possible to derive normative ethical conclusions deductively, or, if not deductively, then at least inductively, from non-ethical statements of fact. And in the final section I shall argue briefly that even if one were to hold that ethical reasoning is neither deductive nor inductive, as the good reasons approach holds, it is still possible to maintain the naturalistic thesis that ethical disagreement can in principle be resolved by reaching agreement on relevant non-ethical matters of empirical fact.

In response to the suggestion that factual and evaluative statements differ in kind, one might ask "But are they exclusive: isn't it a fact, for example, that torturing people for the fun of it is wrong? The suggestion that it is not a fact is one we would ordinarily find somewhat puzzling. A natural interpretation of the suggestion that it is not a fact that torturing people for the fun of it is wrong is that it is being suggested that it is not wrong but sometimes right or at least excusable. That interpretation would be mistaken: what is intended is a meta-ethical remark about the sentence "It is wrong to torture people for the fun of it," not a moral judgment about torture. But the fact that it would be natural to interpret it as a moral judgment suggests that we at least sometimes suppose that we are stating facts when we make moral judgments. Again, while we might ordinarily consider as open to discussion the suggestion that any given evaluative statement does not state a fact, we would consider the assertion that no evaluative statement states a fact as a highly paradoxical one. Perhaps we would not regard it as a paradox to suggest that it is not a fact that torturing people for the fun of it is wrong, although we might think that only a person with unusual moral principles would make that suggestion. But we would regard it as paradoxical to say that it is never a fact that something is right or wrong, good or bad, beautiful or ugly. That suggestion seems equivalent to saying that all evaluative statements are mistaken, and that there is really no such thing as rightness or wrongness, goodness or badness, beauty or ugliness. Doubtless this would again be a mistake: the philosopher who asserts that no evaluative statement is factual is not really asserting that nothing is right or wrong, which is itself an evaluative statement. He is only making a statement about the kind of statement we are making when we say that something is right or wrong. But the fact that it would be natural to misinterpret his suggestion is, I am arguing, evidence that we do ordinarily regard evaluative statements as in at least some cases statements of fact.

It might be held that although we do ordinarily consider it natural to say in some instances "It is a fact that X is wrong," we do not really mean by "it is a fact that" what we mean by "it is a fact that" in the case of statements considered factual by those who consider the distinction between factual and evaluative statements a distinction in kind—e.g. in "It is a fact that water expands when it freezes." What is intended by the latter statement, it may be held, is that something is the case regardless of what anyone thinks or feels or believes, whereas that is not intended in "It is a fact that X is wrong." "It is a fact that X is wrong" could just mean that the wrongness of X is to be considered as something settled and beyond reasonable doubt or argument, not that X's wrongness is something independent of human belief or feeling. The natural resistance to the suggestion that no evaluative statements state facts may therefore result from a simple verbal misunderstanding, and would vanish when one explains in what sense of "factual" it is being denied that evaluative statements are factual. But would it? The answer to that question depends on just what is meant by "factual" by those who regard factual and evaluative statements as differing in kind, and it is not easy to say what that is. The above suggestion, that a factual statement is one that states something to be the case independently of what people think or feel, hardly seems adequate: what about statements which themselves state something about human thoughts or feelings or beliefs? And while it is plausible to say that *part* of what is meant by saying it is a fact that X is wrong is that "X is wrong" is to be regarded as settled beyond reasonable doubt—a fact as opposed to a theory or a tentative suggestion—more is intended. It is commonly intended in some cases that X *is* wrong and would still be wrong even if everyone were to think it not wrong. Nor can "factual" as opposed to "evaluative" be understood easily in terms of the method of verification of the former as opposed to the method of verification, if any, of the latter. There is no particular method of verification common to all statements generally called "factual": there are vast differences, for example, between the method of verifying an everyday statement of observable fact such as "There's no more beer in the icebox" and a highly theoretical statement in science such as the statement that air is a mixture of oxygen and nitrogen, or $E = MC^2$. In regard to certain kinds of factual statements, it is even inappropriate to speak of the method of verifying them at all, e.g. "My foot hurts." Yet all these as well as many other kinds of statements would all be classified as "factual" by those who regard factual statements and evaluative statements as two distinct classes of statements. It might be suggested that when factual and evaluative statements are so regarded, "factual" just means "non-evaluative." But that would trivialize the claim that factual and evaluative statements are mutually exclusive. Doubtless there is a distinction to be made between evaluative and non-evaluative statements, but surely something more than that is intended. Hence, I think it is at least not obvious that the disagreement between the view that evaluative statements are never statements of fact, and the ordinary belief that some evaluative statements are statements of fact, is only a verbal disagreement.

Some readers may be impatient with the kind of argument just presented. The very most the argument shows, they might say, is that it is part of our ordinary naive conceptual framework that some evaluative statements are factual in the same sense as statements that by common consent are factual, such as "It's raining." But what reason is there for thinking that this naive conception is true? Indeed, the very fact that it is a view held by ordinary unreflective persons may be a reason for thinking it isn't true. And in any case, there are serious philosophical considerations that strongly suggest that it isn't true— that there is good reason for separating statements into two distinct non-overlapping classes, factual and evaluative. I fully accept the point that our ordinary conception of evaluative statements as sometimes factual might have to be abandoned in the light of philosophical considerations. But I shall argue that no philosophical considerations have yet been set forth which show conclusively that this conception need be abandoned altogether, although it may have to be somewhat revised. For purposes of exposition, I shall consider four possible meta-ethical arguments which might be thought to show that the conception of evaluative statements as sometimes factual must be abandoned: (a) what I shall call "the sceptical argument", (b) the version of subjectivism which, to distinguish from another version of subjectivism, I shall call "subjectivism $_1$", (c) subjectivism $_2$, and (d) the prescriptivist argument. In all four cases I shall argue that, while there may be something to the argument in question, it does not convincingly show the desirability of making "factual" and "evaluative" names of two separate classes of statements. My conclusion will be that we need not altogether abandon the naive conception of normative ethical statements as sometimes factual. Rather than thinking of "factual" and "evaluative" as predicates picking out two separate classes of statements, these predicates (I shall suggest in conclusion) designate ways of assessing statements in terms of their relative position on one of several possible scales of assessment.

(a) What I will call for lack of any better expression "the sceptical argument" is briefly as follows. What is involved in the distinction between factual and evaluative statements is an ontological distinction. In the case of factual statements, there are objectively real entities—facts, in the sense of states of affairs—which correspond to the statement when the statement is true and by corresponding to which the statement is true. In the case of evaluative statements, there simply are no such entities and perhaps could not conceivably be. We would not even know what it would be like for there to be an entity, the wrongness of stealing, say, to which the statement "Stealing is wrong" could be thought of as corresponding, whereas we can literally see the state of affairs to which "It's raining" corresponds. Hence, the sceptical argument concludes, there is a real and quite clear distinction between factual and evaluative statements, however much that may be obscured by our ordinary use of expressions such as "is a fact that" and "is true that." It may well be the case that we do speak of evaluative statements as true and false, for example. But not (so the sceptical argument runs) in the same sense in which "It's raining" is said to be true. Statements like "It's raining"—genuinely factual statements—are true because they correspond to facts, which is never the case with evaluative statements.

The sceptical argument as I have briefly sketched it raises many basic philosophical issues which I cannot hope to deal with. I shall simply mention here some of the difficulties I find with it. (1) If the sceptical argument were to be carried through to its ultimate conclusion, one would have to say that, strictly speaking, all affirmative evaluative statements are false—false, that is, when viewed as statements which purport to have truth values in the strict sense of truth and falsity. For so viewed, all affirmative evaluative statements represent the world, so to speak, as containing states of affairs corresponding to the statement in question. But there are no such states of affairs. And that makes the evaluative statement false, just as a factual statement such as "It's raining" is made false by virtue of the non-oc-currence of rain. Aside from its generally paradoxical air, this conse-quence yields a paradox in connection with evaluative arguments, that is, arguments with affirmative evaluative statements in the premises. If all affirmative evaluative statements are false, then no arguments of that kind would ever have true premises and a false conclusion: hence all such arguments would be valid, according to the logician's way of counting as valid an argument in which it is never the case that the premises are true and the conclusion false. The sceptic would, of course, say that it is a mistake to view affirmative evaluative state-ments as asserting the existence of facts or states of affairs. He would say that in the strict sense evaluative statements lack truth values al-together. But one could equally well deny the premise that all evalua-tive statements are false, holding either that since there are in some cases facts or states of affairs corresponding to evaluative statements, such statements are sometimes true, or, simply rejecting the notion of truth in the strict sense of correspondence with a fact or state of affairs conceived as a separately existing entity.

(2) The notion that there are facts or states of affairs, while in a way unproblematic, does raise a question if take seriously as an onto-logical commitment of a philosophical kind. When I say "John is tall" am I saying there is an entity, John's being tall, which is separate from John? If so, then much of the objection to ethical facts vanishes; stealing's being wrong may be a queer entity, but it is not altogether clear that it is any queerer than John's being tall. If, on the other hand, one were to deny that there is any such separate entity as the fact that John is tall, as distinct from John, then one could use the sceptical argument against the factual character of "John is tall" as well as against "Stealing is wrong." But no argument whose conclusion is that statements such as "John is tall" are not factual is likely to be widely accepted.

(3) Even those who accept facts, as distinct from things and proper-ties, as G. E. Moore did, do not want to say there are such entities corresponding to all true statements that by general consent are fac-tual. Thus, statements of scientific laws would generally be regarded as factual as contrasted with evaluative (not, of course, factual in the sense in which we contrast fact and theory). But it is difficult to think of there being *a* fact corresponding to, say, the statement that metals

expand when heated. If anything, it corresponds to an indefinitely
large set of facts. Again, there are problems with statements about the
past or future: "It's going to rain tomorrow" could be a statement of
fact, but is there now a fact, the fact that it's going to rain tomorrow?

In sum, then, while the sceptical argument raises basic issues of existence and truth that go far beyond the scope of a book on ethics,
there are enough initial difficulties in it to warrant scepticism about
scepticism in this case. At the same time, the argument does suggest a
way of distinguishing factual and evaluative statements not as two mutually exclusive and exhaustive classes—as a classificatory type in the
sense explained by Carl Hempel in his article "Typological Methods
in The Social Sciences"—but as marking relative position on a scale
ranging from what could be called "hard" statements of fact at the
bottom to statements which lack literal truth values at the top (as an
extreme type in Hempel's sense). At the bottom might be statements
ascribing directly observable properties to objects, e.g. "This book is
red," where it seems most plausible, if it ever is, to regard the statement as true by virtue of its correspondence to a fact or state of affairs
conceived as an entity—the book's being red. Somewhere in the middle might be statements commonly called factual, such as "Water
boils at 212° F" which employ concepts that do not in any obvious
way merely designate observed properties, and which go beyond anything that can in principle be directly observed. Evaluative statements
such as "Stealing is wrong" occur toward the upper end of the scale.
And to indicate this, one could say that they are not factual, i.e. less
like hard facts than like statements which lack literal truth value altogether. But on this conception the distance from hard facts to many
ordinary factual statements is much greater than the distance from
these ordinary factual statements to evaluative statements: that is, evaluative statements are more like many factual statements than many
factual statements are like basic "hard" statements of fact. (Using a
distinction between the "material" and the "notional," suggested by
Julius Kosevi in his book *Moral Notions,* one could say that evaluative
statements such as "You acted wrongly in stealing that money" are
like ordinary descriptive statements such as "You stole that money"
in that both employ notions such as "acted wrongly," "stealing," and
"money" which cannot be reduced simply to directly observed properties: both contrast with what could be called material judgments such

as "This book is red"—or, insofar as "book" is also a notion, with simply "This is red." In these terms "factual" could be understood to mean the relative approximation of a statement to a purely material statement; saying that evaluative statements are not factual could be viewed as a way of saying that they are relatively formal or notional.) In short, a distinction can be made, but it is really a distinction between the relatively more factual ("factual") and the relatively less factual ("evaluative"), and not a distinction in kind.

(b) A distinction in kind between factual and evaluative statements can be made, it might be argued, by defining "factual statement" as one which states what is the case regardless of the speaker's own desires and preferences. The paradigm of a factual statement, by this argument, is something like "The boiling point of water at sea level is 212° F," which does not state or imply anything about the speaker's or anyone else's desires or preferences, whereas the paradigm of an evaluative statement, something like "Torturing people for the fun of it is wrong," does state or at least imply something about the speaker's desires and preferences. Such a statement, it may be said, certainly says in some sense that the speaker disapproves of torturing people for the fun of it, would seek to prevent sadistic torture, feels aversion toward people who approve of or practice sadistic torture, and so on. For the sake of convenience I shall call a statement "subjective" when it asserts something about the speaker himself: "It terrified me" or "I detest asparagus" are in this sense subjective. An objective statement by contrast makes no assertion about the speaker himself: the above example, "Water boils at sea level at 212° F," would ordinarily be an objective statement in this sense. The argument in question, in these terms, is that evaluative statements are subjective and, in particular, assert something about the speaker's desires and preferences, whereas factual statements are objective.

Granting the above distinction between subjective and objective statements, clearly not all subjective statements in this sense are evaluative: "I have a headache" is not an evaluative statement. Nor could one plausibly hold that all statements about the speaker's desires and preferences are evaluative: "I don't care for more dessert," or "I prefer my steak well done" do not seem to be value judgments. There may be epistemological differences between first-person reports of desires and preferences, and objective statements: the former may be incorrigible whereas the latter are not. And these differences might incline one to say that they are "factual" in somewhat different senses. But in a reasonable broad sense of "factual," the person who answers the waitresses' question "How do you prefer your steak?" by saying "I prefer my steak well done" is making a factual statement. In general, if by calling a statement "factual" one means that it is primarily intended to convey information, there is no reason for excluding many subjective statements from the class of factual statements. Hence one cannot equate the distinction between factual and evaluative statements with the distinction between subjective and objective statements, and still maintain that "factual" and "evaluative" are mutually exclusive.

Apart from the problem indicated above, there are many well-known difficulties in the view that evaluative statements are always subjective. One difficulty that seems to me especially great is the following. If the statement "X is wrong" were *simply* an assertion about the speaker's own attitudes, feelings, preferences, etc. then we would have to accept as evidence that X is wrong whatever goes to show that the speaker does have these attitudes. And that is not the case: the evidence that abortion is wrong is vastly different from the evidence that would go to show that the person who says "Abortion is wrong" is speaking sincerely. This argument shows that it is not even *part* of what I am asserting, when I assert that X is wrong, that I have certain attitudes and feelings toward X. If it were even *part* of what I am asserting, I could not be said to have established that X is wrong until I have established that I do have these feelings and attitudes. And that is not the case. If, moreover, my statements about my own feelings and attitudes are, as some philosophers hold, incorrigible, it would be a mistake to ask for the evidence for such statements at all. I make the statement "Abortion is wrong" on the basis of what I consider evidence; it is not clear I make the statement "I feel negatively toward abortion" on the basis of anything that could be considered evidence. However that may be, it does seem clear that showing that one does indeed have certain feelings and attitudes toward X is not even a part of showing that X is wrong, and if it is not, the statement "X is wrong" cannot be a subjective statement in the sense in question. Again, it is not contradictory to say "Abortion would be wrong even though no one disapproved of it" whereas it would be contradictory to say "Abortion would be disapproved of by me even though no one disapproved of it." The statement "Abortion is wrong" cannot therefore be equivalent to the statement "I disapprove of abortion." It is perhaps true, as G. E. Moore suggested, that a statement of the form "X is wrong" implies, in a sense, "I disapprove of X." It would be odd for a person to say "X is wrong but I don't disapprove of it." In general, it is a reasonable expectation that when a person says something is wrong, he has certain attitudes and feelings toward it: if he does not, we regard his statement as insincere. But in the same way, as Moore pointed out, the factual statement "It's raining" implies that the speaker believes it is raining. That does not make us regard the statement "It's raining" as subjective: why, then, should the fact that statements of the form "X is wrong" imply something about the speaker's feelings and attitudes make us regard that statement as subjective?

It could be held that evaluative statements are subjective in the sense that they assert something about the feelings, desires, preferences, attitudes, etc. not of the speaker himself, but of all or most men of a certain description, e.g. all or most men in the society or social class to which the speaker belongs, or all or most educated men, or by ideally qualified judges as in the "ideal observer theory." One might hesitate to call such theories "subjectivist." The mere fact that a statement is about the feelings, desires, attitudes, etc. of some person does not make it subjective as opposed to objective: few would deny that "Many children fear the dark" is an objectively true statement. But one could, simply as a matter of terminology, use "subjective statement" to mean any statement about human feelings, desires, attitudes, etc.: the proposed view is that evaluative statements are subjective in this broader sense, whereas factual statements are objective in the sense that they are not about human feelings, desires, attitudes, etc. Such a view, however, has some of the same problems mentioned in connection with the previous view as well as problems of its own. Clearly, not all subjective statements in this sense are evaluative. And "subjective" here cannot reasonably be contrasted with "factual": it is surely a fact that many children fear the dark, or that a majority of persons in the United States approved of the war against Hitler. Hume, who can be construed as holding a kind of social approval theory according to which "X is bad" means all or nearly all men disapprove of X, has been criticized for making normative ethical statements equivalent to statements of sociological fact. Again, it is doubtful that the evidence one would cite to prove that something is disapproved of or an object of aversion to all or most men of a certain description is necessarily a reason for thinking that thing to be wrong: one might well agree that most men in the society or social class of which one is a member disapprove of abortion, but still one might maintain without contradiction that abortion is not wrong. Or, reversing the case, it is hard to believe that a person is not entitled to claim to know an action is wrong even though he has no statistical data showing it would be disapproved by most people in his society.

All these and other difficulties are avoided by the ideal observer theory, since it does not equate moral judgments with statements about actual feelings, desires, attitudes, etc. but with statements about what the attitude of a possibly non-existent ideal observer would be. But while I would not deny that approval by an ideal observer is a test of moral rightness, there are well known difficulties in this theory too, understood as an analysis of what moral judgments mean. There is no way to prove that all ideal observers would approve the same things: it is logically possible for an action to be approved by some and disapproved by others. But if approval by an ideal observer strictly constituted a thing's rightness, one would have to conclude it is logically possible for an action to be at the same time right and not right. And while a good method of deciding whether something is right may be to ask oneself whether an ideal observer would approve of it, it is hard to maintain that one is not qualified to claim to know that something is right unless one has used this method. In general, I conclude, evaluative statements are not wholly subjective in the sense that they are statements about human feelings, preferences, desires, attitudes, etc. Hence no very promising way is open to make a distinction in kind between factual and evaluative statements by interpreting "factual" as meaning "objective" and "evaluative" as meaning "subjective."

(c) In the above discussion I have understood the distinction between subjective and objective statements as a distinction between the things the statements are about. But "subjective" and "objective" could be understood not as a distinction of subject matter, but as a distinction between ways or methods of establishing statements. An objective statement could be understood as a statement which is made on the basis of some reasonably rigorous, well established, and reliable method, in particular on the basis of scientific method. A subjective statement, in contrast, could be understood as a statement that is not so based, but is made on the basis of personal impression, whim, prejudice, or some other relatively non-rational or irrational basis. Thus, my statement "Smith dislikes me" could be called "subjective" not meaning that it is about someone's attitudes or feelings, but meaning that I have arrived at the belief I am expressing on the basis of a few impressions, and cannot support the statement in a rationally satisfactory way. Clearly, a statement could be subjective in this sense and not be about anyone's feelings, desires, beliefs, etc. at all, e.g. "Winters are not so cold as they used to be." All evaluative statements, it could then be argued, are subjective in this sense, and equating "objective" with "factual," one could say that all evaluative statements are non-factual.

The argument sketched above does, I think, state correctly what is often intended by those who make a distinction in kind between factual and evaluative statements. But it is doubtful whether such a distinction can be defended in these terms. There is again the problem that not all subjective statements in the above sense would commonly be called "evaluative": few would regard as evaluative a statement such as "Winters are not so cold as they used to be." Further, the distinction between subjective and objective statements in the present sense is clearly a matter of degree. Few of the statements we accept as true are accepted entirely on the basis of rational considerations: factors such as acceptance of authority are involved in our acceptance of statements we regard as highly objective, e.g. "Water boils at sea level at 212° F." On the other hand few statements are accepted with no rational justification whatever: the person who says "Winters are not as cold as they used to be" has at least some impressions to go by in making his statement, and it is not entirely non-rational to use these as a basis for making a statement. And there are a large number of statements somewhere in between, which we might hesitate to call either subjective or objective. A statement such as "Women are shorter on the average than men" as commonly made is not based on any extensive precise measurements, and is therefore to a degree subjective. But insofar as it is based on some observations, it is objective. We call "subjective" in the present sense statements which fall in the lower range of rigorous rational justification; "objective" statements are those which occur relatively high in the scale. The fact that we speak of statements as "very subjective" or "highly subjective" suggests that this distinction is one of degree. But the distinction between factual and evaluative statements I am questioning is a distinction in kind. Again, granting that some evaluative statements are subjective in the present sense, not all evaluative statements are. "He's a wicked man" said of a complete stranger on the basis of a single impression is subjective, but few would say that "Hitler was a wicked man" said by someone who has made a thorough study of Nazi Germany is subjective in an equivalent sense. But if the distinction between subjective and objective statements can be made among evaluative statements themselves, that distinction cannot be used to distinguish evaluative statements from some other kind of statement. Hence, while a distinction certainly can be made between statements that are subjective in the sense that they are not arrived at or tested by a rigorous exact method, and those that are so arrived at or tested, this distinction cannot well serve to establish a difference in kind between factual and evaluative statements.

(d) A last possible way of making a distinction in kind between factual and evaluative statements might be in terms of the distinction between descriptive and prescriptive statements. A descriptive statement simply reports that something is the case without recommending, advising, encouraging, commanding, etc. anyone to take any course of action. A prescriptive statement, by contrast, is one which does not, or at least does not *simply*, report that something is the case, but does advise, urge, order, request, etc. the listener to take some course of action. What it means to say that ethical and in general evaluative statements are not factual, it could be argued, is simply that they are prescriptive rather than descriptive statements. And, in this connection, one might argue that evaluative statements cannot be descriptive since if they were, evaluative judgments would not have any necessary connection with conduct, whereas, as William Frankena states the argument in his book *Ethics,* "it would seem paradoxical if one were to say 'X is good' or 'Y is right' but be absolutely indifferent to its being sought or done by himself or anyone else."

The descriptive–prescriptive distinction undoubtedly helps to clarify the factual–evaluative distinction. At the same time there are problems in understanding the factual–evaluative distinction in these terms. One obvious problem is that it is clear that evaluative statements are at best a subclass of prescriptive statements. Mere commands, such as "Shut the door," or requests, such as "Pass the salt," are not value-judgments. A moral judgment of the form "X is wrong" may well involve a request, command, etc. not to do X, but it seems to involve more: how, otherwise, could we distinguish the physician's advice not to have an abortion from the moralist's claim that having an abortion would be morally wrong?

A further problem in understanding the factual–evaluative distinction in terms of the descriptive–prescriptive distinction is that it simply is not clear that evaluative statements must in all cases be prescriptive, or that factual statements cannot be to some degree prescriptive. As regards the first point, there are evaluative statements which do not in any obvious way recommend, order, urge, advise, etc. any particular course of action, e.g. "Caesar was a great general," or "John was a bad king." The prescriptivist might reply that "John was a bad king" does prescribe against conduct like King John's: it says that if you are a king, do not act like King John. But those of us to whom the statement is made are not remotely likely to be kings: what would be the point, therefore, in prescribing how we should or should not act if we were? And while "John was a bad king" is doubtless a mere conventional statement in the sense that repeats what is commonly said, it does not follow that it is a mere report of what others have said and so not a genuine evaluative statement. It would, to be sure, be odd to say "John was a bad king: be like him if you are a king." But it does not follow that the statement actually prescribes against conduct like that of King John. In general, it is odd to prescribe doing something said to be bad or wrong, but it does not follow that saying something is bad or wrong always prescribes *against* seeking or doing that thing. As regards the second point, there is no reason why statements generally considered factual could not be used with the intention of recommending, advising, encouraging, warning, etc. and so be, to a degree, prescriptive. One who says to a doubtful child "You've climbed that high before" is encouraging him, not simply reporting that something is the case. It is true that the factual statement "You've climbed that high before" supports a further prescriptive statement, "Try to climb to the top" for example. But "You've climbed that high before" also has its own prescriptive force, which is not the same as "Try to climb to the top": the former merely encourages, while the latter requests, urges, or even commands. But if factual statements can be to a degree prescriptive, the factual–evaluative distinction cannot be equated with the descriptive–prescriptive distinction, important as that distinction may be.

I mentioned above Frankena's argument against the view that "an ethical judgment simply is an assertion of fact"; I shall conclude this section by trying to explain the sense in which I am maintaining that view and the sense in which I am not. Frankena argues that a value judgment cannot simply be an assertion of fact in the following way:

> When we are making merely factual assertions we are not thereby taking any pro or con attitude toward what we are talking about; we are not recommending it, prescribing it, or anything of the sort. But when we make an ethical judgment we are not neutral in this way; it would seem paradoxical if one were to say "X is good" or "Y is right" but be absolutely indifferent to its being sought or done by himself or anyone else. (*Ethics,* 2d ed., p. 100)

Frankena is right, I think, for the reason he gives, in holding that an evaluative statement cannot be simply an assertion of fact, if "simply" means that all one is intending to do, and is in fact doing, is to convey a piece of information. But it seems to me a mistake to think that "simply asserting a fact" in that sense is something we frequently or ever do. One does not frequently or perhaps ever make a statement merely with a view to communicating information. At the very least one is communicating information which one thinks is desirable that the listener should have, and which would in some sense be in his interest to have. One's intention, that is, is to alter the listener's state in a way one thinks desirable, not simply to alter the listener's cognitive state for its own sake. Usually more than that is intended: we make statements to warn people, to encourage them, to dissuade them from or persuade them to some course of action, to rebuke them, and so on. Yet, the statements we make in the course of doing these things can often be called "factual" and even "simple statements of fact." The historian's account of some set of past events would generally be considered factual; yet, there is surely a purpose in what he is saying beyond simply informing us of truths about the past. His purpose, one supposes, is to inform us of something he thinks we will benefit from knowing. In general, we do not simply report a fact for the sake of reporting a fact: why report this fact rather than another? We come close to simply reporting a fact, in the sense in which that is an extreme rarely if ever instanced, in connection with, say, teaching some factual branch of knowledge, say the geography of South America. But in such cases, while a particular statement, e.g. "The highest mountain is Aconcagua," may be made with no purpose except to inform, there is some aim in regard to the subject as a whole, some reason for thinking this subject is worth knowing as contrasted with the other things one might learn instead. The idea of simply asserting a fact, if that means asserting a fact with no purpose whatever but to inform, is a kind of limit which we may approach but never actually reach: generally in asserting a fact we are doing something in addition. Hence the admitted fact that evaluative statements are not simply assertions of fact does not warrant a sharp distinction between factual and evaluative statements, if it is understood as a distinction between two mutually exclusive classes of statements which between them divide up all or most of our actual statements.

To summarize, there are several possible ways of distinguishing factual from evaluative statements: as statements reporting hard data as contrasted with more or less interpretative statements, as statements about the non-human world as contrasted with statements about the world of human feelings and attitudes, as statements arrived at in a rigorous and precise way as contrasted with statements made on the basis of personal impressions, and as statements intended to communicate information as contrasted with statements intended to influence the listener's attitudes and actions. These are certainly all valid distinctions. But they are also all distinctions in degree, not distinctions in kind. Statements commonly considered evaluative fall relatively low in the scale in each of these dimensions, as compared with other statements commonly considered factual. To that extent there is some reason for questioning the common view that evaluative statements sometimes state facts. But, again, there is not a difference in kind, only a difference in degree.

3 "Is" and "Ought"

I have argued in the previous section that the distinction between factual and evaluative statements, taken as a distinction between two mutually exclusive classes of statements, is an untenable dualism: if it is, then one possible argument for holding that it is impossible to derive normative ethical conclusions from non-ethical factual premises, deductively or inductively, is without force. In brief, the argument I have in mind is that since ordinary logical relations can only hold among factual statements, and since normative ethical statements are not factual, therefore no such logical relations can hold. The argument is valid and I am not disputing the truth of the first premise. But if I am right, the second premise is either false or so misleading as to destroy the force of the argument. I have not, however, argued positively for the thesis that one can arrive at normative ethical conclusions from non-ethical factual premises by ordinary deductive or inductive reasoning. In the present section I shall offer some considerations to suggest this is not impossible. I shall first discuss John Searle's derivation of an "ought" statement from an "is" statement, arguing that it is a valid argument, contrary to some recent objections—if not deductively valid, then at least inductively valid. And I shall then suggest some general considerations that go to show that if one is sufficiently tolerant in what one takes to be a normative conclusion, there is no general logical problem in deductive or inductive derivations of normative ethical conclusions from non-ethical factual premises.

Searle's derivation of an "ought" statement from an "is" statement in his article "How to Derive 'Ought' From 'Is' " may, closely following Searle's own statement, be stated as follows:

1. Jones uttered the words "I hereby promise to pay you, Smith, five dollars."
1a. Under certain conditions C anyone who utters the words (sentence) "I hereby promise to pay you, Smith, five dollars" promises to pay Smith five dollars.
1b. Conditions C obtain.
2. Jones promised to pay Smith five dollars [From 1, 1a, and 1b

by the principle that if p implies that if q then r, and p and q, then r].

2a. All promises are acts of placing oneself under (undertaking) an obligation to do the thing promised.

3. Jones placed himself under (undertook) an obligation to pay Smith five dollars [From 2 and 2a by the principle that if p implies q, and p, then q].

3a. Other things are equal.

3b. All those who place themselves under an obligation are, other things being equal, under an obligation.

4. Jones is under an obligation to pay Smith five dollars [From 3, 3a, and 3b by the principle that if p implies that if q then r, and p and q, then r].

4a. Other things are equal.

4b. All those who are under an obligation to do an action ought, other things being equal, to do that action.

5. Jones ought to pay Smith five dollars [From 4, 4a, and 4b by the principle that if p implies that if q then r, and p and q, then r].

One objection, made by Hare in his discussion of Searle's argument in Hare's article, "The Promising Game" (*Revue Internationale de Philosophie,* 1964), can, I think, be answered. Hare argues that "the argument will be simplified" if we combine 1a and 2a into the following single statement:

1a* Under certain conditions C anyone who utters the words (sentence) "I hereby promise to pay you, Smith, five dollars" places himself under (undertakes) an obligation to pay Smith five dollars.

But, Hare argues, 1a* is an evaluative statement—"a synthetic moral principle," in fact. Hence, Hare concludes, Searle's argument contains an "ought" statement as a premise and is not therefore a case of deriving an "ought" statement from an "is" statement. Hare is right in calling 1a* a moral principle. But he is wrong in saying this is a *premise* in Searle's argument. Hare's 1a* is not a mere conjunction of Searle's 1a and 2a. Searle's 1a and 2a conjoined would have the form if p, then if q then r; and if r, then s. Hare's 1a* has the form if p, then if q then s. That is a logical *consequence* of Searle's 1a and 2a conjoined, but it is not its logical equivalent.† Searle would not deny that his 1a and 2a conjoined would have as a logical consequence an evaluative statement; that is precisely his point. Hare's objection is thus beside the point: unless he can show that the logical equivalent of 1a and 2a conjoined is evaluative, which he does not show, he is only pointing out what Searle himself is calling attention to, namely, that premises that to all appearances are "is" statements have an "ought" statement as their logical consequence.

Another objection to Searle's derivation, that by James and Judith Thomson in "How Not to Derive 'Ought' From 'Is' " can also, I think, be answered, although not without somewhat revising the derivation. The Thomsons point out that 4a in Searle's argument can be interpreted in two ways, the "weak" interpretation in which 4a only says that those of us considering Jones's case see no reason or know of no reason why he ought not or need not pay, and the "strong" interpretation in which 4a says that there *is* no reason or at least no conclusive reason why he ought not or need not pay. But, the Thomsons argue, on the weak interpretation of 4a, 4a and 4b do not entail 5, since there could *be* some reason why Jones ought not to pay which we do not know about, whereas on the strong interpretation 4a is evaluative. In either case the point of the argument is destroyed. The Thomsons' point is correct. But the difficulty they point out could be met by revising the argument so that it is not a strict entailment, but an inductive argument. This could be done by restating the step from 4 to 5 as follows:

4. Jones is under an obligation to pay Smith five dollars.
5' Jones probably ought, in the absence of any reasons we know of to the contrary, to pay Smith five dollars.

Or, one could keep the argument a strict entailment by restating the step from 4 to 5 in the following way:

4. Jones is under an obligation to pay Smith five dollars.
5' ' If there are no reasons or no conclusive reasons against it, Jones ought to pay Smith five dollars.

† The point that Hare evidently confuses a statement equivalent to the conjunction of 1a and 2a with a statement that is a logical consequence of their conjunction was brought to my attention by William Tolhurst.

Understood in the second way the conclusion would be a very weak one, but it would still be an evaluative conclusion, and would follow strictly from 4. The Thomsons suggest that 5' ' is an analytic statement in that it is an instance of the Law of Excluded Middle, and is hence not evaluative but logical. But that is a mistake. The instance of the Law of Excluded Middle would be the statement that either there are no conclusive reasons against Jones paying Smith five dollars, or there are conclusive reasons. But the statement that either there are no conclusive reasons against his paying, or he ought to pay—5' ' in other words—is not an instance of Excluded Middle and not analytic. There is the third alternative that it is morally indifferent whether he pays or not. In general, it is not the case that the mere absence of conclusive reasons against my doing A entails that I ought to do A: there are no conclusive reasons against my now going into the kitchen for a cup of coffee, but it is not the case that I ought to. Searle's derivation can therefore still be made, although the conclusion is a weaker one than the one originally stated: weaker in the sense that it only follows with a certain degree of probability, as in 5', or weaker in that it only establishes a *prima facie* or hypothetical "ought," as in 5' '.

If Searle's argument is valid, it ought to be in some way generalizable. I think it is. The general principle involved in the argument is that while it is perhaps never possible to argue deductively from non-ethical factual premises to a categorical normative conclusion of the form "X is right" or "Y is obligatory," it is very often possible to so argue to a hypothetical conclusion of the form "X is *prima facie* right" or "Y is *prima facie* obligatory" where *"prima facie"* right or obligatory means that the act in question is right or obligatory unless there is some overriding reason why it ought not to be done. Thus, the argument from "X caused Y's death" to "It is *prima facie* right to hold X morally responsible for Y's death" is a valid deductive argument. The conclusion, to be sure, is very weak. But it is not trivial: it is not trivial to say that unless there is some conclusive reason for not doing so, I ought to be held morally responsible for so-and-so's death. If, to be sure, one believes that a genuinely normative conclusion must be categorical, not hypothetical, one might prefer to make the hypothesis that there are no conclusive reasons against doing A one of the premises in such arguments. That is, one might prefer to give the argument the form if p and q, then r, instead of if p, then if q then r, where p is the non-evaluative premise, q is the statement that there are no conclusive reasons why an act would not be right or obligatory, and r is the evaluative conclusion. Thus if one wants the conclusion to be the categorical statement "It is right to hold X morally responsible for Y's death," one could make the premises "X caused Y's death" and "There is no conclusive reason against holding X morally responsible for Y's death." But it would be a great mistake to think one has, by restating the argument in this way, shown that the argument from "X caused Y's death" to "If there is no conclusive reason against doing so, it is right to hold X morally responsible for Y's death" really contains an evaluative premise which has gone unnoticed. It makes no difference whatever from a purely logical point of view whether the argument is given the form if p, then if q then r, or if p and q, then r: these are logically equivalent. The real objection would be simply the belief that genuine evaluative statements must be categorical. And I see no compelling reason to hold this belief.

In general, whenever a non-evaluative factual statement is a part of a normative ethical statement, as for example "You stole that money" is a part of "You acted wrongly in stealing that money," it is possible to construct a deductive argument (or an inductive argument if one prefers) with the non-evaluative statement as the premise and a hypothetical evaluative statement as the conclusion. Thus, since "You stole that money" is a logically necessary condition of the truth of "You acted wrongly in stealing that money," one can argue that if you stole that money, then if all the other necessary conditions of the truth of "You acted wrongly in stealing that money" obtain, then you acted wrongly in stealing that money. If, that is, a statement of non-ethical fact is a logically necessary condition of the truth of an ethical statement, as it always is when the statement of non-ethical fact is a part of the ethical statement or is entailed by the ethical statement, then the truth of the non-ethical statement is a logically sufficient condition of the hypothetical statement that if all other necessary conditions obtain, then the ethical statement is true. But normative ethical statements often do contain as parts non-ethical statements of fact. (There is an even simpler way of showing that an "ought" can be derived from an "is" if one considers the negation of an evaluative statement as itself an evaluative statement. When a statement of non-ethical fact is a logically necessary condition of the truth of an evaluative statement, the falsity of that non-ethical statement is a sufficient condition of the falsity of the ethical judgment. Thus, if "You stole that money" is a logically necessary condition of "You acted wrongly in stealing that money," then "You did not steal that money" is a logically sufficient condition of "It is not the case that you acted wrongly in stealing that money.")

The reply may be made that statements such as "You acted wrongly in stealing that money" are not pure evaluative statements, but mixtures of pure evaluative statements—"You acted wrongly"—and factual statements—"You stole that money." What has to be shown, it might be said, is how to derive a pure evaluative statement from a purely non-evaluative factual statement. There is something to this reply. Taking it together with the point made in connection with Searle's derivation, that his and analogous arguments do not show how to derive a categorical "ought" from an "is," one could say it has not been shown how to derive a pure categorical evaluative statement from a purely non-evaluative statement of fact. But what this amounts to, I should say, is that it has not been shown how to derive what might be called an atomic "ought" statement from non-evaluative statement. (More exactly, it has not been shown how to so derive an evaluative statement in an interesting way: Arthur Prior, as mentioned earlier, has shown how to make such a derivation in a vacuous sense). That is hardly surprising: I should say it is obviously true and even analytic that an atomic "ought" statement cannot be derived deductively from any statement at all except itself or a more complex statement that includes it as one of its parts. That is what "atomic" as ascribed to statements means. The thesis of the non-derivability of an "ought" from an "is," in the sense in which it is defensible, is a tautology. As such it is doubtless true, but not something that a naturalist need deny. A naturalist would, if he is what I previously called an analytic naturalist, hold that some pure ought statements are identical in meaning with a statement of fact not containing any evaluative expression, so that in the kind of limiting sense in which a statement can be said to be derivable from itself, he would say that a pure "ought" statement can be derived from an "is" statement. Other naturalists, Dewey for example, would not, I think, regard pure categorical "ought" statements as identical in meaning with "is" statements, and so would not even maintain their derivability in that limiting sense. They would, however, hold that *some* evaluative statements can be derived deductively or inductively from non-evaluative factual premises. If the preceding discussion is right, that is a defensible thesis. If one is reasonably tolerant in what one takes to be an evaluative statement, I see no objection to the thesis that evaluative statements can sometimes be derived by ordinary deductive and inductive procedures from non-evaluative factual premises.

It is true that in the kind of example I have given of a deductive derivation of an evaluative statement from a non-evaluative factual statement, the validity of the derivation is not a matter of the derivation's conforming to some standard deductive inference form, such as *modus ponens*. Nor is it a matter of entailment in the sense in which entailment requires that the meaning of the conclusion be contained in the meaning of the premise—as, for example, "John is unmarried" could be said to be included in the meaning of "John is a bachelor." It is not that "A ought *prima facie* to be held morally responsible for B's death" is contained in the meaning of "A caused B's death" in the sense that one could not understand the meaning of the former without accepting the truth of the latter. However, I should still maintain that the relationship is a deductive one. There is a necessary connection between "A caused B's death" and "A ought *prima facie* to be held morally responsible for B's death" in the same way as there is a necessary connection between "That was a lightning flash" and "That was an electrical discharge in the sky" or between "It's a whale" and "It's a member of the order *Cetacea.*" The connection is not a priori in the sense that it cannot be known just by knowing the meanings of the terms involved, but it is still a necessary connection. Hence I think the connection can properly be called "deductive," although it does differ from what are most commonly thought of as deductive connections. One might prefer to call it non-deductive but still logical, in which case my position would not differ significantly from the good reasons approach. The important point is that there is nothing mysterious and special in the logical relations holding between evaluative statements and non-evaluative statements of fact.

To summarize, I have argued that when the truth of an "is" statement is a logically necessary or sufficient condition of the truth of an "ought" statement, it is possible to derive, inductively if not deductively, an "ought" from an "is," at least assuming a reasonably lib-eral interpretation of what counts as an "ought" statement, and as-suming that Searle's derivation of an "ought" from an "is" is a case in point. There are doubtless difficulties and objections I have said nothing to answer, but I hope that the preceding discussion will to a degree meet some of these. Thus, it might be objected to Searle's derivation of a statement of the form "A ought to give X to B" from "A promised to give X to B" that there is not even a prima facie obligation to keep a promise, when to keep the promise would be to commit an immoral act: e.g., there is not even a prima facie obligation to keep a promise to kill one's best friend. I would answer that while it may well be that there is not even a prima facie obligation to keep a promise in such a case, it is still the case that the fact that a person has promised to do an act is some evidence that he ought to do it; and that it is therefore a valid inductive inference, in the absence of any other information, that one ought to keep a promise even though it turns out, on further information, that the action in question is grossly immoral.

Again, I have not in my discussion made any use of the notion of an "institutional fact," a notion Searle himself emphasizes both in his 1964 article and in his discussion of the derivation in Chapter VIII of his 1969 book, *Speech Acts*. Searle maintains that an essential feature of his derivation of an "ought" from an "is" statement is that in the case of promising, the conventional institution of promising is gov-erned by the "constitutive rule" that if one says "I promise to do X," one automatically undertakes an obligation to do X: one is committed by this rule in the same way that in playing a game one is committed to accept decisions applying the rules of the game. Without denying that promising can be seen as a conventional insitution governed by rules, in a manner analogous to a game, I do not think that is the es-sential point about the derivation of an "ought" from an "is." If it were, the "ought" in question would not be a moral ought at all: one could derive in a similar way the conclusion that one "ought" to challenge a certain person to a duel from the fact that he has insulted one in a certain way, on grounds that there is a widely accepted (at certain times and places) convention to the effect that if you are in-sulted in a certain way, your duty is to challenge the insulter to a duel. If the obligation to keep a promise were similarly simply a matter of what is required by conventional rules, it too would not be a moral obligation—a point Searle evidently acknowledges when, in *Speech Acts,* he remarks that he is not concerned with "ought" in the sense of "morally ought." And, on the other hand, there appear to be derivations of an "ought" from an "is" where conventional rules of an institution play no essential role at all; e.g. the derivation of "A ought to be held morally responsible for B's death" from "A caused B's death." Hence the fact that what may be called a conventional "ought" follows from an "is" is neither sufficient nor necessary to show the derivability of a moral "ought" from an "is." But I have tried to suggest there are reasons for thinking there are no insuperable logical objections to the derivation of a moral "ought," and that Searle's derivation, despite his own disclaimer in *Speech Acts,* is an instance. I certainly have not proved the derivability of an "ought" from an "is": as I said above there are doubtless many difficulties and objections I have not tried to deal with at all. But I hope to have at least shifted the burden of proof to an extent onto the non-naturalist who would maintain as a matter of principle that in no case can what may reasonably be called an "ought" statement be derived from an "is" statement.

4 Can Ethical Disagreement be Resolved?

In discussing Stevenson's theory of ethical disagreement in Chapter IV, I distinguished between merely *terminating* an ethical disagreement by non-rational or anti-rational methods, and *resolving* an ethical disagreement by bringing about agreement through rational discussion and argument. Clearly, an ethical disagreement can always be terminated, as for example totalitarian regimes end disagreement by imprisoning, killing, or otherwise silencing all those who disagree with their policies. But the important question both for ethical theory and for practical ethics is whether ethical disagreement can be resolved, and to what extent. Are ethical disagreements the kind of disagreement which can typically be resolved? Or is the opposite the case: must we have to expect to resort to non-rational methods to end ethical disagreement? In many ways this question brings together and focuses most of the issues in ethical theory discussed throughout this book. One specific question, certainly, concerns the nature of ethical disagreement: whether, to use Stevenson's terms, ethical disagreement is primarily disagreement in belief or disagreement in attitutde. It may seem natural to think that if ethical disagreement is primarily disagreement in attitude, then it cannot be resolved, on grounds that while we can of course use various means to seek to change our opponent's attitudes, we cannot strictly speaking argue him into a different attitude: attitudes as opposed to beliefs cannot in any clear sense be the conclusion of arguments. Hence it might seem that the presupposition of the view that ethical disagreement can be resolved is that such disagreement is not primarily disagreement in attitude, but, rather, disagreement in belief. But on closer reflection this line of thought, while it may be natural, is open to doubt. Nor does it express Stevenson's own view. Stevenson's view is that while ethical disagreement is primarily disagreement in attitude, it can be resolved to the extent that it is rooted in disagreement in belief, where "rooted in" means roughly "produced by" in a causal psychological sense. If an ethical disagreement is caused by some factual disagreement, then if we can resolve the factual disagreement, we will have removed the cause of the ethical disagreement and so end it. And we will have done so by rational methods of argument and discussion. Thus, if A opposes violence because he thinks it causes social instability, and B favors it because he thinks it will produce an ultimately more stable society, their disagreement, while in itself it may be a disagreement in attitude, can in principle be resolved by means of a sociological investigation of the effects of violence. The more important question, therefore, which is the question Stevenson himself raises, is whether ethical disagreements, whatever their nature is, are always rooted in disagreement in belief or not.

At the same time the question of the nature of ethical disagreement does have some importance too: it may be that the tendency to think that ethical disagreements are not rooted in disagreement in belief is itself to a degree rooted in the belief that ethical disagreements are primarily disagreements in attitude. In any event, I shall consider both these questions in the following discussion. I shall first discuss the question of the nature of ethical belief, whether, as Stevenson holds, it is primarily disagreement in attitude, or is to be viewed rather as disagreement in belief. Second, I shall discuss the question whether or to what extent ethical disagreements are rooted in disagreement in belief. Third, I shall consider critically the argument that ethical disagreement cannot be resolved without reaching agreement on ultimate ethical premises, and that disagreement concerning such ultimate premises can itself in no sense be resolved. And fourth, I shall consider very briefly (it quickly leads off into general philosophical questions) this question: supposing ethical disagreement is always or is typically rooted in disagreement in belief, are these beliefs of a sort which permits consensus as to their truth or falsity to be reached by rational discussion and argument? The general thesis I shall be defending in discussing these questions is that ethical disagreements are to an important degree resolvable by rational methods and, although certainly not in all cases completely resolvable, do not in this respect differ from many factual and scientific disagreements which, too, are not always in practice and not even in principle completely resolvable.

1. The question whether ethical disagreements are primarily disagreements in belief or in attitude is closely related to the more basic question as to whether ethical statements can be said to be true or false, an issue that comes up repeatedly in recent ethical theory. It may seem that the view that ethical disagreements are disagreements in attitude follows necessarily from the view that ethical judgments lack truth values. Yet, the issue of the nature of ethical disagreement is not quite the same as the issue of cognitivism versus non-cognitivism. One could take the position that although ethical judgments themselves have truth values, it is still the case that ethical disagreement is primarily disagreement in attitude. One might hold that what is primary in ethical disagreement is conflict in attitudes, and that we assert our ethical beliefs as a way of justifying or even rationalizing our attitudes. If this were the case, one could be a cognitivist in the sense of "cognitivism" used in this book and still hold that ethical disagreement is primarily, as Stevenson holds, disagreement in attitude. (Along similar lines, one could hold that what might appear to be disagreements on straightforward factual questions, such as whether there are racial differences in intelligence, are in fact primarily disagreements in attitude).

In general, the fact that two opposing statements have conflicting truth values—that the parties to the dispute hold beliefs both of which cannot be true—does not really decide the question whether the dispute is to be viewed as a disagreement in belief, primarily, or a disagreement in attitude. (One may prefer to make this point in terms of the causes of disagreement rather than in terms of the nature of disagreement. The point would then be that just as disagreements in attitude are sometimes rooted in disagreement in belief, so disagreements in belief are sometimes rooted in disagreement in attitude. If the latter is the case, the disagreement may not be resolvable even though it is itself a disagreement in belief. An example of such disagreement might be religious disagreement, which is certainly disagreement in belief, but resists resolution by rational argument and discussion.) Even though one maintains (as I have tried to do) that ethical judgments have truth values, the question of the nature of ethical disagreement is still an open one. It does seem clear that ethical disagreements do very often involve disagreement in attitude, in the sense that the parties to the dispute do have conflicting feelings and attitudes, and are advocating incompatible courses of action—as in a dispute between a person who asserts that abortion ought to be forbidden and one who asserts it ought to be permitted. Yet, something more is involved in an ethical disagreement than simply the advocacy of incompatible courses of action: there is no *ethical* disagreement between two persons who disagree over whether to go to the beach or the museum this afternoon. Disagreement in attitude is not sufficient to characterize an ethical disagreement: if A says "Let's invite Smith: I like him" and B says "Let's not: I can't stand him" their disagreement is not an ethical disagreement, although clearly a disagreement in attitude. Nor is disagreement in attitude a necessary condition of an ethical disagreement. If A says "We ought to invite the Joneses" and B says "I don't think we are obligated to" there need be no disagreement in attitude; they may both share the same feelings toward the Joneses. No doubt they have conflicting feelings of obligation. But the mere existence of conflicting feelings does not show a disagreement to be a disagreement in attitude. In the case of most if not all disagreements in belief, there are conflicting feelings too: if nothing else, each person wants his belief to be proved true, desires which cannot both be satisfied. The truth is that the distinction between disagreement in attitude and disagreement in belief is best viewed, as I argued that the distinction between factual and evaluative statements be viewed, as an extreme type in Hempel's sense rather than a classificatory type. Probably there is no such thing as disagreement in belief which is only a disagreement in belief and not to some degree a disagreement in attitude. Ethical disagreements are no doubt closer to the extreme of pure disagreements in attitude than most non-ethical factual and scientific disagreements. But they certainly are not pure disagreements in attitude, nor does Stevenson hold that they are.

2. I suggested above that a disagreement might be a disagreement in belief, but be caused by disagreement in attitude, and that if this is the case with ethical disagreements, they may not be resolvable even though they are primarily disagreements in belief. I should say this is in fact the case: ethical disagreements are very often rooted in, in the sense of caused by, disagreements in attitude. But this is not a unique feature of ethical beliefs. Disagreements in science, too, are often caused by differences in attitudes. Further, while it is doubtless true that our ethical beliefs (like many other beliefs) have been produced in a psychological causal sense by non-rational factors, that does not mean we have no rational basis for them, or do not hold them in a rational way. Most of us do hold our ethical beliefs in a rational way in the sense that if certain non-ethical factual beliefs turned out to be false, we would change our ethical beliefs. It is widely believed that Stalin was an evil man, and no doubt this belief is rooted in, in the sense of having been causally produced by, attitudes produced at an early age. But if it came to be widely believed that Stalin did not do the acts he is commonly thought to have done, the belief that he was an evil man would change. Hence, while there is no question about the fact that attitudes do have an important role in shaping our ethical beliefs, there is no reason to be more sceptical on this account about resolving ethical disagreements by rational argument and discussion than about resolving other kinds of disagreement.

3. I have argued above that ethical disagreements, while often rooted in disagreement in attitude rather than disagreement in belief in the sense of being causally produced by conflicting attitudes, may still be resolvable. But a question might be raised here concerning our ultimate ethical beliefs, beliefs which in the nature of the case cannot be argued for in the usual way, and which yet might be subjects of disagreement. One could hold that while ethical disagreement within a community of persons who share the same ultimate ethical premises

can be resolved, this cannot be done when there is disagreement about ultimate ethical premises themselves. If we shared the premise that all persons have the same innate moral worth, we might be able to resolve our disagreement about a guaranteed annual income; if this premise is not shared, we may not be able to do so. There is an important element of truth in this line of thought, but it is not a reason for special scepticism about the resolution of ethical disagreements. We are in the same situation in science too: if someone denies the validity of induction, or refuses to accept sensory data as evidence about an objective reality, we cannot hope to convince him of the truth of scientific theories. In ethics too, there are types of argument which involve assumptions that, if challenged, cannot be proved by any further ethical argument. One such assumption is Sidgwick's axiom of equity, that what is right for one person is right for all similar persons in similar circumstances, a premise involved, as Marcus Singer has shown, in the "What if everyone did it?" argument. Another is the assumption that my happiness is not worth more than the happiness of another, or that what causes unhappiness in anyone should *prima facie* be avoided. There is this much truth in Sidgwick's view that such principles as these are among the axioms of ethics which cannot be proved and must be regarded as known directly, without proof: there is no clear sense in which we can speak of proving or giving evidence for them, without circularity, and yet they are implicit in most people's actual ethical beliefs. We could say that just as acceptance of the principle of induction in some form constitutes rationality in factual and scientific inquiry, so acceptance of such ethical principles as the above constitutes rationality in ethics. It will be said that "rationality" has an evaluative meaning. But the same can be said of "rationality" in other areas too. Ethical disagreement, I conclude, can be resolved in much the same way and subject to the same limitations as non-ethical factual disagreement: in ethics, as elsewhere, there is even an obligation to rely on rational argument and discussion. Can we in any sense establish the rationality of accepting this obligation itself? The question "Why ought I be rational?" is in ethics as elsewhere one of the limiting questions which cannot be argued for without begging the question at issue. Perhaps the best one can say is that commitment to rationality is a way of life, an ultimate value about which only those who have experienced and practiced it are in a position to judge. In

any event it is important to support the conviction that we can in a coherent and meaningful way speak of rationality in ethics. I hope the
preceding discussion is a contribution making this conviction itself a
rational one.

(4) I suggested above that while ethical disagreements often are rooted
in disagreement in attitude, in Stevenson's sense of "rooted in" as
meaning "caused by" in a psychological sense, it may also be the
case that the disagreement has a rational basis in the sense that the parties to the disagreement would change their ethical beliefs if they came
to hold different non-ethical factual beliefs—and that if this is so, an
ethical disagreement may still be resolvable in spite of the fact tha' 't
is not in Stevenson's sense rooted in a disagreement in belief. Thus, it
may well be that what *causes* disagreement about the morality of capital punishment, say, is conflicting attitudes towards criminals and
crime. But it may also be the case that if the parties to the disagreement were to reach agreement on certain non-ethical matters of fact,
such as the deterrent effect of capital punishment as measured by statistical studies, they might come to agree about the morality of capital
punishment even though their conflicting attitudes might remain. Stevenson points out that ethical disagreement tends to disappear when
the parties to the disagreement come to share the same attitudes, even
though some disagreement in belief may remain; while not denying
this point, it is also true that there is a tendency for ethical disagreement to vanish when the parties to the disagreement come to agree on
non-ethical matters of fact even though some disagreement in attitude
still remains. In general, what is important as far as the resolution of
ethical disagreement is concerned is not so much the actual source of
the disagreement in a causal sense, as it is a mutual willingness to
revise ethical beliefs in the light of (often hitherto unknown) matters of
non-ethical fact. In this connection, however, a final question can be
asked—a question I said I would only discuss briefly—which is the
following: granting that in general an ethical disagreement can be
resolved if the parties to the disagreement can reach agreement on certain matters of non-ethical fact, could it not sometimes be the case that
there is disagreement on these matters of non-ethical fact themselves,
disagreement which itself cannot be resolved in a rational way? I suggested earlier that the abortion controversy may be a case in point: if

we could reach agreement on the necessary and sufficient conditions for being a human being, perhaps the controversy could be resolved; but can we resolve the present disagreement about the necessary and sufficient conditions for being a human being? Not, it seems, without first solving what philosophers call "the mind-body problem." (My own view is that one's position on the mind-body problem reflects to some degree one's position on ethical questions such as euthenasia and abortion: I see a possible circle here.) I said that this question quickly leads off into general philosophical questions. What I mainly had in mind is this. If one is generally committed to rationalism, in a very broad sense of rationalism in which "rationalism" is the thesis that all truths are in principle knowable, and only knowable by the use of our ordinary faculties of sense-perception and thought (a sense of rationalism in which both rationalism in its narrower technical sense— the view that there are synthetic propositions which can be known *a priori*—and empiricism, are forms of rationalism) then it is reasonable to think that all disagreements about non-ethical matters of fact can in principle be resolved in a rational way. But to the extent that the use of our ordinary cognitive faculties, the faculties we use in daily life and in science, cannot give us access to the truths needed for the resolution of ethical controversies, those ethical controversies may not be ultimately resolvable. We may simply have to wait for everyone to have the mystical experience, or revelation, or whatever non-rational form of knowledge is thought to be required, before we can hope to resolve the ethical disagreement.

The crucial question is whether it makes sense to say there are truths which cannot in principle be known by the use of human reason. Clearly, there are many matters which cannot be so known in practice, such as the exact size of the world's population a thousand years hence. But can there be truths which are *in principle* so unknowable? Probably the majority of academic philosophers in the English speaking world at the present time would say no. To the extent that naturalism is opposed to supernaturalism, as it often has been, naturalists would certainly say no; a naturalist need not deny there is non-rational access to truths (by clairvoyance, say, or mystical insight) but he would, I think, have to hold that for such non-rational access to count as "knowledge," its results would have to be independently verified by ordinary methods. Again, many philosophers would be strongly inclined to say there cannot in principle be knowledge of future contingencies that depend on human choice, as in the above example of the future world's population. But they would deny there is a "truth" here to be known. In general, academic philosophy in the English-speaking world at the present time is strongly committed to rationalism, as opposed to a theory of knowledge which holds there are truths which can only be known by such non-rational methods as mystical experience or revelation. Whether that commitment is ultimately defensible, and whether, even though it be defensible, it will continue to be defended, may itself be a subject of considerable philosophical discussion in the years to come.

REFERENCES

Ayer, A. J. *Language, Truth, and Logic*. London: Victor Gollancz, 1936; revised edition, 1946. Chapter VI, "Critique of Ethics and Theology," is partially reprinted (omitting the discussion of theology) in Sellars and Hospers, *Readings in Ethical Theory*, 1952; second edition, 1970. A section of the Introduction to the revised 1946 edition of *Language, Truth, and Logic*, entitled "The Emotive Theory of Ethics," is reprinted in Sellars and Hospers, *Readings in Ethical Theory*, second edition, 1970, under the title "Ethical Judgments."

Brandt, Richard. "Some Merits of One Form of Rule Utilitarianism." *University of Colorado Studies in Philosophy*, No. 3, January, 1965. Reprinted in The Bobbs-Merrill Reprint Series in Philosophy, Phil-30.

Dewey, John. *The Quest For Certainty*. New York: Minton, Balch & Co., 1929. Chapter 10, "The Construction of Good," is reprinted in Sellars and Hospers, *Readings in Ethical Theory*, 1952 edition.

——. *The Theory of Valuation*. International Encyclopedia of Unified Science. Chicago: University of Chicago Press, 1939.

Firth, Roderick. "Ethical Absolutism and the Ideal Observer." *Philosophy and Phenomenological Research* XII, March, 1952. Reprinted in Sellars and Hospers, *Readings in Ethical Theory*, 1970 edition.

Foot, Philippa. "Moral Beliefs." *Proceedings of the Aristotelian Society*, Vol. 59, 1958–59. Reprinted in *Theories of Ethics*, edited by Philippa Foot, Oxford University Press, 1967.

Frankena, William. *Ethics*, second edition. Englewood Cliffs, N.J.: Prentice-Hall, Inc., 1973.

——. "The Naturalistic Fallacy." *Mind* 48, 1939. Reprinted in Sellars and Hospers, *Readings in Ethical Theory*, 1952 and 1970 editions.

——. "Obligation and Value in the Ethics of G. E. Moore," in *The Philosophy of G. E. Moore*, edited by Paul Arthur Schilpp. New York: Tudor Publishing Co., 1942.

Hampshire, Stuart. "Fallacies in Moral Philosophy." *Mind* 58, 1949.

Hare, R. M. *Freedom and Reason*. London: Oxford University Press, 1963.

——. *The Language of Morals*. London: Oxford University Press, 1952. Pp. 95–97, 111–119, 121–133, 148–150 are reprinted in Sellars and Hospers, *Readings in Ethical Theory*, 1970 edition, under the title "What is a Value Judgment?"

——. "The Promising Game." *Revue Internationale de Philosophie*, No. 70, 1964. Reprinted in *The Is/Ought Question*, edited by W. D. Hudson (Controversies in Philosophy, General Editor A. G. N. Flew). London: Macmillan and Co., 1969.

——. Review of Stephen Toulmin's *An Examination of the Place of Reason in Ethics*. *The Philosophical Quarterly* (St. Andrews), July, 1951; pp. 372–375.

Hempel, Carl. "Typological Methods in the Social Sciences," in *Philosophy of the Social Sciences*, edited by Maurice Natanson. New York: Random House, 1963. Reprinted in Carl Hempel, *Aspects of Scientific Explanation and Other Essays in the Philosophy of Science*, New York: Free Press, 1965.

Kosevi, Julius. *Moral Notions*. New York: Humanities Press, 1967.

Moore, G. E. "The Conception of Intrinsic Value," in *Philosophical Studies*. London: Routledge and Kegan Paul, 1922.

——. *Ethics*. London: Oxford University Press, 1911.

——. "Is Goodness A Quality?" Aristotelian Society, Supplementary Volume VII, 1927. Reprinted in *Philosophical Papers*, London: Allen and Unwin, 1959.

——. *Principia Ethica*. Cambridge: Cambridge University Press, 1903. The Preface and Chapter I are reprinted in Sellars and Hospers, *Readings in Ethical Theory*, 1952 and 1970 editions, under the title, "The Indefinability of Good."

Paton, H. J. "The Alleged Independence of Goodness," in *The Philosophy of G. E. Moore*, edited by P. A. Schilpp.

Perry, Ralph Barton. *General Theory of Value*. Cambridge: Harvard University Press, 1950. My discussion is mainly based on Chapter V, partially reprinted in Sellars and Hospers, *Readings in Ethical Theory*, 1952 and 1970 editions, under the title "Value as Any Object of Any Interest."

Prichard, H. A. "Does Moral Philosophy Rest on a Mistake?" *Mind* 21, 1912. Reprinted in Sellars and Hospers, *Readings in Ethical Theory*, 1952 and 1970 editions.

Prior, Arthur. "The Autonomy of Ethics." *Australasian Journal of Philosophy*, 1960.

Rawls, John. *A Theory of Justice*. Cambridge: Harvard University Press, 1971.

Ross, Sir David W. *The Right and the Good*. Oxford: Clarendon Press, 1930. Excerpts are reprinted in Sellars and Hospers, *Readings in Ethical Theory*, 1952 and 1970 editions.

Russell, Bertrand. "The Elements of Ethics," in *Philosophical Essays*. London: Allen & Unwin, 1910. Reprinted in Sellars and Hospers, *Readings in Ethical Theory*, 1952 and 1970 editions.

Santayana, George. *Winds of Doctrine*. London: J. M. Dent & Sons, 1915. Santayana's discussion of Russell's "The Elements of Ethics," on which the discussion of Santayana's theory in this book is based, is contained in *Winds of Doctrine*, pp. 138–154 ("The Philosophy of Bertrand Russell"). This part of *Winds of Doctrine* is partially reprinted in Sellars and Hospers, *Readings in Ethical Theory*, 1952 and 1970 editions, under the title "Hypostatic Ethics."

Searle, John. "How to Derive 'Ought' From 'Is.' " *The Philosophical Review* 73, January, 1964. Reprinted in Sellars and Hospers, *Readings in Ethical Theory,* 1970 edition.

——. *Speech Acts.* Cambridge: Cambridge University Press, 1969.

Sellars, Wilfrid, and John Hospers, eds. *Readings in Ethical Theory.* New York: Appleton-Century-Crofts, 1952; second edition, 1970.

Sidgwick, Henry. *The Methods of Ethics,* 7th edition. London: Macmillan, 1901 (Chicago: The University of Chicago Press, 1962). See especially Book I, Chapter III ("Ethical Judgments"), and Book III, Chapter XIII ("Philosophical Intuitionism"). Book I, Chapter III is reprinted in Sellars and Hospers, *Readings in Ethical Theory,* 1952 and 1970 editions.

Singer, Marcus. *Generalization in Ethics.* New York: Random House, 1961.

Stevenson, C. L. "The Emotive Meaning of Ethical Terms." *Mind* 46, 1937. Reprinted in Sellars and Hospers, *Readings in Ethical Theory,* 1970 edition (with added footnotes).

——. *Ethics and Language.* New Haven: Yale University Press, 1944.

——. *Facts and Values.* New Haven: Yale University Press, 1963.

Strawson, P. F. "Ethical Intuitionism." *Philosophy* 24, 1949. Reprinted in Sellars and Hospers, *Readings in Ethical Theory,* 1952 edition.

Thomson, James and Judith. "How Not to Derive 'Ought' From 'Is.' " *The Philosophical Review* 73, October, 1964. Reprinted in Sellars and Hospers, *Readings in Ethical Theory,* 1970 edition.

Toulmin, Stephen. *An Examination of the Place of Reason in Ethics.* Cambridge: Cambridge University Press, 1950.

Urmson, J. O. *The Emotive Theory of Ethics.* London: Hutchinson, 1968.

Wellman, Carl. *Challenge and Response: Justification in Ethics.* Carbondale: Southern Illinois University Press, 1971.

White, Morton. "Obligation and Value in Dewey and Lewis." *The Philosophical Review* 58, 1949. Reprinted in Sellars and Hospers, *Readings in Ethical Theory,* 1952 edition.

BIBLIOGRAPHICAL NOTE

THE PRECEDING LIST of references gives only those books, articles, and reviews which have been mentioned and discussed in the text of this book. This, it should be said, is only a small and to an extent arbitrary selection from the very extensive literature in the general field of British and American meta-ethics since 1900. An excellent bibliography covering the general period and subject dealt with in this book can be found in Sellars and Hospers, *Readings in Ethical Theory*, 1970 edition, pp. 769–780. Richard Brandt's *Ethical Theory, The Problems of Normative and Critical Ethics* (Prentice-Hall, 1959) contains useful bibliographical suggestions at the ends of individuals chapters; the lists of "Further Readings" in Chapters 1–10 cover most of the issues dealt with in this book. There is an excellent bibliographical essay in Paul Edwards and Arthur Pap, eds., *A Modern Introduction to Philosophy*, at the end of Part IV ("Moral Judgments"), covering much of the period and issues dealt with in this book. Marcus Singer's *Generalization in Ethics* contains a great deal of bibliographical information in the "Bibliographical Notes," pp. 343–351. Shorter bibliographies can be found in Philippa Foot, ed., *Theories of Ethics*, pp. 185–187, and in Joseph Margolis, ed., *Contemporary Ethical Theory* (New York: Random House, 1966). Among all the works that might be singled out for special notice, several might be worth special mention as dealing with much the same material with a similar purpose as this work. These are: Mary Warnock, *Ethics Since 1900* (London: Oxford U. Press, 1966); G. A. Warnock, *Contemporary Moral Philosophy* (London: Macmillan, 1967); G. Kerner, *The Revolution in Ethics* (Oxford, 1966); and W. D. Hudson, *Modern Moral Philosophy* (Anchor Books, 1970).

INDEX

Accompaniments: of actions, 54-55

Analytic: ethical judgments as, 29, 119, 179, 186

A priori synthetic knowledge: notion of in Moore, 24-25; notion of in Prichard, 48; Ayer's denial of, consequences for his ethical theory, 90

Attitudes: Stevenson's conception of, 113-14

Autobiographical aspect: of ethical judgments, in Stevenson, 103

Axiom of benevolence: Sidgwick's view of, 9, 43

Axiom of justice: Sidgwick's view of, 8-9, 42

Ayer, A. J.: limitation of ethical theory to meta-ethics in, 5-7; emotive theory of ethics as held by, 88-97; theory of truth, 94; theory of meaning in, 99, 106

Bentham, Jeremy, 44

Brandt, Richard, 11, 151, 158-59

Choice guidance: role of ethical judgments as involving, in Hare's theory, 120-23, 127-30

Cognitive claim: problem in regarding intuition as, 52-53

Cognitivism: defined, 12-13; two types of, 13-14; argument for, 93-94; as related to the nature of ethical disagreement, 123

Commending: Hare's account of, 120 ff.

Conduction: ethical reasoning as, in Wellman, 154

Consequences: of actions, 54-55

Contextualism: defined, 78-79

Correspondence: of moral judgments with facts, 148-49, 201-3

Criterion: absence of in intuitionism, 52-53; notion of in Hare, 105-6; need for, of morally essential features, 141

Deductive: ethical reasoning as, 152-53, 213-21

Definitions: of ethical terms, descriptive as contrasted with prescriptive, 83-84

Descartes, R., 35

Description: of actions, as contrasted with evaluation, 53-54; Moore's notion of, 63-64

Descriptivism: defined, 27; Hare's characterization of naturalism as a form of, 60-64; as contrasted with prescriptivism, 124 ff., 209 ff.

Dewey, John, 11, 15, 26, 74-80

Disagreement in attitude, see Ethical disagreement

Disagreement in belief, see Ethical disagreement

Emotive meaning: Stevenson's account of, 98-99; problems in Stevenson's account of, 106-8

Emotive theory of ethics: 11, 12; as held by Ayer, 88-89; problems in as held by Ayer, 93-96; difference between Ayer's version of and Stevenson's, 97-102; problems in Stevenson's version of, 102-9

Entailment: Hare's criterion of, 132

Ethical disagreement: nature of, whether disagreement in belief or disagreement in attitude, 2, 67-68, 110-11, 223-25; problem of explaining, in Moore's theory, 36-37; as a problem in naturalism, 86; resolution and termination of, 112, 190

Ethical knowledge, 12-13; problem of in Moore, 33 ff.; in subjectivism, 92

Ethics of Motive: Prichard's criticism of, 47-48

Evaluative statement: Hare's definition of, 126; distinguished from factual statement, 197 ff.

Facts: ethical judgments as stating, 197 ff.

Firth, Roderick, 11, 80

Fittingness: of feelings of moral approval and disapproval, 96

Foot, Philippa, 60-62

Frankena, W. K., 24, 209, 211

Generalization argument, 165-76

Generalization principle, 165 ff.

Generalized principle of consequences, 166 ff.

Good: meaning of as the basic question in ethics, 4, 19-20; Moore's conception of as a simple non-natural property, 33-34; Stevenson on the descriptive meaning of, 102-6: Stevenson on the emotive meaning ot, 109; Hare's attack on naturalistic definitions of, 120-21; Rawls' definition of as rationality, 182-86

Good Reasons approach: defined, 16, 144; suggested by Hampshire, 146-49; as held by Toulmin, 150-52; as held by Wellman, 152-54

Hampshire, Stuart, 145-49

Hare, R. M., 6, 8, 12, 21; conception of naturalism, 60-64; notion of criterion in, 105-6; refutation of naturalism in, 119-23; theory of ethical judgments as prescriptive, 123-33; conception of universalizability and its basis, 134, 142-43; criticism of Toulmin by, 156-60; criticism of Searle, 214-15

Hartmann, Nicoli, 1

Hedonism, 30-33, 63, 195

Hempel, Carl, 189, 203, 224

Hobbes, T., 63, 117

Homonym: "good" as a, in Stevenson's theory, 105

Hypostatization: of good, 64-65

Ideal observer theory, 11; as a form of naturalism, 80-81; problems in, 81-82, 207

Imperatives: ethical judgments as containing, 16, 123-33

Incorrigibility: of first-person reports of desires and preferences, 205

Inductive: ethical reasoning as, 153-55, 215, 217

Interest: notion of in Perry, 68 ff.; use of notion by Stevenson, 113-14; in Toulmin, 150

Internal property: Perry's notion of, 70-71

Intrinsic value: Moore's assumption concerning, 22; ordinary meaning of, 22-23; meanings of in Moore, 23-24; and obligation in Moore, 24-25; criticism of Moore's conception of, 25-26; and intrinsic nature, 38, 64; Perry's conception of, 70-71; Dewey's criticism of, 79

Intuitionism: two senses in Sidgwick, 42-43; problems of in wider sense, 52-53; problems of in narrow sense, 54-56; Ayer's criticism of, 89-90

Judgments of prudence: as distinct from moral judgments, 79

Kant, Immanuel, 7, 47, 94-95
Kosevi, Julius, 203-4

Leibniz's law, 177
Logical Positivism, 10, 99

Method of isolation, 37-38
Mill, J. S.: principle of utility in, 7; principle of utility as meta-ethical, 9, 91
Moore, G. E., 2; anticipation of normative ethics/meta-ethics distinction by, 4; classification of theory as teleological, 15; characterization of naturalism in, 18-27; refutation of naturalism in, 29-32; theory of indefinability of good, 33-34; problem of verification of ethical judgments in, 34-39; conception of intuition in, 35-37; problem of ethical disagreement in, 36-37
Moral dilemmas: Ross's analysis of, 51-52

Natural intrinsic properties: Moore's conception of as distinct from non-natural properties, 63-64
Naturalism: defined, 1, 13-14, 58-61; Moore's refutation of, 28-32; assumptions in Moore's characterization of, 60-64; problems in definitional naturalism, 84-86; Ayer's refutation of, 97; Hare's refutation of, 119-23; three theses associated with, 197-98
Non-cognitivism: consequences for ethical theory, 7; defined, 12-13
Normative ethics: defined, 2-4; recent return to, 167

Objectivism: defined, 14
Obligations: Prichard's view of as known directly, 50; Ross on prima facie, 51-52; three kinds distinguished, 171

Open question argument, 27 ff., 186
Ought: Sidgwick on irreducibility of, 46; Prichard on underivability of, 46-49; Searle's derivation of, 213-16

Paton, H. J., 26
Perry, Ralph Barton, 11, 16, 68-74
Persuasive definition, 10, 16, 73, 104
Plan of life: notion of in Rawls, 184-86
Pragmatic theory of meaning: in Stevenson, 99, 106-7
Prediction: value-judgments as, in Dewey, 61, 75-77
Prescriptive: ethical judgments as, in Hare's theory, 124 ff.; in Hampshire, 146-47; distinguished from descriptive statements, 209-11
Prichard, H. A., 11, 15, 46-50, 53
Principle of consequences, 165 ff.
Principles: moral, as distinct from rules, 43; status of in Singer, 177-81

Rationalism: broad sense of, defined, 228
Rawls, John, 182-86
Relational: ethical judgments as, as distinct from relativistic, 67, 69-70
Relativism: defined, 45; problem of in Santayana's theory, 67; problem of in R. B. Perry's theory, 69-70; problem of in Rawls' definition of "good," 185-86
Right: knowledge of in Moore, 39-40; Sidgwick and irreducibility of, 43-46; Prichard and underivativeness of, 46-49; notion of prima facie in Ross, 51, 55-56; empirical characterizability of, 58
Ross, W. D., 11, 15, 50-56, 70
Rules of inference: moral principles as, in Toulmin, 156-57, 158-59
Rules of relevance: notion of in Hampshire, 148; notion of in Toulmin, 149-52
Rule-utilitarianism, *see* Utilitarianism
Russell, Bertrand, 64

Santayana, George, 11, 14, 58, 64-68, 74
Scepticism: as a consequence of Moore's theory, 35; as a basis for a fact-value distinction, 201-4

Scheler, Max, 1
Searle, John, 153, 213-16
Self-contradictoriness: problem of determining, 92
Sidgwick, H.: ethical axioms in, 8-9, 42-43; meaning of "intuitionism" in, 42; indefinability of "right" in, 43-46
Singer, Marcus, 135, 167 ff.
Social approval theory, 44; Sidgwick's criticism of, 45
Spencer, H.: definition of "good" as an example of naturalism in Moore's sense, 13, 14, 28, 104
Stevenson, C. L., 2; conception of meta-ethics in, 5-6; concept of persuasive definition in, 10, 16, 104; theory of meaning and conception of emotive meaning, 98-99, 106-7; theory of ethical disagreement, 109-17, 223-25
Strawson, P. F., 55-56
Subjectivism: defined, 14; Santayana's theory as an example of, 65-67; Ayer's criticism of, 91, 92-93; two kinds of, 200; criticism of, 204-9
Synonymity: criterion of, 121-22

Teleological theory of ethics: defined, 15
Theological theory of ethics, 44, 45
Tolerance: Santayana's view of as encouraged by scepticism, 65-66
Tolhurst, William, 215n
Toulmin, Stephen, 145, 149-52, 156-60

Truth and falsity: of ethical judgments, 12-13, 36-37; Ayer on, 88-89, 93-94; Stevenson on, 106; Hampshire on, 148-49; 201-3, 223

Universalizability, principle of, 8-9, 133-40; alleged triviality of, 140-42; basis of, 142-43
Unverifiability: of ethical judgments in Moore's theory, 35-37; see also Verification Principle
Use: of expressions as contrasted with meaning by Stevenson, 100-1; dynamic as contrasted with descriptive by Stevenson, 119 ff.; as contrasted with mention, 195-96
Utilitarianism: as a meta-ethical theory, 9-10; ideal, 11; criticism of classical utilitarianism by Sidgwick, 44; Prichard's criticism of, 48-49; whether a form of descriptivism, 61; Dewey's theory as a version of, 85; Ayer's criticism of, 91; rule utilitarianism, 151-52, 158-59, 174

Value: generic notion of in Perry, 68 ff.
Veracity: obligation of, 172-74
Verification Principle: in Ayer, 90
Voting: obligation of, 167-71
Voucher system, 116

Wellman, Carl, 152-55
Westermarck, Edvard, 2